D0926713

Martin Buber's Philosophy
of Interhuman Relation

Martin Buber's Philosophy of Interhuman Relation

*A Response to the Human
Problematic of Our Time*

Alexander S. Kohanski

Rutherford • Madison • Teaneck
Fairleigh Dickinson University Press
London and Toronto: Associated University Presses

Associated University Presses, Inc.
4 Cornwall Drive
East Brunswick, N.J. 08816

Associated University Presses Ltd
69 Fleet Street
London EC4Y 1EU, England

Associated University Presses
Toronto M5E 1A7, Canada

Library of Congress Cataloging in Publication Data

Kohanski, Alexander Sissel, 1902–
    Martin Buber's philosophy of interhuman relation.

    Bibliography: p.
    Includes index.
    1. Buber, Martin, 1878–1965. 2. Interpersonal
communication. 3. Philosophical anthropology. I. Title.
B3213.B84K64   128   80-70626
ISBN 0-8386-3085-5   AACR2

Printed in the United States of America

To my wife
Dorothy
and our sons
Daniel and *Ronald*
In whose midst I wrote this book

Contents

Preface

Buber's Philosophical Goal

This book is an exposition of Martin Buber's philosophy of communication centered in his principle of dialogue. Whether communication is viewed as a problem of technological media, of the sociology of intergroup relation, the psychology of individual association, or the theology of man's searching for God, its foundations must be sought in man himself as a communicating being. This is the theme of Buber's investigation into the act of dialogue, which always leads him back to the question "What is Man?" The ancient dictum "Know thyself" he would transform into "Know thyself as a communicating being." For in the living act of communication or dialogue he sees not only how man can know himself but also how he can fulfill himself as man—and in no other way.

There are two prominent features in Buber's writings, one his acute awareness of the crisis that prevails in all human concerns of the present age, and the other his deep sense of the power of speech as the essential act of man's relation to the world around him. The bulk of his philosophical output is devoted to the overcoming of this crisis, at the root of which he finds "the destruction of confidence in existence in general," or "the mistrust of eternity," a mistrust that has dominated modern science and technology as well as religion. He hopes this crisis may be resolved through a renewal of the primary act of speaking, which he designates as the "dialogical principle" of man's encounter with reality. How to highlight his specific contribution to a solution of this problem presents some methodological difficulty.

A mere discourse about his ideas on religion, ethics, socialism, politics, and the like may give us an insight into the diverse aspects of his philosophy, yet fail to show the goal of his philosophizing, which to him is the essence of his thinking as living experience *(dem erlebenden Denker diktiert)*. My method is to treat his philosophy as a *response* to the human problematic of striving to communicate with fellowman and the world of things through scientific knowledge and technological devices, and to examine how his "pointing of the way" meets this problematic and gives it *direction* toward real communication. In order to bring this out fully I have emphasized the *dynamic* and *alogical* aspects of his mode of thought.

Buber's dynamism stems from the primary act of relating, which is the ground of his philosophizing. Methodologically this must be shown through an analysis of his concepts, such as spirit, the between, meeting, faith, freedom, destiny, good and evil, and the like, all of which are functional forces of entering-into-relation. It is not enough to describe these terms in the language of accepted philosophical connotation. We must determine their precise meaning in Buber's own mode of thinking and, more important, ascertain the role he ascribes to them in the actualities of man's relation to fellowman, nature, and the Absolute. This runs through my entire study. The second aspect, his alogical mode of thought, I have considered in a special section, contrasting it with the logical mode of natural science and philosophy in general.

The Three Areas of Communication

To give a systematic presentation of a philosopher we must find its anchor in his writings. This is not readily available in the works of Martin Buber, who cannot be rightfully regarded as a systematizing thinker. "What I had to say did not fit into a systematic," he wrote of his philosophizing. One may therefore ask, By what right may we bring him under the control of system thinking? My approach to his works is by the method of what I would call "philosophical analysis." By that I mean: while all that Buber had to say was not constructed by him in systematic form, it nevertheless constitutes a "self-contained communicable thought compound" *(ein in sich schlüssiger transmittierbarer Denkzusammenhang)*, which is discernible at the root of all his writings and may, upon philosophical analysis, be brought under a system. There is a subconscious intellectual storing up and organization of ideas and concepts in the mind of a philosopher which find expression in his writings even though they are not couched in systematic language. By the method of philosophical analysis we can delve into the innermost fissures of his works and bring forth their overt and covert conceptual interconnections within a systematic frame of reference. What comes to light in Buber's case is a structure not of categories of the understanding, as for example in a Kantian system, but of interrelated thought forms which manifest a consistent orientation in reality. This is basically what the *Geisteswissenschaften* (cultural sciences) are about, and Buber can be best understood within this kind of frame of reference. Thus he may engage in *Religionswissenschaft* without resorting to metaphysics or to natural science. Nonetheless, he has a *Wissenschaft,* and like all science it has a structure. In order to comprehend it, his concepts must be analyzed in their structural interrelations and also compared with similar concepts in the general sciences.

My treatment of this area centers on Buber's concept of "the between," which is essentially a scientific principle of gauging reality, going back to Aristotle. My task here is to ascertain its nature in the field of the general sciences and how Buber conceives it as the central issue of the crisis of modern man. That is, in order to have a better understanding of how he gauges reality, we must learn to know the elements of his "between" and how he transforms them from an ordered world, or the natural sciences of experience *(Erfahrung),* into a world order, or a spiritual science (a *Geisteswissenschaft)* of spontaneous experience*(Beziehung).* This is the thrust of chapter 1 of this book, which brings my entire study of Buber's philosophy of communication into the mainstream of the modern age.

Besides a specific science, Buber also has a specific technology with reference to man's relation to man. I consider it a technology, because it undertakes to answer the question of how man may build or rebuild his social order in which he may realize his human destiny. Buber maintains that the philosophical-scientific orientation which modern man has inherited from the Age of Enlightenment, coupled with the physicotechnological instruments he has since then perfected to a high degree, cannot solve his crisis in relation to nature and fellowman; on the contrary, they are the chief contributors to this crisis. Yet he does not advocate a return to the prescientific and pre-technological age, but undertakes to show the way toward a new approach to the world order and toward a restructuring of the social order. The latter is discussed under the topic of his social technology in chapter 2.

In both these areas the dominant factor is Buber's religious world view as differentiated from a purely philosophical-scientific outlook which prevails in modern thought. His chief contribution, therefore, lies in his teaching about man's relation to God as the basis of genuine dialogue in all spheres of human life. This is presented in chapter 3, which ends the first part of the book, entitled "The Reality of Communication." The second part, entitled "Judaism: A Living Experience of Relation," runs parallel with part I, also in three chapters, and is considered here as the source from which Buber drew his basic ideas of the principle of dialogue.

In the Jewish Mode of Thinking

Buber gained his religious experience through the Jewish faith, which he came to recognize as a paradigm of dialogical speaking. It is from this faith that he took his first steps into the world of philosophical thought, and it is to this faith that he always turned and returned for renewal and confirmation of his ideas. Basically, his general philosophy follows the development of his Jewish mode of thinking in form as well as in method. He draws a distinction between the Western way and that of the Orient and regards the Jewish spiritual creations as the most representative of the latter way. While the Jew, he says, has lived among Western nations and been greatly influenced by their civilization, he has remained at heart an Oriental. This is perhaps truest of our philosopher himself, whose tendency to lean toward the East is quite pronounced in his writings. It may be difficult at times to separate this blend into Jewish and general components; but in my analysis of his thoughts on Judaism in comparison with his general religious views, I find the Jewish to be primary in his orientation and serving as a reservoir for his philosophy as a whole.

This blend of Buber's general and Jewish philosophy is presented in two parts not in order to separate them in thought or goal, but, on the contrary, to emphasize the confluence of two currents in the mainstream of his thinking process and their singular direction toward the same end: the establishment of a true human society on earth. The principle of dialogue or communication runs through the entire book in parallel strands. In the first part its concern is with human life in general, in man's relation to the world (science), to fellowman (social technology), and to God (religion). The same concern is expressed in the three phases of Judaism (substance, relation, and essence) in the second part, and in the same relationships: the Jewish people and the world, its communication with God, and its striving for a true community. The very title of this part expresses Buber's conviction that essentially the Jewish way of realizing the human goal is that of communication with God, which, he says, is "the strongest witness for the primacy of the dialogical known to me."

Sources of Reference

My main sources are Buber's works in German published under the following titles: *Werke* in three volumes (Heidelberg: Verlag Lambert Schneider, 1962, 1963, 1964), *Der Jude und sein Judentum* (Köln: Joseph Melzer Verlag, 1963), *Hinweise* (Zürich: Manesse Verlag, 1953), *Nachlese* (Verlag Lambert Schneider, 1966), and *Briefwechsel aus sieben Jahrzehnten,* in three volumes (Verlag Lambert Schneider, 1972, 1973, 1975).

All my quotations from the German and Hebrew originals are my own translation, unless indicated otherwise. Where I feel that the German or Hebrew text may lend itself to different interpretations, or where the fullness of meaning is difficult to transmit in any translation, I also cite the original for comparison. For further comparison I refer the reader to Buber's works published in English translations. Buber's language is rich in nuances, which require the reader's, not to speak of the interpreter's, meticulous attention. For consistency and clarity of his vocabulary I have provided an Index of Terminology at the end of this book, giving the sources in the English editions of his works.

Acknowledgments

I gratefully acknowledge the permissions granted to me by the following:

Mr. Rafael Buber of Haifa, Israel: To quote from the works of Martin Buber in the German original and in my translation.

Jewish Social Studies: To use my article "Martin Buber's Restructuring of Society into a State of Anocracy," published in the issue of January 1972 (34:1).

The Princeton Seminary Bulletin: To use my article "Martin Buber's Approach to Jesus," published in the issue of Winter 1975 (67:1).

Judaism, A Quarterly Journal: To use my article "Martin Buber's Philosophy of Judaism," published in the issue of Winter 1975 (24:1).

Passaic, N.J., 1980   ALEXANDER S. KOHANSKI

Martin Buber's Philosophy
of Interhuman Relation

PART I
The Reality of Communication

Introduction

The Crisis of the Between

Martin Buber has characterized the crisis of modern man as "the crisis of the between."[1] It may be viewed as a threefold issue manifested in the spheres of science, technology, and religion.

The scientific issue deals with the universe as an organized totality. According to Buber's philosophy, the universe constitutes a *world order* in which man interacts with all other beings in a primal ontic relationship. We know of its existence through our spontaneous experience, but we don't know the essence of its constitution or the organization of its inner forces. From our living experience we can only learn that the world order has an underlying primal duality, as it manifests itself in our very act of relation *(Beziehung)*.

Now when man the scientist starts to investigate the world around him, he tries to understand it in terms of forces that determine each other in an ordered sequence of cause and effect, thus constituting an *ordered world* in an organized, self-contained unity. We know this ordered world and its inner forces because its order takes the form of our own logical mode of thinking, of our concepts of matter, energy, motion, and other factors which enter into the universal system of natural phenomena. This scientific way of looking at the world enables man to orient himself in nature as he strives to uncover its hidden laws and gain an understanding of their operations. However, when man the scientist begins to stretch the bounds of the ordered world with total disregard for his living experience of the world order, the two worlds come into conflict with each other and there ensues what may be called a scientific crisis, that is, natural science ceases to be a true guide of human orientation in reality.

The technological issue is essentially a social one, insofar as man uses technical instruments, which he has created for the improvement of his condition, without regard to the need for social change which those instruments dictate. Buber calls it the problem of man being behind his works, that is, man is so overwhelmed by his technological proliferation that he becomes its slave rather than its master. As the technical instruments continue to undermine his social structure but are not used for a restructuring of society, there arises what may be regarded as a technological crisis, because the social order cannot contain the instruments which it has produced.

In the sphere of religion, the issue is one of faith, which embraces all aspects of human life and thus also permeates the other two spheres. "Religion," as Buber views it, "is essentially the act of holding fast to God," or "the self-binding of the human person to God,"[2] which gives meaning to all of man's partial, incomplete, or finite activities in everyday life. This is experienced through faith in the presence of God when man goes forth to meet Him. The man of faith does not question, and hence does not try to prove, God's existence or Providence. In his relation to God he finds the center of all his other relations to fellowman and the world. But when faith is undermined through whatever forces that may act against it, man loses his anchor in reality and all his activities become meaningless. This is what we call the religious crisis of our time.

In all three spheres as described above, the problem centers on man's living relation with others. In science, the relation is with the world of nature including the human species; in technology it is with fellowman in regard to the formation of a social structure which is uniquely human; and in religion the relation is with the Absolute Being or between the finite and the Infinite. In all these spheres, then, the crisis takes place in what happens *between* man and others with whom he relates. Accordingly, Buber calls it "the crisis of the between." In order to resolve it, he first has to establish a principle of entering-into-relation which produces a "between" in all those spheres. This principle Buber calls dialogical.

The Dialogical Principle of Relation

Method of Philosophical Anthropology

When asked to characterize his philosophy, Buber said it was grounded in his personal experiences of faith *(Glaubenser-*

fahrung), not in tenets derived from traditional revelation. However, in order to transmit these experiences, he further noted,
they had to be given a logical exposition and this entailed a
certain method, which he designated as the method of
philosophical anthropology. It is not metaphysical or theological, as it does not deal with things, as such, but with the human
relationship with things.[3] The anthropological question is not
"How are judgments possible?" but "How is man possible?"
and the answer lies in the reality of man's twofold communication with the world. Buber wants to avoid splitting the world into
two realms, one phenomenal and the other noumenal, as, for
example, Kant did. As a humanist, he starts with man as a being
endowed with a double movement, one of distancing and the
other of relation. Buber calls it "the principle of being human,"
or the question about his "beginning" *(principium)* as category
humanum. In the first movement man sets things over against
himself as separate existents, and in the second he establishes a
relationship with them. But his approach to these independent
existents may manifest itself through "experience" *(Erfahrung)*
of the distanced beings as objects of use toward various ends, or,
on the other hand, through an act of entering into a relationship
(Beziehung) with no intention of using them.[4] These two manners of man's approach to others have their basis in his twofold
communication with them.

The Primary Words and Genuine Dialogue

"To man the world is twofold, according to his twofold
communication."[5] With this opening statement in his essay *I
and Thou* Buber raises the anthropological question of man's
existential relation to the world as distinguished from a rational
comprehension of it. The problem is not to prove the existence
of the I (as for example Descartes tried to do), but to ascertain
how man takes his stand in the world as a living human being,
not merely as a thinking, willing, or sensing subject. Man's
existential question is how existence is established in reference
to the world or, more accurately, how his existence is revealed
through his communication with the not-self. Buber says this
occurs through speaking in two ways. Man may address the
other or not-self by speaking I-Thou or I-It. The other may be
the same in both instances, but the communication established is
not the same, nor is the I who speaks I-Thou the same as the one
who speaks I-It. Buber designates these two ways of speaking as

primary words *(Grundworte),* not single words, but word pairs: I-Thou and I-It. The word "He" or "She" may take the place of "It." Each word pair represents a specific relationship of man to the world, and the relationship of one word pair is not like that of the other. Accordingly, when man says I, he means either I-Thou or I-It, for whenever I is spoken, the second word of one or the other word pair is implied.

In the act of speaking I-Thou one must be willing to step into relation with the other without holding himself back, without putting the other in doubt, without reservation whatsoever. This is the true state of dialogue. On the other hand, one who cannot step out of his confined selfhood even in the company of others is in a state of monologue, in the sphere of I-It. He is the total individual who cannot recognize the exclusiveness of another besides himself. His reaction to the other is not a turning away from him *(Abwendung),* which is the opposite of turning toward *(Hinwendung),* but a recoiling *(Rückwendung)* from the other, whom he regards as a thing, an It, an object of possession and control, to which he may direct his monologue but not listen or respond. This difference between monologue and dialogue is what distinguishes the individual from the person. The latter is one who enters into relationship with others without reservation, who says what he has to say at the time he says it *(was ich jeweils zu sagen habe),* who gives of himself fully whatever he has to give, without semblance, affectation, or injection of his self. This is genuine dialogue.

Dialogue and Dialectic

In order to clarify Buber's meaning of dialogical relation as an act of speaking, it will be well to draw a distinction between dialectic and dialogue in general. Referring to Ludwig Feuerbach's aphorism, "True dialectic is not a monologue of the lonely thinker with himself; it is a dialogue between I and Thou," Buber asks a rhetorical question, "When will dialectic of thought become dialogic, . . . a strictly thinking dialogue with the man present at the moment?"[6] He does not elaborate on it in this particular context, but the contrast he draws is instructive to our understanding of his dialogical principle.

Both dialectic and dialogue seek to establish a relationship between the I and the not-I or an other. But in the former it is through an act of positing *(thetic)* whereas in the latter it is one of meeting *(encounter)*. We may take Johann Gottlieb Fichte as the first to suggest that the I has an ontological capacity of positing itself and the not-I in reality. This duality, which all thinking presupposes, he finds in consciousness where it has been posited by the pure I (pure activity) through dividing itself into an I and another or not-I. In order to dwell together in consciousness, the two elements must limit each other; otherwise, the unlimited action of the pure I will exclude or annihilate the other, that is, the contradiction between the pure I and the not-I will be devastating to the I.[7] This is what actually takes place in dialectic interlocution. The dialectician aims at overcoming his opponent by completely negating his views or by absorbing them *(aufheben)* into a new synthesis. In contrast to this process, dialogue does not presuppose any positing of an I and a not-I by an absolute or pure I. Here the I is not intelligence-in-itself but a real living man who encounters another living being actually. In their mutual relationship they recognize each other's exclusiveness and do not try to limit each other, for they fear not being annihilated by each other or being absorbed into a higher unity; their relationship is one of mutuality. Instead of negation or partial negation, dialogue seeks affirmation of one I by another, a not-I, who is Thou.

In dialectic communication, two individuals treat each other as intelligences and thus try to set a common ground of reasoning by agreeing at the outset on acceptable propositions which are to govern their argument.[8] The rule here is the well-known dictum that one does not argue with anyone who denies all principles. The discussion must follow in accord with the agreed-upon propositions and with due regard to logical reasoning. In dialogue, on the other hand, the partners in speech have no prearranged propositions to talk about; nor do they seek a common ground to base their conversation on, but each speaker is just concerned with what the other has to say and with the ground on which he stands as an other. Each wants to affirm the otherness of the other and be affirmed by him. Any topic may serve as a starting point, which is pursued as long as each has something to say, or may be modified and dropped. Neither one tries to convince his partner or to overcome his argument. They speak, each standing on his own ground, which the other is trying to understand. To quote a few passages from Buber, "Dialogue is communication." It "is no privilege of intellectual activity like dialectic." "Genuine dialogue cannot be arranged beforehand." It "does not presuppose agreement," nor does it try to convince. Rather, the way to it is by "showing interest and understanding for what the other has to say" (BMM 35, KnM 87, PW 222).

The Reality of Relation

Buber investigates the reality not of being but of what occurs between beings in their mutual relation of spontaneous experience *(Erlebnis)*. His problem is to find this reality *(Wirklichkeit)* and to recognize it as such. It is not a question of whether man, fellowman, animals, or things in themselves are real. These are all beings whose reality comes into view when the inquiring person, not just the inquiring mind, stands in some communication with them. The question of reality is thus not metaphysical but ontological, and can be answered only by a being who stands over against *(entgegnet)* another being in an ontic relationship. One who observes another from a distance does not know him in reality, but constructs a system of metaphysical or natural science to *explain* his existence as an object of observation. But the inquiring person who enters into relation with an other steps forth spontaneously and unsystematically where he can meet the other and *understand* him through "being there" in the reality which occurs between them.

The distinction between explaining and understanding is of particular importance in Buber's philosophical method and requires some elucidations. Buber seeks to establish man as the category of being who knows himself as a human being and not as a set of concepts. That is, man is to understand himself through his own existential category which makes him human but not through conceptual categories of reason. The latter, such as causality, substance, spatiotemporal elements, or even spiritual concepts, can only explain his existence with reference to entities other than human. This kind of explanation is the goal of natural science or metaphysics, but man's explanation of himself as man is the quest of philosophical anthropology.[9] Accordingly, to understand himself, man reflects on the I in the word pair I-Thou, which involves himself and another. This is not the same as the introspection of the I upon itself, in which one forms a concept of himself as mind in psychology, body in physiology, or soul in metaphysics, in comparison with his own I as a self. That way he *explains* his I as an object of psychology and so on, but does not *understand* himself as man. The human problematic, therefore, does not arise from a conceptual I but from man's ontological existence insofar as it is related to an other. This is what Buber designates as the category *humanum,* which consists of two distinct ways of communication, one of distancing and the other of entering-into-relation.

Four Potencies of Communication

Philosophical anthropology considers man as a unique being inasmuch as he communicates with the world as no other creature does. Its ground *(Seinsgrund),* according to Buber, is that man alone is a being who distances the world as a whole, as a universe, separating it from his own being, and also enters into relation with it. In this double movement he exercises four potencies, which are not drives, psychic and social states, or faculties reacting to contingent situations, but prime forces of his being as a whole which become manifest as he "takes his stand" in communication with others. Buber does not negate or minimize the human drives and faculties of biological self-preservation but considers them insufficient motivations to satisfy man's striving for relation with reality. The four potencies are *cognition, art, love,* and *faith* through which man strives to fathom the world, to unveil its hidden being, to overcome its strangeness, and avert his alienation from it.[10] Buber calls them potencies rather than faculties, because they do not reside ready-made in psychology but are realized only whenever there is an act of confrontation with others. This act is what makes man a human being, for no other animal can act this way. This may be best illustrated by Buber's example of considering a tree.

In the case of distancing, I may regard a tree as a picture, a movement of foliage, a species or sample of a certain plant, or in terms of given laws of nature. I may further conceive it as a number of mathematical relation or even as a figment of the imagination. In all these observations the tree remains an object of my empirical knowledge and possible use, with its fixed time and place, conditions and qualities. In the case of entering-into-relation, on the other hand, I may regard the tree only as an exclusive being as I become involved in confrontation with it as a whole. In this involvement, to be sure, my other experiences of observing the tree are not eliminated but become enmeshed in the relationship of my being with its being. My act of establishing this relation occurs regardless of the fact that a tree has no consciousness similar to mine; I do not meet in it a dryad, I meet the tree itself.

The potency of cognition as a way of knowing reality, then, actualizes itself in the form of subject-subject relation (I-Thou) through a noncausal and nonspatiotemporal immediacy. In this form I am aware of the tree as a whole, not of its space, time, or cause and effect, even though they are there under a different aspect. Similarly, the potency of art actualizes itself through the act of forming an image of the relation which I have established with the tree as whole. The artistic image is not a representation of the tree but a product of the artist's meeting it as an other.[11] It is the embodiment of the *between* in the form of an image representing the artist's response to the tree in their mutual encounter.

Love, according to Buber, is the specific potency actualized in interhuman relations, in which fellowman is met as "Thou" (as a subject), not as an "I" (an object of observation, use, and the like). Love in such an encounter is not an affection one has for another or a feeling bestowed on the other, but rather an acceptance, a confirmation of the other as he is and even as he might become.[12] Again, love is realized not in "I" nor in "Thou" as states of feeling (though feelings are involved), but between them. "Feelings," says Buber, "dwell in man, but man dwells in his love."[13]

Faith is the potency that prevails in man's relation to God. Buber considers this potency as the highest of all, because it embraces also the other three. As in the case of love, faith is not a feeling of assurance that God exists (the believer neither questions nor tries to prove His existence), but the very act of entering into relation with the Absolute, as this occurs when the human being is realized most fully as a whole, that is, most complete. Here, too, the act is one of taking a stand in the between of the relation, in the occurrence of the confrontation.

Philosophy and Religion

While man thus faces two realms of knowledge, these do not constitute two separate unbridgeable worlds, one real and the other phenomenal or illusory. On the contrary, one realm passes into the other and back again, as every Thou *must* become an It when relation ceases, and every It *can* be turned into a Thou through entering into relation again.[14] Human destiny fulfills itself through a constant "swinging between Thou and It." As man gets to the threshold of Thou, he can tarry there but for a moment, lest it be too consuming; he must step out of the relation into the world of It, the world of empirical knowledge and use. His fulfillment comes when he bestows the glimpses he caught in the world of I-Thou on the things of I-It in everyday life, not rejecting those things as if they were evil, but serving them with his whole being. These glimpses are of the divine sparks that light up the things and help man not to succumb to the burden which they place on him in his everyday existence.[15] Through the interaction of his two ways of communication with reality, man attains wholeness as a human being, which is his freedom. But what are the ontic forces that prompt him to go in this direction?

Buber finds in man two closely connected dispositions, the origin of which, he says, is unknown. One is a dissatisfaction with being confined to a condition of merely observing, possessing, and using others in the movement of distancing, and the other is a desire for completion in the movement of relation. This accounts, on the one hand, for man's oscillation between his ordered world and the world order and, on the other, for his striving to actualize his potency of faith as the only way of completing his self-realization. Man cannot rest in the ordered world of conceptual knowledge where he tries to attain certainty of a well-constructed system. He always ventures into spontaneous experiences of the world order, which may not be expressed in propositional knowledge, yet has the certainty of meeting others through immediate relation. This taking a stand in immediacy Buber calls the "narrow ridge" of his philosophical anthropology.

I have on occasion described my position as the "narrow ridge," [he writes in his essay "What is Man?"]. By this I wanted to express that I did not stand on a broad elevated plateau of a system which comprises a set of sure statements about the absolute, but on a narrow rocky crest between precipices where there is no sureness of propositional knowledge, yet the certainty of meeting the One who remains concealed.[16]

Meeting with the Absolute, the "One who remains concealed," is the goal of man's striving for his completeness as a human being. His twofold way of communicating with fellowman and the world converges in his relation with God, which can only be an I-Thou communication, never an I-It. This religious world view will be brought out fully in the course of my discussion of Buber's science of religious knowledge. For the present I will indicate the general distinction he makes between religion and philosophy.

Buber differentiates a religious world view from one that constitutes a philosophical system.[17] Philosophy, he says, believes in the supreme power of reason and, as Kant realized, knows only what "was heretofore discovered in our thought." While this is legitimate for natural science, it does not render a knowledge of the concrete person, because in scientific explanation the person is taken apart into sundry elements of observation and torn away from his category *humanum* as well as from God. Such knowledge is especially unable to account for the relation between the finite and Infinite, or between man and the Absolute, because it takes them both as objects of rational knowledge and not as different, independent subjects. It does not ask, "What is *man* who knows?," only "What are the *things* he may know?" On the other hand, philosophical anthropology, which sees man in his twofold way of communication, can understand him as a finite being relating with another finite being in a knowledge of the limited, and also relating with the infinite in a knowledge of the unlimited. Indeed, from the religious viewpoint, knowledge of the finite is impossible without participation in the Infinite.

> This participation [Buber writes] is given in order that knowledge may at all be possible. This is to say that, *simultaneously* and *together* with man's finitude we must also recognize his participation in the infinite, not as two concomitant qualities, but as a duality of the processes in which the existence of man as such is recognizable. The finite works in him and the infinite works in him; he participates in finitude and he participates in the infinite.[18]

An Atypical Philosopher

In answer to a question whether his position was philosophical or theological, Buber wrote: "It is often argued whether I am a philosopher, a theologian, or whatever else. . . . As far as I know myself, I would call myself an atypical man."[19] By this he meant that he was not concerned with systematic philosophy or metaphysical speculation and theology, but with the act of philosophizing such as any man who is involved with his whole being in personal relations with fellowman, nature, and the divine Being would be.[20] As a philosopher, then, Buber is not a system builder, not by design, that is, for he does not try to erect a closed-in structure or, as he would call it, a metaphysical "home" where man may lodge every one of his doubts under a sheltered roof. He does not see the problem of man so much in his homelessness as in his lack of readiness to accept his status in the open, which is his human destiny. For an "open world" man needs an "open-end" philosophy anchored at one pole in his own being and from there going forth to meet others in genuine dialogue. As a humanist philosopher, and like all humanists, Buber starts with man. But unlike other humanists, he does not end with man as an absolute, even though he recognizes him as a being sui generis; his absolute is the eternal Thou, not the human Thou.

Can this be considered Buber's terminus of thought and, if so, did he not abandon philosophy and embrace theology? One cannot speak of his thought terminus, because he does not posit an end point to his thinking. This is what he means when he speaks of his collected works not as "works" fully ending within, but as essays pointing without in a never ending essaying forth toward meeting. Neither can one speak of Buber as a theologian, if by that is meant a systematizer of religious speculation. Not that he is not consistent in his religious concepts, but rather that his religious world view is not rounded out in a theology with God as its object. His religious outlook stems, as he states, from two main convictions. One "is the primal experience that God is wholly raised above man, that he is beyond the grasp of man, and yet that he is present in an immediate relationship with these human beings who are absolutely incommensurable with him, and that he faces them." The other "is the basic consciousness that God's redeeming power is at work everywhere and at all times, but that a state of redemption exists nowhere and never."[21] Here is where the philosopher of spontaneous experience merges with the man of faith. For Buber philosophizing about God is a matter of faith, not to question God's existence, but to trust in His presence; this also implies man's ability to enter into relation with Him.

In an address delivered in July 1963, in Amsterdam, on the occasion of his receiving the Erasmus Prize, Buber stated: "If I were to designate my own basic view by a concept, it could be only the one we designate as Erasmus's view: the concept of a believing humanism."[22] Then he made an essential distinction. In Erasmus's view, he pointed out, there are two principles in man's life which have nothing in common, one of "natural humanity" which is to be cultivated in man's life on earth, and the other "faith" in which man is torn from his human aspect and raised to the divine. In his own view, Buber said, there is no such separation in man's life on earth but, on the contrary, the one is inconceivable without the other. Accordingly, man's reaching out to God is not through some spiritual faculty which is separated from his natural impulses, but through his whole being or rather with his being-as-a-whole. This, in essence, is Buber's principle of dialogical relation as it is also the substance of his philosophy of religion.

Signs of Direction

Buber envisaged a magnificent edifice in an open field ascending toward heaven and invited man to enter into it with his whole being, for only by being whole may one tarry there even for a while. This edifice is of the spirit, and the spirit is of the between which comes into existence through relation. However, Buber does not present the actual structure, only its architectural design, because the former cannot be reduced to perceptual configurations or conceptual functions; it may be known only through living experience *(Erlebnis)* as and when one encounters the Absolute. Therefore, all Buber has done is, as he says, "point the way" to it. Can modern man, to whom he addresses himself, recognize his signs and find direction?

There is dramatic tension in Buber's writings. Starting with the unknown, he may lead the reader through uncharted byways in expectation of some startling discovery, when he suddenly tells him that there is nothing for him to discover but only to search in his innermost whether he wants to go forth, for the going forth is what counts. At another time, when he points to the life of spirit, the reader tenses up with anticipation of something extraordinary, only to be advised that the spirit is found in ordinary happenings of everyday life; whatever may be extraordinary about it comes from man's own deeds. Again, at times, when the reader feels ready to follow this advice and take his daily events into outer, heavenly spheres, he is warned of having lost direction, for it is all right here on earth. This tension in Buber's manner of writing reflects certain contending forces in his relation to reality, which, though not stated explicitly, break through the formation of his thoughts. This is especially felt in the distinction he makes between philosophy and religion in his hyphenated religious-philosophical outlook, and in the conflict he sees between the individual and society in a community that is essentially the product of individuals. But all these tensions and conflicts are signs pointing in the direction of man's living experience in encounter with fellowman, with the world of nature, and with God.

1

A Science of Religious Relation

Scientific Knowledge and the Problem of Freedom

Unfulfilled Promise of the Natural Sciences

Man is intent on shaping his world. In this he asserts his freedom, which is the essence of his being human. Centuries may pass before his handiwork comes into full view. But then he may discover that, although his structure is magnificent in form, he cannot find a place in it for himself as man. And not being able thus to place himself in the world he has shaped, he learns to his dismay that he has forfeited the very freedom which he thought he had gained as a world builder. That is how Western man lost his sense of freedom when the scientific-philosophical world of the Greeks disintegrated at the beginning of the Christian era; again, when the medieval logicometaphysical universe split apart in the early days of the Renaissance; and once more, when the world shaped by the natural sciences began to break up in our day. Each man-made world began to show signs of decay just when it appeared to be most perfect in form but devoid of content. But what is the content of a world structure if not man himself? A world without him in reality does not hold together either objectively or subjectively. Hence, no matter what universe man constructs, he must always be able to see himself in it as its content. Yet as often as man has tried to build his universe as a self-contained closed system of causal relations, he has found himself unable to fit into it in reality, i.e., as an actual living being. Such a world builder is like an artist who, having painted the universe in the form of a landscape bounded by a frame, cannot paint himself into it, because, as its painter, he does not see himself in the landscape. He then paints another universe into it in a smaller frame and puts himself outside of it in the universe of the larger frame. But he still cannot find himself in the one he has just painted; so he paints a third universe within the second and puts himself outside of it in the second frame, and so on, making each universe smaller and smaller but never being able to find himself in the ultimate one.[23] This is how man has become estranged from the world, not realizing that he has kept himself out of it by his own design.

At the dawn of the modern era, man began to speculate that perhaps he and the universe are made up of the same natural elements and that, if he could discover their eternal laws, he would find himself and the world in one and the same frame. During the middle ages and early Renaissance, he reasoned, he was hampered by metaphysical and theological doctrines, but with the advent of modern science he felt liberated from those restraints and thought he could build a new kind of world of which he would be a constituent part and at the same time be distinguishable from it as a free, willing and thinking being. The scientists produced many new building blocks and new methods of construction and, although still tied to some of the old forms, hoped to assure human freedom through their newly created instruments. In the words of one of their pioneers, Francis Bacon, they anticipated "the entrance into the kingdom of man, founded on the sciences, being not much other than the entrance into the kingdom of heaven."[24]

In the ensuing three centuries science continued to probe into man's nature, his physical and mental as well as moral qualities, trying to coordinate him with the rest of nature so that he might find his rightful place in a physicomathematical world scheme. In our century, this scheme has been reduced almost entirely to mathematical functions, or a world of pure form without content. Psychological and social phenomena, the media of communication, the very operations of the human mind, emotions, and will are explained now in terms completely deprived of human qualities. Instead of giving man his personal freedom, the newly fashioned world has freed itself from man. It has closed itself up within a physicomathematical universe, permitting nothing human to break in, lest it disturb its system of coordinates. If man is to enter this universe at all, he must pass through a narrow gate and filter through hidden channels in fragments "translated" into nonhuman "bits" or "bites" of information.

In the early stages of modern science, there was still room in the natural scheme of things for a human "soul," a "mind," or a "will," even for a sensuous "self." Now the world is completely dehumanized and man is a total stranger in it.

Upon examining the nature of man's estrangement from reality in modern times, Buber proposes a different approach to a knowledge of the world and, thus, a new direction toward freedom.

The Specter of Alienation

Buber observes that man, instead of finding his own self through an encounter with others, often seeks it through reflection upon himself as an I, that is, without having before him an outside Thou or It. Little does modern man realize how much this kind of reflection alienates him not only from the world but also from himself. Basically, Buber says, man wants to realize himself as a Thou in the presence of someone else; he wants to be confirmed as an exclusive being by another exclusive being. Buber calls it each person's potential or "inborn Thou" which can be actualized only through another Thou; man realizes his own exclusiveness by confronting the exclusiveness of others. Even when he steps out of the I-Thou encounter into the realm of I-It and reflects on that erstwhile encounter, he still is in touch, though indirectly, with the reality of relation to that other. But if he reflects on his own self, his I becomes abstracted or separated both from the I-Thou and the I-It, thus losing contact with a real other. He then mistakes his "inborn Thou" as an outside other but cannot confront it in actuality. His I appears as a ghostlike existent *(Dasein)* or an impersonal self-existent *(Selbstsein)*. Such an I runs into self-contradiction with the real I of the word pairs I-Thou and I-It.[25]

Now when this I, which man has conjured up like a ghost through reflection on himself, faces the world, the latter escapes it, because a ghost cannot reach reality. Having broken the primary connection of I-It by splitting off his I from the word pair, man is unable to connect the world and feels alienated from it. In order to regain the connection, he must decide first to renew his primary relation of I-Thou (since I-It comes into view when the Thou is turned into an It). However, this ontic act entails a risk of losing for a moment the comforts of the world, and modern man, Buber notes, shuns risks; instead, he opts for a rational solution.

Trembling at Alienation

At the end of part 2 of his essay *I and Thou,* Buber describes man's vain attempt to save himself from alienation by a rational representation of the world of It. At times, he says, when man trembles at the alienation between his I and the world, he thinks something must be done about it. He is like a man in a dream who, facing an abyss, sees a possibility of getting across to life but does not know the direction. He could find it in his inner depth through return and sacrifice, but rejects it as too uncertain and, instead, appeals to reason to reshape for him a more comfortable world image. The rational artist in him designs a picture, or rather two pictures, on two opposite walls. One, which moves before him like a cinema, is the *Universe* with man being carried along through history on a tiny globe, always trying to reconstruct the anthills of civilization which had been trampled down. The inscription under the picture reads "One and All." On the other wall there is a picture of the *Soul.* A spinner spins, and the spheres of all stars, the lives of all creatures, and the whole history of the world are woven out of the same thread and are called not by their familiar names, but sensations and representations, experiences and psychic states. The inscription under this picture also reads "One and All."

When man sometimes happens to shudder at his alienation, he may look at one of the pictures, either at the Universe or the Soul, and see the world or the I according to his rational scheme whereby one dissolves into the other, and the abyss may seem to fade away. *If the world frightens him,* he converts it into psychic states of the abstracted I and constructs all things as a mental process. The world then disappears and he feels satisfied. *If the I frightens him,* he decomposes it into material particles and reconstitutes them into a world process. Then the I disappears, and he feels satisfied. As long as he views the world and the I in separation on opposite walls, he is not aware of this double disappearance and he feels relieved of his trembling. But should he happen to see both pictures together, as in a flash, he would tremble exceedingly, for they would both vanish simultaneously and he would face an abyss of expanding nothingness.

Direction toward Freedom

In the above description of man's scientific predicament Buber demonstrates that by reducing the self to physicalism or the world to psychologism, man not only fails to overcome the abyss of alienation but pushes himself deeper into it. Instead, he suggests, one must find direction in relation to the world and fellowman through all modes of communication taken together and not merely through cognition of a world and an I in schematic form. Direction may be found not in a closed world system but rather in an "open field" of spontaneous experiences in a relationship *with* the world and fellowman. For only through such relation does a world order and an ordered world come into existence. "With man," says Buber, "with his being human, there is a world."[26]

This does not mean that man creates the world, as such, but rather sets it up as an ordered reality opposite himself. In Buber's words, "Only when a structured existent is independently opposite a living being does a world, as an independent opposite, exist."[27] That is, a separate world is meaningless unless there is a living being from whom it is separated, and this can come only through the primary act of *distancing* (separation), which is peculiar solely to the human being. Similarly, a world order starts with man, insofar as he enters into *relation* or takes direction toward fellowman, nature, and the Absolute. The two movements of distancing and relation swing back and forth in a pendulum, the former always presupposing the latter. By his decision for direction, man can return from the ordered world (of I-It) to the world order (of I-Thou). He is never alienated in the world of It, because the world of Thou may permeate it through his own act of entering into relation; and if he does at times feel alienated, it is because he despairs of returning to the I-Thou relation. But as long as he strives to realize his human potencies, the possibility of return is always there. This ability of man to "return" and his actual exercise thereof is what Buber regards as his true freedom.

All these phases of Buber's world view will be developed fully in the following pages. In this chapter our particular concern is the manner in which he reshapes concepts of science as a guide to man's way to reality. This is the prospect of what may be designated Buber's science of religious relation.

A Philosophy of Science

Ontology without Metaphysics

When Buber separates himself from the philosophers, he means the philosophers of natural science and the metaphysicians, and when he espouses philosophy again, he aims at a science of religious relation without metaphysics. In his view, the subject of philosophical investigation is not religion but the living experience of the I-Thou relation with the Absolute. The kind of knowledge obtained through such experience is not empirical cognizance as in the natural sciences, not concepts of rationalistic epistemology, nor speculations of metaphysical theology. It is not man's permanent possession but is acquired continually through his renewal of the encounter. This knowledge may be expressed in philosophical discourse through reflection on the relational event after its occurrence. What is then investigated is not the nature of the experiencing I, which is psychology of religion, nor the attributes of the Absolute Thou, which is metaphysics of religion (or theology, strictly speaking), but the ontic reality of the encounter, that is, the ontology of the between. In this respect, the investigation becomes a science of religious knowledge *(Religionswissenschaft).*[28]

The Possibility of a "Religionswissenschaft"

I use the German term in the title of this section, provisionally, in order to emphasize the connotation of *Wissenschaft* in its broadest sense of covering all knowledge that may be acquired through a scientific method. In one of his short essays, entitled "Über Religionswissenschaft,"[29] Buber raises the question whether the field of religion may be investigated by the scientific method. The reality of religious life, he notes, consists of a reciprocity between the Divine and the human, which involves the human act of entering into relation with God. It is this entering-into-relation, when detached from the reality of the reciprocity, that may become the subject of scientific investigation, but always bearing in mind that we must not trespass the boundary which the detachment has created for us. What lies beyond that boundary line can only be revealed divinely, not probed scientifically. That is, we must remember that we are not dealing here with God's reciprocity, but only with man's entering-into-relation, for it is only the latter that we can possibly hope to know. This relationship is established by man as and when he goes forth to a meeting with the Divine. He therefore may investigate the conditions under which such a meeting may take place, the nature of the relation, that is, of the between created under those conditions, and how it affects his human destiny. He can do it not while he experiences the reciprocity, but after he steps out of it and reflects on the relations which he himself had entered into.

To bring Buber's original meaning of *Religionswissenschaft* closer to our scientific way of thinking, we may render this term in English as "a science of religious relation." Religion, by Buber's own definition, "is not human thinking about the Divine," but the relation between man and God within the living experience of their reciprocity. As a science, it concerns our knowledge of this relation, and since the relation is religious, we are dealing here with a knowledge of religious relation.[30] We shall follow Buber's investigation of the nature of this knowledge in the third chapter of our study. Here we want to delimit the concepts which he employs in his science and in what respects they correspond to the same concepts in the scientific mode of thought in general.

Science Is of the Between

As we have seen, Buber's science, like all science, has to do with relation or the between. This holds true not only of the natural sciences but also of what is generally called cultural or spiritual *(Kulturwissenschaften* or *Geisteswissenschaften).*[31] What differentiates one scientific field from another is the kind of relation each deals with. We may trace this principle back to Aristotle, who taught that the scientist who wants to know how two things are related to one another, or how one thing generates from another, must look for that which occurs *between* them as their mediator. This between or "middle," as Aristotle calls it, is the "cause" that explains one thing through another thing. And, says Aristotle, "the cause through which a thing is . . . without qualification . . . and the cause through which a thing is . . . [with] qualification . . . are both alike the 'middle' " *(Post. An.*

90a9). For example, if we want to know how steam is *generated* from water, we examine the middle term "generated" and find it to be "evaporation." We may continue to look for the "cause" of evaporation and discover another middle, fire, and so on, indefinitely.

The problem, as we can readily see, is to find a final middle term that is produced by something which is itself not a middle. In the natural sciences this is impossible, unless we invoke a metaphysical power which is the prime generator or "prime mover" of all events, but is itself ungenerated or "unmoved." Buber, however, as noted above, shuns metaphysics. His chief concern is with man as a living being as a whole; the relationship of this being to others must emanate from its particular mode of existence, without dependence on a power beyond. Buber's science, therefore, investigates the elements of the between which occurs when man goes forth to meet others: fellowman, nature, and the divine Absolute. In general, this kind of between is characterized by two main features: its relation is immediate, and its representation is alogical.

The Logical and Alogical Modes of Thought or the Triad and the Dyad

When the natural scientist studies man in relation to someone or something else, he presents him as a subject connected with an object formulated in a logical proposition of the form "S is P." His aim is to explain man as an entity constituted of certain qualities, or as a product of impersonal factors, or as he is interrelated with other entities in a larger unity. Thus the psychologist presents man as a unity or complex of instincts, emotions, volitions, and a variety of mental states or reactions; the physicist, chemist, or biochemist sees him as a component of certain forces reducible to physicochemical or biological elements; and the sociologist regards him as an individual interacting with other individuals in a social group. What these scientists have in common is that they all try to explain man in terms of categories which may apply not just to him as a human being but to many other beings as well. That is, they interpret man through concepts and things which are not exclusively human. The relation which they thus establish between him and other beings, whether with animate, inanimate, or even with fellowmen, is through the medium of concepts and objects which they find in common on both sides of the relation.

A simple example of this procedure is the well-known proposition "Man is a tool-making animal." "Man" is here related to the general class "animal" through the medium of the concept "tool-making." This medium may be applied to both the subject and the predicate, for if "animal" were not tool-making, there would be no point in designating man as an animal. It means that there is a tool-making quality in the genus animal which is found specifically in man-animal. We are not concerned here with the truth of this proposition, only with its mode of judgment, which is in the form of a *triad:* a subject connected with an object through a copula or middle term. This is the basic form of logical mediation and it is operative only if the subject and object have certain elements in common which may be subsumed under the middle term. Historically, this manner of thinking and mediation goes back to the ancient Greek dictum that "only like knows like." Thus, according to Aristotle, Empedocles teaches, "by earth [in us] we see earth, by water water, by ether godlike ether, by fire wasting fire" (*Met.* 1000b7), and "Plato, in the *Timaeus,* fashions the soul out of his elements; for like, he holds, is known by like" (*De An.* 404b16).

In contradistinction to this way of looking at man and nature, Buber asserts that man is totally *unlike* all other creatures and that a knowledge of him as a human being cannot be gained through the medium of the elements of nature or the qualities of other creatures. "Man," he maintains, is "separated by a primal abyss from all that is merely animal"; and in reference to the Divine he says, "God is God and man is man, and the distance between them is absolute."[32] Now if this be the case, how can we find a real relationship between this unique creature, who stands apart as a being sui generis, and all other creatures? More important, how can we learn to know him if we cannot relate him with others? Buber's answer is that we, as outside observers, that is, as natural scientists, indeed cannot find any real relationship between man and others; but man himself, the human being as a whole, can enter into it through his potencies and can also learn to know himself and the others insofar as they meet in this relationship. This kind of relation is immediate and the knowledge of it is not represented in a logical triad of subject-copula-object, but in an *alogical dyad* of subject-subject. The between thus established is not a given concept or thing, but an act of spontaneous communication. Its form of expression, as was brought out above, is not discursive reasoning or dialectic, but responsive speaking or dialogue. The basic difference, then, between the triad and the dyad is that in the former the between is established by an outside observer who subsumes man (through predicative judgment) under categories which are essentially not-human, whereas in the latter, man himself as the category *humanum* is the subject who creates the between by taking his stand *with* another subject. The "between" is his "being there" responding to an other.

The World Order and the Ordered World

In Buber's world view, the two manners of communication and their corresponding representations are both valid ways of looking at reality. This twofold way has its ground in man's primary movements of distancing and relation, discussed above, which Buber regards as the category *humanum*. Some further insight into this category will bring to light a twofold view of reality which man envisions through his twofold communication. The movement of distancing "creates a presupposition for the second" movement of entering into relation; for in order to relate with an other, the other has to be set apart from the one who relates.[33] However, the distancing, as such, does not create the source of the relation. On the contrary, this source is in the human potencies not in the distanced world. The latter stands apart from man as an independent existent, as another, with which he may communicate in one or the other of his twofold way. He can set "things which he uses at a distance [in I-It]. . . . In this way the first movement of the principle is satisfied but the second is not" (KnM 66). That is, he "can set at a distance without coming into real relation [I-Thou] with what has been set at a distance. He can fill the act of setting at a distance with the will to relation, relation having been made possible only by that act" (ibid. 64). The world as a whole comes into our view not through distancing, as such, but rather through our entering into relation with it, a relation in which man attains his own completeness "over against" the completeness of the world. In the first movement, then, the world is comprehended as an *ordered world*, as "an aggregate of qualities that can be added to at will," and this is not a real unity. In the second movement it is a *world order,* "a genuine wholeness and unity" (ibid. 63).

These two types of world are not two worlds, but one and the same reality which comes into our purview as differently ordered. Neither is man composed of two distinct entities but is one human being who can act with his being as a whole or in part. In the first case he communicates with reality as a world order, in the second as an ordered world. This means that, in any of his I-Thou relations, be it with fellowman, with beast, or with inanimate things, each living experience bears the characteristic of a world order in its wholeness. To be sure, "the encounters do not order themselves to become a world, but each is for you a sign of the world order" (*I and Thou* 83). This relation is immediate and may be represented in the form of a dyad or subject-subject, expressed through dialogue, more correctly, *is* dialogue. In the ordered world, that is, the world of I-It, we see things in their parts, composed of properties. Events are measured, compared, and explained in terms of cause and effect, arranged and ordered according to some function or purpose. Our connection with them is that of subject-object, mediated through images, concepts, or mathematical formulations, represented in propositional triads. This, in general, is the ordered world of the natural sciences and of all human interactions in "practical," everyday affairs. The distance set between man and things cannot be overcome in this kind of world. However, the world of Thou and the world of It, or the world order and the ordered world, are in continual interchange. Man may tarry in the first only a brief moment, because it is too consuming (*I and Thou* 85); when he steps out of the relation, the Thou becomes an It. Then again, at moments when he returns to relation, the It may be turned by him into a Thou (see above, note 14). The question we are concerned with most is how human destiny is affected by this "swinging between Thou and It." This question has its poignancy in the fact that in going back and forth, the Thou *must* become an It, because of the consuming fire of a prolonged relation, whereas the It *may* be turned back into a Thou, depending on man's own strenuous effort to forego the world of It, though he may stay there as long as he desires, and to seek communication with others through relation again.[34] We must look for an answer to this question in Buber's principles of philosophical anthropology.

Man's Place in the World

From the point of view of philosophical anthropology, man may be confirmed as the category *humanum* only insofar as he directs himself to the world order. Even when the moments of relation cease and the Thou is turned, as it must, into an It, man still remains under the impact of those moments as they serve him as signposts for the construction of his ordered world. However, the question is whether man, abiding in the comforts of the world of It, will heed those signposts or even notice them. For they are lodged in his own being, and whether he will return to relation as often as he ought to, or at all, will depend on what he sees in those signs and how much he is willing to give up the things of It even for a moment. He may well regard the signs as figments of his imagination or, at best, as images of his objects of use, and try to make use of them too. That is, he may hear the call of the Thou as a psychological product of his imagination or just another object of familiar "experience," and not bother to exchange it for a real Thou. As Buber forcefully poses the question, "Why, if one cannot bring himself to say Thou to his father, wife, friend, why not say Thou and mean It?" intending to "experience" and use them. This would be much easier and more reassuring than to risk the uncertainties of the world of Thou. Our philosopher's reply is that those who ask this kind of question see man only as a psychological entity *reacting* to his natural surroundings, and not as the ontological human being that he is, *acting* with his whole being to enter into mutuality with nature. Indeed, Buber says, "Without It man cannot live. But he who lives with that alone is not man."[35]

Overcoming Subjectivism

In the above reply to the psychologists Buber intends to overcome subjectification of the I (as a subject without relation) as well as the objectification of the Thou (as an object of the knowing I). A psychologist may contend that the I-Thou is not an active, ontic word pair, and that the I reacts to an object not as to a real outside Thou, but only calls it Thou. Buber argues that, since the I-Thou relation is between two independent subjects, the one who enters into such a relation cannot be subjectified as an I (of the I-Thou) without a real other (a Thou);

neither can be regard the other as his object (an It), because in that case the other becomes dependent on him and the relation cannot occur (see above, "The Specter of Alienation" section).

While Buber may thus dispose of the problem of objectification of the Thou, he cannot altogether escape the subjectivism or psychologism of the I. The signs of the encounter are in the subject who enters into relation (the other may not even be aware of it) and they may readily be interpreted not as primary ontic acts but as psychic reactions to another's behavior or to a given situation. If subjectivism is to be ruled out, there must be specific signs in man's relational experience which are unmistakably ontological, indicating that they come from one's being as a whole and not in partial reaction. However, such signs cannot appear in their purity in moments of relation with finite beings, not only because there are psychological concomitants on both sides of the encounter, but also because the reflection on the occurrence takes place after it ceases and the Thou is turned into an It. The only relation, therefore, that may show pure ontic signs is one with the Absolute, who cannot be turned into an It. Here God summons man-as-a-whole, not just some of his psychic states or any other part of him, to respond to the call of every one with whom he may come into contact. This summons, Buber maintains, is active in all human encounters with finite beings as well, because the primary word pair I-Thou, when spoken in truth in any relation, addresses itself through that relation also to God. Or, as Buber puts it, "The extended lines of relation intersect in the eternal Thou."[36] In this we may recognize the essence of his science of religious relation.

Nevertheless, the signs of the encounter with the Absolute, too, are found only in man, and he may easily subjectify or objectify them according to his psychological approach. What, then, are these signs and how may they be recognized as a summons from above? This question, among others, will be discussed in the third chapter, below. Here we shall consider further the condition of man insofar as he may enter into relation with the world. What is his destiny with regard to this?

Longing for Completeness

Buber's science of religious relation is in effect a science of man, a subject which has occupied a prominent place in modern philosophy since the days of Hume and Kant. Without going into a comparative study, it may just be mentioned that Buber, like Kant, puts his emphasis on the principle of completeness. However, whereas Kant seeks to establish a complete science of man's knowledge of the world, Buber aims at completeness of man himself. The person, he says, is characterized by what he would "call the longing for complete relation or for completion in the relation. . . . In this the genuineness of the person becomes manifest."[37] To be sure, man is one being, but he is driven by an inner duality to approach the world in two conflicting ways. As said, he is "swinging between Thou and It," and this tears him apart, often leading him to distraction. His destiny, therefore, is to seek an avenue through which he may realize his *humanum,* that is, become a human being-as-a-whole.

Now man can start out on his way to self-fulfillment by exercising his potencies of entering into relation or moving toward nature and fellowman, since this movement, as such, is an act of his being-as-a-whole. But inasmuch as his relation is with finite creatures, even though he himself may act with his whole being, he cannot attain fullness, because their Thou must constantly turn into It. Ontologically speaking, the "other" in each of these encounters is only a relative Thou as it always harbors an It, and one who communicates with such a Thou must continually step out of the relation and communicate with him also as an It. Thus the inner human duality is not completely overcome even in moments of relation. This duality is reflected in man's approach to the world of nature and to fellowman, but not to God, for God, as said earlier, cannot become an It. Therefore, man may find completeness only through his encounter with the absolute Thou. This matter will be dealt with in the third chapter. Our concern now is how man's striving for completeness affects his knowledge of the world as a whole.

Cosmic and Metacosmic

All science deals with experience and Buber's is no exception, only his science differentiates between two kinds of experience, which, as discussed earlier, are called "living experience" or relation and "experience" of use. The first kind yields a knowledge of the world order and the second of an ordered world. But it is the former from which a real knowledge of the world emanates, because real knowledge is attainable only through the living experience of relation. Now every science that relates man to the world as a whole reaches the boundary of human experience without completing itself. The scientist or philosopher may then venture into speculation about what lies beyond that boundary and try to find some connection with it. Buber faces the same problem when he considers man's relation to the world order through living experience. Can man ever have a complete knowledge of it and, if not, how does he know there is such an order as a whole in reality? Obviously, the answer must be in the negative, because human knowledge of the totality of the world terminates at the boundary of experience. And human experience, whether of the first or second kind, is by nature incomplete.

This condition is especially true of the living experience in which, according to Buber's own account, every encounter is unique and never repeats itself. In order to gain a knowledge of the universe as a whole, a philosopher-scientist would have to go beyond experience into metaphysical speculation. Looking at the world, then, from the human side, we find that Buber's cosmos is only surmised to be a world order, inferred from the character of man's living experiences with the various creatures in it; that is, each relational event is only a sign of a world order, which is presupposed by the distancing (see above, "The World Order and an Ordered World" section, note 33). But if man is to seek a complete knowledge of the world order he must enter in relation with it as a totality, for only through his relation as one whole being with another whole being can he possibly know it in reality. This, however, he cannot do, because all his experiences are *in* the world, and he can never place himself as other-than-world "over against" it, which he would have to do if he attempted to enter into relation with it as a whole.

Buber seems to have recognized this gap in his world view, but instead of speculating on the existence of some "world being" lying beyond our experience, he suggests a kind of relation that surpasses our experience of things in the cosmos. Issuing from his principle that real knowledge is obtained through entering into relation, our world as a totality might be known to someone "not-world," through an act of relation similar to our act, perhaps constituting an original duality. Buber calls it a "metacosmic relation," which is enveloped in mystery, beyond our ken. In this respect, he may be justified in his claim that he is "no metaphysician." For he does not build a metaphysical superstructure or metacosmos, but rather rests his case in the cosmos in which we all live. "I have, indeed, no doctrine of a primal ground [*Urgrund*] to offer," he says, but merely a primal relation.[38] Beyond that he does not speculate, but only has this to say:

> In the great privilege of pure relation, the privileges of the world of It are annulled. By virtue of it there is the continuum of the world of Thou: the isolated moments of the relations combine themselves in one conjoint world-life. . . . By virtue of it we are not exposed to an alienation from the world and to an unreal I. . . . To return is to know the center again, to direct-oneself-again. In this essential deed man's subdued power of relation is revived, all the waves of the spheres of relation surge up in living torrents and renew our world. Perhaps not ours only. For we must divine this double movement as metacosmic, a primal form of duality that inheres in the relation between the world as a whole and that which is not world.[39]

The human experience of this duality is expressed in a turning from the ground and back toward it. In the first act the world as a whole is preserved in its *becoming,* and in the second it is returned or redeemed in its *being.* Buber sees it as "the paradox of the primal mystery," of which nothing further can be said.

The Mystery and the Mystics

Since Buber leads us up to an ineffable primal mystery, does he not follow the way of the mystics? We may answer this question prima facie that, as he neither speculates about its nature nor claims any special knowledge of it, he may not be counted among the mystics. However, there may be other grounds on which his entire approach to reality could be judged as mystical. This calls for clarification.

In his student days and early gropings, Buber showed some mystic tendency, but, according to his own testimony, he abandoned it long before he developed his *Denkzusammenhang* (comprehensive thought structure). That stage, he said, he "had to pass through before [he] could enter into an independent relationship with being. One may call it the 'mystical' phase."[40]

Its influence is still felt in the style of some of his writings, but not in the mode of his thinking as manifested in his philosophical output since the publication of his transitional work *Daniel* (1913) and his basic essay *I and Thou* (1923). However, instead of weighing sundry statements of his which may have some mystical connotation, we shall do better if we present an overview of his approach to reality in contrast with the ways of the mystics. We shall then find that neither his method nor his goal is the same as theirs.

To begin with, there is a fundamental difference between Buber and the mystics in their modes of thinking, similar to the difference we have found between the logical and alogical modes. The mystics move in a triad of mediation, whereas Buber thinks in the dyad of immediacy. The former see reality as a unity but man as a duality which he must overcome through identification with the absolute One. Buber, on the contrary, sees reality as dual but man as a unity relating to the Absolute as one independent, exclusive being, though limited, to another independent being, though unlimited. For Buber the mystery is *in the duality* of the finite and the Infinite, not in their *unification* or identity. Both see it as a paradox, but while Buber finds it in the exclusiveness-inclusiveness of the primal relation with the Absolute, the mystics look for it in oneness-and-separation of the Absolute itself. The latter is a logical paradox of oneness of being with not-being; the former is an alogical paradox of duality of being with being.

"For practical purposes," says Alan W. Watts, "mystical religion has always tended to insist that man and the world must be utterly united with God, must in some sense *be* God"; and the freedom man seeks to attain, he further indicates, is the overcoming of man's and the world's duality, "the transcending of dualism, the realization of union with God."[41] Buber does not set such a goal for man, as he does not find in him a duality of body and soul or flesh and spirit that needs to be overcome. Neither does he regard the duality which exists between man and God as a hindrance to their mutuality in relation; on the contrary, it makes this relation possible.

As Buber differs from the mystics on the goal to be attained, so does he differ from them on the way of attaining it; and like their separate goals, their respective ways reflect the difference between the logical and alogical modes of thought. The complementarity of logic and mysticism was first brought to light by

Parmenides, the father of Logic, who separated the way of logos from the way of mythos and posited truth or identity only in the former. As long as the two run parallel, he said, they may be regarded as complementary, even though only the way of logos is salvation and that of mythos is illusion. But, he warned, when naïve persons try to combine the two ways, they run into a double way and thus face grievous error.[42] It is this kind of double way that has led to the paradox of the mystics in all generations. In reference to modern mysticism, Wilhelm Windelband writes: "When knowledge of the true essence of the world and of the final ground of reality is denied to rational thought, then the metaphysical drive finds its license in satisfying itself by all means of irrationality."[43] But, he points out, instead of acknowledging the limits of reason to reach the Absolute, irrationalism finds in these limits the right of paradox. It maintains that the unlimited is certain because limited reason cannot attain it, thus substituting a logic of irrationality for a logic of reason. The mystic confronts the Absolute as an object with which he seeks unity through a mystic experience. Not being able to express such experience either in terms of sense perception or reason, he posits a supersensate and superrational faculty—intuition or extrasensory intellection—as a mediator between himself and his object. This is the familiar logical triad of subject-copula-object, but without a rational ground for the necessary existence of the copula (intuition) either as being or not-being (is or is-not), except to say that it *must be,* because reason fails to provide its own mediator. The paradox consists in giving a rational necessary ground for an irrational cause. To bridge the gap between the human subject and its divine object, the irrational medium assumes a superhuman character but is lodged in man for the explicit purpose of unifying him with God. Having no other human or divine function, its existence, source, and nature remain a mystery.

This is not Buber's way. For him the rational and irrational are both human ways of relating to reality, neither one possessing superior powers over the other, or functioning to the exclusion of the other. All the perceptual and intellectual capacities are included in the immediate relationship, because man may enter into it only with his whole being, that is, with all his potencies of cognition, art, love, and faith, which also function in mediated relationships.[44] Accordingly, man does not strive to fuse some spiritual part of himself, his soul, with a spiritual being outside of himself, the Absolute. On the contrary, he tries to bring all of himself in direct relation with the Absolute. He has no need for a supersensate or superrational medium to know God, as he needs no medium of any kind in meeting Him. For ultimately he cannot know God, only his own relation to Him.

Another difference between Buber and the mystics is with regard to man's limitations. Buber acknowledges man's finitude as an ontic reality of his potencies. Man cannot *be* God in any human sense of the word. "God," says Buber, "is wholly raised above man, . . . he is beyond the grasp of man, and yet . . . he is present in an immediate relationship with these human beings who are absolutely incommensurable with him, and . . . he faces them."[45] "God in heaven" means he is in complete hiddenness, in a "darkness" which man cannot reach, but out of which God reveals Himself. This darkness or hiddenness is the *mysterium* that Buber speaks of, but man, who is wholly a creature, does not possess any mystic powers, whether supersensate or superintellectual, to break through it.

Although the mystics also recognize man's limitations of being and knowing, they attribute them to his sensate and rational functions. In the final analysis, the mystics do not accept man as entirely a creature of God. They search for something in him, which is of a divine essence and has the potential of becoming God. In their view, man may exercise his perceptual and conceptual faculties for a knowledge of physical things but must divest himself of these earthly media so that his supernatural faculty may unite his divine essence with the essence of the Absolute. Since there is an unbridgeable gulf between these two faculties, the mystery lies in man's divine capacity to break through the earthly bounds of his own being and to unite with the absolute Being. Buber's *mysterium,* on the other hand, is not in man but in transcendent reality. It sets a limit to his being and knowing, but sets no bounds between him and God. This is Buber's paradox of the between.

Finally, Buber's *mysterium* differs from that of the mystics in their accounts of how the individual finds his way to God. We need not be concerned here with the theological implications of this problem, only with the distinction between the two views. The main feature of mysticism is its emphasis on the possibility of direct individual experience of unity with God. One who strives for this unity is advised not only to divest himself of all sensory-intellectual awareness but also to isolate himself from his fellowmen and all worldly things. He must face God alone, and when he reaches unity with the One, his individuality fades away into pure Nothingness, into the Godhead or Darkness, or other such designation. In contradistinction to this absorption of man in the Darkness, the "darkness" which Buber speaks of does not absorb man and does not abolish his individuality. Man may meet God in loneliness but not in separation from fellow men or the world; for to meet God at all, one must bring within himself the fullness of his actual relations with others: he stands with this fullness in the meeting over against the Absolute. In sum, Buber's science of religious relation does not operate with mystic intuitions but, on the contrary, his concepts of the between are in keeping with the same concepts of modern science in general.

The Elements of the Between

Signposts in an Open Field

Buber envisions a world order of I-Thou relations as an "open field" in which man is roaming around, looking for signposts of orientation. It is remarkable that he uses signs to designate the between almost identical with those of the natural scientist, only he endows them with different meanings. But insofar as he and the other scientists deal with pure form, their similarity or identity in terminology is not accidental; the terms in a coordinated system of the *ordered world* may be applied, in a translated notation, to the interrelations of the *world order*.

We said earlier that science, whether physical or spiritual, is of the between. Speaking of the physical between, Sir Arthur Eddington notes:

> The primary interval relation is of an undefined nature, and the g's contain this undefinable element. The expression G_{mn} is therefore of defined form, but of undefined *content*. By its form alone it is fitted to account for all the physical properties of matter; and physical investigation can never penetrate beneath the form. . . . We cannot expect the form to explain the activities of the content.[46]

Similarly, when Buber investigates the religious or spiritual between, he seeks its characteristic forms that may account for all spiritual relations of man with reality. He may differ from the physical scientist in operation, but their problem is the same, and that is to establish the permanence of the forms through their recognizable signs. In Buber's terminology the question is: when man goes forth to meet God, fellowman, and nature, what are the signs which identify the between of relation? In terms of natural science the question is: since, according to Buber, each relational moment does not repeat itself and hence cannot be known as a fact (a past experience), in what form does it become manifest so that, upon reflection, it will show that the relation has occurred? What is its locus and what are its earmarks?

This problem is further complicated by the fact that the religious scientist can account for his relational experience only as a being-as-a-whole and cannot detach his person from it in a manner in which the natural scientist can. He cannot do it even in the manner of the psychologist who may analyze his own mental reaction to an outside stimulus, because such analysis requires both a description of the stimulating object and of the reacting subject. In the dialogical relation the description is only of the subject who enters into it, but not of the other who influences it. Therefore, the religious scientist, reflecting on his act of meeting, can describe only what took place in *himself* and not really *between* him and the other. As Buber emphasizes, "The man who feels himself alone is the most readily inclined and most suited for the self-reflection of which I am speaking; he is the man . . . who succeeds . . . in discovering man in his own self."[47] This then is the paradox of the relational occurrence: one who has been involved in a spiritual between may find its signs only in himself. If he interprets them as his own mental states, he falls into the trap of subjectivism, and if he sees them as issuing from the other, he runs the risk of converting the other into an It, thus failing to grasp the relation. Against these two possibilities Buber posits a third one, namely, an ontological explanation of the signs of the between as coming into existence through the very act of entering-into-relation. Once they are recognized as such, they cannot be mistaken either as subjective or objective but must be relational, that is, of the between.

The Spheres of Movement

The identity in terminology used by Buber and the physicists in describing the elements of the between stems from the fact that both deal with movement, except that the physicists deal only with physical locomotion, whereas Buber recognizes a twofold movement, one physical and the other spiritual. A further distinction is in the locus of power that generates the movement. The modern physicist, under the influence of relativity, eliminates force and locates all properties of motion in a field, such as the gravitational or electromagnetic field. Whatever the final cause of such a field may be, it lies outside of it, metaphysically or metamathematically. Buber, on the other hand, locates both movements in man, who is ontologically the kind of being that moves toward and away from. This sets up a duality of physical and spiritual ways of motion (communication), but not a duality of man's being. Man is not composed of mind and body. He is neither mind nor body, but wholly man, who may find himself in both a spiritual and a bodily sphere of communication, according to one or the other aspect of his twofold movement. Hence the same elements of the between may be found in both spheres, but each bestows on them a different quality or meaning and thus a different aspect of the world. One is a movement in a *world order* of immediate relation, and the other in an *ordered world* of mediated connection. Both are accounted for by the same between, but the first is the spiritual sphere of entering-into-relation and the second the physical sphere of distancing. A brief examination of the major elements of this kind of between will reveal that in form they may pass from one sphere to the other only in a continuum of spiritual relation. That is, in contrast to the natural sciences, the continuum is here not physical (space-time) but spiritual (dialogical).

The Continuum

The problem of natural science to establish a universal continuum that will account for discontinuity of movement has not been resolved by modern physicists, and, despite their concerted efforts, it appears to be insoluble on the level of physical theory.[48] Buber views the continuum as a dynamic movement toward the Absolute. It is neither *in* space and time nor *of* space-time, but has a metacosmic quality in which "the isolated moments of relation combine themselves in one conjoint world-life." And while he speaks here, in the manner of the physicists, of a crossing of world lines, these lines are not of distance but relation, that is, not separation, but combination.[49]

The closed field in which the physicist measures his distances through tensor analysis is the same universe which, according to Buber, man establishes through his movement of distancing himself from the primal ground. In both cases, in order to build a world structure, man has to remove himself from the observed conglomerate of things and set up a system of coordinates for their unification. This is the kind of world all scientists deal with, whether in physics, biology, psychology, or politics. But it is also the same world with which man may enter into relation, except that in such a moment its continuum is not held together by *coordinates* but through spiritual *correlates*. Even when relation ceases and the distancing brings the physical universe in view, the spiritual continuum is not abrogated but only suspended until man decides to return and again take his stand in relation. Man-as-a-whole is never entirely out of either movement, the physical or spiritual, but is continually in both, oscillating back and forth without having to cross boundaries beyond physical reality. That is, man does not live in a metaphysical continuum but in this world here and now where he takes his physical experience into his living act of relation, and where his spontaneous experience permeates his everyday life. To be sure, both spheres are circumscribed by human limitations, but the limits too must be experienced and cannot be set in advance. Neither sphere forms a boundary to the other; each combines the finite and the infinite without insurmountable barriers or unbridgeable gaps.

Inertia and Direction

Two other concepts which Buber has adopted from physical science are inertia and direction. In Newton's physics, inertia reigns as a natural innate force in every material object, a *vis inertiae,* which gives direction in a straight line, resisting an outside gravitational pull. In Einstein's general theory of relativity inertia loses its independent status as a force, inasmuch as it is made equivalent to a gravitational field which becomes the "guiding influence" of motion.[50] Buber's concept of inertia is akin to Einstein's in that it is not an inner force and does not direct movement. But whereas Einstein eliminates it as a separate factor, Buber retains it as a privative state of the act of relation, as the condition in which man does not respond to the call of an other and refuses to enter into relation with him. Thus, one who enters into relation is in a state of direction; one who refuses to enter, or simply does not respond, is in a state of inertia or nondirection. Like the gravitational field in physical motion, the relational act "influences" man's movement toward an other. Though this movement is bipolar—man responding to the call of the other—the power which gives direction comes as a free act of decision on the part of the one who responds. But the response must be with one's whole being; if one responds partially only with his intellect, sense faculties, passions, or technological devices, his movement is splintered and to that extent directionless.

Potency and Potential

Man's decision to respond comes as an act of faith which is a human potency, similar to a physical potential. As a power directing motion, it must have a locus of operation. The human potency operates in man's spontaneous experience expressed in correlative terms. The physical potential operates in observed data measurable by a system of coordinates. While both are realizable in a between, the physical potential cannot be traced outside the between, not even to matter from which it presumably issues, because it and matter are measured by the same interval.[51] The spiritual potency, although acted out in a between, has its source in man who creates the between but is not measured by it. Furthermore, the path of the particle in the physical interval is determined by the space-time configuration or geodesic that fills the interval's continuum. But the path of the spiritual relation, though it can lead only to God, does not follow its course through an inner necessity but out of man's free choice, out of his being human. Any other determining factor, Buber says, would have to be posited metaphysically within a closed system of categories, leaving out the category *humanum*. In answer to the question of how man may know himself as *humanum*, Buber presents a philosophical anthropology which maintains that the very *ontic act* of entering-into-relation is the *humanum*, for no other being can act that way. This distinguishes Buber's humanistic view from the natural scientist's outlook: he places ontology before epistemology.[52]

Return in an Open or Closed Field

The contrast between Buber's open field and the physicist's closed system is most pronounced in their different application of the concept "return." In the physical universe, whether constructed according to Einstein, de Sitter, or Lemaître, a body having run its course in time and reaching the outer bounds of the space-time continuum must of necessity either return to its place of origin or run into nonexistence.[53] In any of these world structures the return or nonreturn, as the case may be, is of a temporal character. In Einstein's Cylindrical Universe a ray of light returns to its temporal starting point, so that the past becomes the future. In the other structures, time stops or vanishes when the expansion has reached its limiting value, so that there is no return. The *fatum* of time, as the ancient Greeks and Hindus conceived it, is here the deciding factor, and its saving grace is the cycle of rebirth of the past into a new future or, according to Buddha, the abolishment of time altogether.

Buber considers return as a renewal of the act of relation but not in time, that is, not reverting to a past or starting point of sinless spirituality. For he does not regard man as a spiritual entity, but rather as a human being who can always return to the spiritual sphere of the between which comes into existence at each moment of his entering-into-relation. Man is not in a cycle of rebirths, but in a continuous between which must be renewed constantly as he oscillates from distancing to relation. With each return he also renews the world of things. "The spirit can penetrate and transform the world of It. . . . To return is to know the center again, to direct-oneself-again."[54] There is no discontinuity in man's world orientation even when he steps out of one moment of relation only to enter into another moment again and again. As a wayfarer, he moves through his ontic act of *humanum* on his way to God. He often loses direction and gets off the path; he then has to decide to get back, not where he started, but where he was sidetracked, and go on. When he gets off, he has no direction and his way fades out of his sight; when he gets on again, his way is renewed and continues.

In the language of modern science, we may say that Buber "translates" a closed system of a field of coordinates into an open field of correlates. He does not exclude or negate the physical world. On the contrary, as said, the spiritual between permeates the physical through the very act which brings man constantly in direction toward God. This is Buber's meaning of the world being redeemed by man: "The occurrence which on the part of the world is called return, is on the part of God called redemption.[55]

Unification: Space, Time, and Causality

Whether man lives in a closed system of the ordered world or in an open field of the world order, his ultimate goal is the unification of his experience and knowledge of this world. In the natural sciences, his goal is to unify all elements of observation under an all-embracing theory of explanation. In the science of religious knowledge it is to attain a unified self so that he may enter into complete relation of the highest order. In the first, the unification constitutes a systematic totality; in the second, it is the bringing together of all partial relations as well as separations into one's being as a whole, culminating in the relation with the Absolute. This unification, however, is not a fusion of elements within the ordered world, or of the self with the world order or the Absolute. Rather, it is what the naturalists call a "Unity of Science,"[56] and what Buber calls exclusiveness-inclusiveness of complete relation. In Albert Einstein's words, "Science is the attempt to make the chaotic diversity of our sense-experience correspond to a logically uniform system of thought."[57] In Buber's mode of thinking, "the chaotic diversity" of *all* our experiences is to be brought into the wholeness of relation with God. In a similar vein, Moritz Schlick, speaking of the organic unity of life, says, "Scientists and philosophers thus have good reason to trust that nature does not consist of two realms separated by an unbridgeable gulf but that it is rather one and the same causality which pervades all its parts."[58] Buber would agree that nature is not split into two unbridgeable realms, but he would say, not "the same causality" but the same noncausal world order pervades all parts of man's life with nature and fellowman even in the ordered world.[59]

According to Buber, space, time, and causality in the world order do not have the same functions that are assigned to them in the ordered world of the natural sciences. In the world order, too, the Thou may be said to be in space, but it signifies the exclusiveness of a being standing out against its enveloping background and confronting another exclusive being; there is no unbridgeable separation between them, such as occurs through spacing (discontinuous cuts) in physical science. Similarly, "the Thou in time" means a self-fulfilled occurrence in a moment of relation, and not a discrete succession of time points. Finally, causality for the Thou signifies an immediate acting and being acted upon in mutuality but not through a chain of causal mediation.[60] In the world of empirical science, then, unification is the impersonal goal of cognitive thought, whereas in the science of religious knowledge it is the goal of man-as-a-whole in every one of his potencies, in cognition, art, love, and faith.

Success and Failure

"Religion," says Buber, "means goal and way. . . . Even in the highest experiences, the religious goal remains only that which gives direction to the mortal way; it never enters into historical consummation."[61] The signs that appear on the way to the goal cannot be recognized in temporal successes, because they cannot be recorded in history books; they can only be lived in spontaneous experiences. The goal is always before us, but the way never ends. As we step back into the world of It, the moments of our encounter with the Absolute assume various forms, such as images, concepts, or ideas. But if we turn these forms into objects of use for temporary ends we corrupt the religious character of their primary effect. Therefore, failure rather than success in using these signs shows us the way to our goal. As Buber states:

> The real way from Creation to the Kingdom is trod not on the surface of success, but on the deep of failure. . . . The way leads through the work which history does not write down . . . [yet leads] toward the final, messianic overcoming of history . . .—history consummated in the whole of reality.[62]

As will be brought out below ("Prophecy" section), it means that the way is to be trod not by individuals alone or by small groups in pursuit of their private ends, but by communities, and ultimately by the community of all nations, which *is* the goal of God's kingdom on earth.

This messianic view of history need not detain us for the present, as our interest here is only to draw a parallel between its concept of success and failure and a similar concept found among natural scientists. The latter, too, envision a "kingdom," though not of God, but of man, which will be attained not through the temporary ends which one scientist or another may set for himself, but through the community of scientists working in concert toward the highest goal—the unraveling of the laws of nature as a whole. In this way, one scientist's failure may lead more readily to the goal than another's success. In the words of Henry Margenau,

> Science is more than a record of results which can be stated with precision; indeed facts can be so fully certain as to be trivial and uninteresting to science, as most facts are. Perhaps the greatest thrill for a scientist comes not when he has demonstrated a conjecture to be valid [success] but when a departure from expectations convinces him that an accepted theory is wrong [failure].

While science, he points out, cannot ignore its purpose of making its findings at every step certain, this is not the final goal of scientific activity.

> A scientific problem is never done. There is a region below every problem which is illuminated and exposed to view by its very solution, and in this region new problems are always found. . . . [Science is not] a predictable and final process. . . . Natural science will go on forever.[63]

This vision of a natural scientist, like Buber's vision of the science of religious knowledge, extends to the kind of experience man encounters in the depth of real existence.

Faith and Uncertainty

What part does faith play in Buber's science of religious relation? This question may be raised by the skeptic who contends that the "hidden one" who is revealed in the meeting is only a psychological projection of the knowing subject. Since the subject can know only his part of the way, what assurance does he have that the Absolute has come the other part to be present in the meeting? Actually, the skeptic is asking two questions: (1) Does the Absolute exist independently of the knowing subject? (2) Assuming that he does, is he really that "other" whom man encounters in the relation? In answer to the first question, Buber holds that the existence of God cannot be proved or disproved and cannot be posited even as an object of belief, because in all these instances God is turned into a thing, and It, and ceases to be the absolute Thou, or is not God. Concomitantly, God's presence in the meeting, too, cannot become a matter of proof or an object of belief. At the same time Buber maintains that man's relation with the Absolute emerges as an act of faith. When man decides for direction (toward God) he exercises the potency of faith which establishes a mutual relationship between him and God. This between *is* the sphere of faith, not in the sense of a preexistent mediator, but as a relation which comes into existence with each decision for direction. Faith, Buber emphasizes, is not a belief that something exists (for this one may demand proof), but rather a trust in God, whose existence is not put in question and who is present whenever man exercises this potency and enters into mutual relation with Him. In other words, "the fundamental experience of faith itself ought to be regarded as the highest degree of the reality of the meeting."[64]

But the potency of faith which enables man to relate to the divine is in man himself. When he exercises any of the other three potencies—cognition, art, love—he establishes a between with an actual other who may also (rather must) be turned into an It, that is objectified in cognition, love, and art on the perceptual-conceptual level. This not being the case in the relation with God (who cannot be turned into an It), the potency of faith may readily be interpreted as a psychological capacity to establish a mutuality of man with his own self rather than with the Absolute. Yet Buber speaks of the "certainty" of man's relation with God and fends off all psychological interpretations of it.[65] Now, in order to be certain in any sense of the word, there must be a permanence or constancy in the process of exercising the potency, and since faith is exercised in encounters which cease momentarily, one cannot be certain that the encounter is really with an other than the self. Again, Buber's reply rests in his philosophical anthropology that man is the kind of being who strives to enter into relation with others; and the certainty of his entering into relation with God, though indeterminate, is authenticated by the constancy of his decision to direct himself toward Him.

Principle of Uncertainty

Such a view in the science of religious relation is not inconsistent with the "principle of uncertainty" or indeterminacy in the science of modern physics. According to this principle, the actual presence of a given state in an atomic process cannot be determined with certainty both as to place and momentum simultaneously. Yet the physicist who calculates the mathematical matrix of the state is certain of its presence in the physical process in time and place. In a sense, such a matrix is a spiritualization of the between in the atomic encounter of particles, as faith is the spiritual between in the religious encounter. Both have two basic ideas in common: (1) that in the world of reality each event is unique, and (2) that this event is not subject to measurement, for the act of measuring breaks off its real occurrence.

Thus, for example, the state of a moving particle in quantum mechanics cannot be measured as to its position and momentum together, because the measuring instrument destroys the system to be measured (through their interaction). Hence, while the physicist may set up the exact conditions (his part of the way) for a particle to move in a certain direction, he cannot know whether the particle is there in a given momentum (the particle's part of the way), but he has "faith" in its "being there" because he is certain of his theoretical calculations of the event each time it is renewed (but not repeated). In physical science as well as in religion, faith and certainty complement each other; in both fields certainty lies in the constancy of renewal.[66]

Faith, the Highest Potency

When we gather all the lines of communication of Buber's science of religious relation, we see them converging on the potency of faith, so that this potency becomes the pivotal signpost of his open field, no matter how far it may extend. And since "all extended lines of relation intersect in the eternal Thou," man can approach God only through faith. This being the highest degree of meeting, faith must be the highest potency as compared with the other three (cognition, art, love); actually, it embraces them all in the consummation of the encounter with the Divine. What guidance does our philosopher offer to one who ventures out to this encounter? When Buber took stock of his philosophical writings on the occasion of the publication of his collected works, he explained that all he had tried to do was to transmit his personal "I-Thou experiences" and insights "which presented themselves in growing measure as *one* great experience of faith." In presenting it in philosophical form, he said, one "must not sacrifice anything of that reality to consistency," that is, it would not "become a system." Nevertheless, he hoped it would result in "a self-contained communicable thought compound *(transmittierbarer Denkzusammenhang)*."[67] Therefore, when he spoke, on other occasions, of having no theory but pointing to reality, or "pointing the way," we must assume that his "pointings" are identifiable signposts in his transmitted thought compound. If we follow him on his way without being able to identify those signs, we shall lapse into psychologism and inevitable skepticism. But here again, we must fall back on his philosophical anthropology.

Buber observes that

> in the course of becoming human, there appear two intimately interconnected constituents of the human person, difficult to grasp in their origin: an insufficiency in being confined to the useful [in the world of It], and a desire for complete relation [in the world of Thou].[68]

He elaborates on these factors with reference to the potencies of cognition, art, and love, but when he comes to faith, which by his own standard "is the highest potency, embracing and enveloping all the others," he says he "can only indicate the connection," suggesting that it "is discernible to everyone who has had to enter into its domain."[69] Ultimately, then, each man must look for this highest potency in his being in the very manner he goes forth to meet fellowman, nature, and God.

> Real faith—. . . it is not a *what* at all, . . . it is not an experience which can be recalled independently of its situation, it always remains the address of that moment and cannot be isolated, it remains an inquirer's inquiry demanding an answer.[70]

Furthermore, faith is not a mere feeling but the very act of entering-into-relation with reality without reduction or curtailment.[71] It is trust in God who exists and is always present when man is in readiness for the Presence. "To believe is to vow," to bind oneself to something. This entails a risk, but is overcome by man through the constant renewal of his faith as he proceeds on the way. The certainty of faith is in the stream of never repeated occurrences, in which lived life is probed and fulfilled; the certainty of knowledge spans across that stream.

Reality of Freedom

Man's freedom, says Buber, is found in the relation in which he shapes his world in partnership with God. Freedom is neither *in* the world nor *outside* of it, but *between* the world and man, a between which he has helped create through his primary encounter with God. In this encounter, man does not overcome sense perception or any of his other faculties associated with bodily behavior. When he goes forth to the meeting with God, he is fully man with all his potencies—perceptual-conceptual, loving, artistic, and believing—and they are all included in the exclusiveness of the relation. This is man's destiny: to act as a being-as-a-whole, and insofar as he decides to act according to his destiny he is free. This is not to be confused with "fate." The latter is conceived as a force outside of man, controlling and propelling him along paths without direction and without hope of self-fulfillment. He is not a partner to it. Destiny, on the other hand, is in man, in his potencies to realize his *humanum*. His self-realization, as such, is freedom inasmuch as he establishes a state of relation between himself and others; for there is no greater freedom than in meeting an other openly, fully, without holding oneself back. The between thus created is freedom, or freedom is in the between. It is not a power man may possess and use to ward off oppression. Rather, it is a flowing action of self-fulfillment through others. To confirm the other and be confirmed by him in mutuality is real liberation, and "only one who establishes freedom in reality, meets destiny."[72]

Man's decision to respond to an other is not a potency like cognition or faith, but comes through these potencies when one has a knowledge of human destiny. One decides for relation if he knows what it is and believes that he can fulfill himself through it. "Only one who is cognizant of relation and is aware of the presence of the Thou, is capable of deciding," thus realizing his freedom in the affairs of everyday life on earth.[73] This, in the final analysis, is the goal of Buber's science of religious relation. Since the dawn of our modern age, the natural scientists have set for themselves the same goal, but have not as yet found its proper direction. Buber, then, undertook to point the way to it in the light of his insights into human destiny.

2
A Technology of Restructuring Society

The Social Issue of Modern Times

The Legacy of the Age of Enlightenment

One of the moments of tension in Buber's thought, as indicated earlier, is the way he relates the individual to society and tries to reconcile their conflicting roles. The issue centers on man's freedom in a social setting which constantly militates against him—a problem which has been growing with increased intensity since the days of eighteenth-century Enlightenment. Buber traces it back to the French Revolution and its policy of social centralism. That, in his opinion, was the beginning of the atomization of society into individuals, with no organic interconnection, held together only by the power of the state. This trend has since undergone many changes, but its basic orientation still prevails.

The Logic of Individuality

"If one wants to understand the direction which social science assumed in the seventeenth and eighteenth centuries," writes Ernst Cassirer, "and if one wants to clarify fully the new methodology which was developed in connection with it, one must relate it directly to the contemporary development of logic."[74] Logical analysis, the new method, reduces everything to its ground or constituent parts; but then it also uses logic as an instrument to construct those parts into a totality. An incongruity sets in when the parts assume an independent existence and refuse to subordinate themselves to the whole. The part, we might say, makes an existential claim against the whole when it

64

is being pressed into it. Such is the paradox of logical individuality: when individuals are reduced to independent entities, freed from social subordination, how can they be united into a social structure without being subordinated to it, that is, without losing their independence? The new method aimed at discovering natural laws in the individual and in his social structure which would account for both on one and the same ground. But this did not obviate the logical paradox of individual freedom. Logically the two are irreconcilable. The scale was then tilted on the side of the individual as he was made the beginning and end of the social order.

The Individual Absolutized

The logic of individuality, which we have inherited from the Age of Enlightenment, has dominated our mode of thinking to this day. The individual, as bearer of thought and as the prime element of society, has now come to claim absolute freedom in both areas, in one under the principle of academic freedom, and in the other under the concept of the rights of man. The philosopher-scientist of today regards it his absolute right to be free not only in his thinking but also in his giving of himself to others as he may determine of his own accord. The method of logical analysis and research, which started as a means to an end, has now become an end in itself. Research, as such, is looked upon as a contribution toward man's salvation. At the same time, specialization has removed the researcher from contact with fellowman, even with fellow academicians in different fields.[75] Kant's dream of ending the conflict among the faculties by evolving one philosophy governed by principles of practical reason and the moral ought has been shattered on the rock of today's "scholarly individualism."[76] Even those who labor to establish a "universal science" do not hold out any real hope for universal communication among scientists, much less between them and the public at large.

When the rights of man were first proclaimed in the Enlightenment period, man was conceived in terms of a specific human quality, either rational or natural, or a combination of both. Subsequently, many such qualities were singled out by political scientists, psychologists, economists, sociologists, and others, each according to his scientific specialty. Each of them sought to ascertain a basic property in man on which he could build a social order that would guarantee the free development and functioning of that property. However, with the advancement of scientific-technological methods in social research, qualitative analysis has been converted into quantitative computation. Man is no longer thought of as a rational animal, a productive human force, or a set of social drives, not even as a fixed biological or physiological entity; he is seen as "just man"—an absolute individual element of a social state, defined by its judicial system. This abstract man-in-general now claims to be the legitimate heir to the "rights of man" proclaimed in the past by all the prophets of individual freedom.

The scientific revolution, which began at the dawn of the Age of Enlightenment, has now reached a stage in which the struggle between individuals is not so much for social and economic position as for gains in science and technology, regardless of the position one may occupy on the socioeconomic ladder. This has given the old slogans of "the rights of man" and "equal rights" an entirely different meaning and a new promise. The modern philosopher-scientist has promoted the idea that man is an *instrument* able to produce other instruments of unprecedented capacity to change nature and himself at will; and the modern technologist, disregarding human qualities and limitations, has put forth the promise that absolute freedom is attainable through an accelerated proliferation of instruments. Freedom now means to be free from all human limitations and natural obstacles. We are thus witnessing a new ideology of man and his social order. Like previous ideologies of this age, it views man not as a human being-as-a-whole, but as a certain function of a given totality. However, while in the past he functioned as a rational element, a psychic urge, or a productive force, his function now is that of pure instrumentality. The "rights of man" which the modern revolutionist or reformer, as the case may be, demands is no longer that of a rational being to think freely, or of a producer to work for himself in freedom, but of an instrument to exercise its functions without restraint. "Equal rights" has come to mean the right of every individual to be *equally unlimited,* to be entitled to the same unrestrained powers as any other man-in-general may have. The goal of the absolutized individual is no longer the wisdom of right living—the wisdom of man as an end in himself, but the breaking of all bounds for the conquest of nature through the ever growing power of technological tools. This is modern man's confrontation with social technology. In the following pages we shall consider Buber's analysis of this problem and its resolution under his concepts of "the restructuring of society" and "moral responsibility."

The Restructuring of Society into a State of Acracy

The Communal Cell

Modern man, as we have seen, strives toward individual self-absolutization. How can a social order be structured or restructured out of such individuals? This is the basic problem which Buber poses before us today. His critical comments on Aldous Huxley's experiment with mescaline, for example, may well offer a good vantage point from which to start our examination of his critique of the technological approach to man as an individual, and of his view on restructuring society out of communal cells. He considers Huxley's experiment with the drug as a demonstration of the kind of individualism which has "the tendency to reach a higher side of existence, indeed 'real' existence, through abandoning communality."[77] The taker of mescaline, he notes, may free himself for a moment from "repugnant surroundings" by seeing their objects transformed into pure being, but he leaves behind his fellowmen who also belong to those surroundings, yet are not transformed along with their objects. The taker avoids the men around him because, like his everyday environment, they become repugnant; he and they have nothing in common.[78] At best, this is a transformation of an individual without a change in the social order or in other individuals. To be sure, Buber holds that both man and his social structure need a transformation, but that will be accomplished neither by science nor by technology but by man himself in actual relation with his fellowmen. An absolutized individual is an abstraction without real content and cannot, therefore, become a constituent element of real society. Nor can a social structure be maintained without the human social ingredient as its social content. Buber calls such a society unstructured or poorly structured.

In a well-structured society the cell tissue is not the detached individual but "far-reaching autonomous togetherness [*Miteinander*] of human beings, forming and transforming itself from within.''[79] The cells have communal content, to begin with, in the form of communes, building themselves up from below into larger associations until they constitute themselves into a large community. Buber differentiates this communal aspect of society from the collective. The latter may be formed to serve a particular temporary or even long-range purpose, such as a labor union, a political party, or a business association. In the social cell, which is the embryonic community, each man is a free person insofar as he participates in the formation of his society—a freedom which all participants confer on each other through their mutual response and responsibility. This act of society building is not a one-time occurrence but an ongoing process of interhuman relations. The social units that are formed by the communal cells must be comparatively small so that the immediacy of personal communication may prevail.[80] Without losing their identity, the small units form themselves into associations of larger entities, such as towns, peoples, nations, all constituting an organic community.[81]

Factors in the Crisis

Throughout history, Buber maintains, genuine human society occurred on the "basis of functional autonomy, mutual recognition, and mutual responsibility, whether of the individual or the group."[82] There were centers of power in these societies for common order and security and, despite inner conflicts, every man felt at home in the clan in which his independence and responsibility were confirmed. In modern times, many factors have contributed to the breakdown of the social order, but in its broadest sense the problem may be viewed as a technical one. It reached a critical stage when the technical instruments which man fashioned for the promotion of well-being began to threaten the existence of his social structure.[83] Buber describes it as "man's lagging behind his works," unable to control "the Golem he has created and to cast it out and make it harmless."[84]

Among the forces determining modern society Buber lists the machine, economic overproduction, and surpassing political power, but he views them mainly as a conflict between what he calls the "political principle" and the "social principle," which he proposes to resolve through a restructuring of the social order.

Religious Socialism

In general, technology has to do with means designed to attain certain ends, and if Buber speaks of restructuring society, he must show by what means this may be done, that is, he has to devise a technology that will lead to the desired end. In the restructured society, he says, interhuman communication must open up so that man may reach fellowman directly, without holding himself back. When the question is raised, "What is one to do?," Buber advises that "one alone," taken as an isolated individual, can do nothing. But, he says, if the question is "What have I to do?" meaning I, who together with my fellowmen can recreate the social order, the answer is "You shall not withhold yourself. . . . Establish directness, formed out of meaning, respectful, modest directness between men!"[85] His advice may be well taken, but this is a time of crisis when strong forces militate against the kind of human relations that he urges. By what means does he propose to overcome those forces? The technological tools of the mechanical and electrical machines as well as those devised by the behavioral engineers only add to man's discomfiture and heighten his crisis. According to Buber, they have turned man himself into a tool for the establishment of a preconceived social order, a perfect predetermined system, rather than making him a part of a living social structure. What "human tool" can man possibly devise that will counteract the machine? For Buber does not advocate a turning back to the pretechnical age of civilization, but to bring technology under human control.[86] Therefore, the technological issue, as he sees it, is not how to abolish the growing technical instruments which affect interhuman relations adversely, but how to derive from these relations such instruments as may help us restructure our society and keep it going that way. To do that, Buber rightly says, we must "know *where* we want to go," and the goal he projects is on the road of what he calls "religious socialism."[87]

In the opening statement of his "three theses" on this subject, Buber emphasizes:

> Religious socialism cannot mean a combination of religion and socialism in such a form that each of the constituents could achieve, independently of the other, its autonomous life, if not its fulfillment. . . . Religious socialism can only mean that religion and socialism essentially point to each other, that each of the two needs a covenant with the other for the fulfillment and completion of its own essence.[88]

This is in keeping with his principle of communality as the formative element of true society. His first thesis, then, is that *religio* or a person's self-binding to God can be realized only through a community of men "communicating" with each other in a circle whose radii converge toward the center of the Absolute or God, and that *socialitas,* or the formation of human fellowship, can come about only through a common relation of all men to that divine center. In the two together man has a living experience of divine revelation, as it expresses itself in true society.[89]

The second thesis is that both the religious and the socialist forms are real only to the extent that man is committed to their realization here and now, not in the beyond or in the distant future. The third thesis is that religion and socialism may meet together only in the concreteness of personal life, and not in dogmas and rituals, in ideologies or doctrines. When Buber speaks of a religious socialism "here and now," he does not mean that there is no social ideal or goal to be attained. Indeed, he recognizes that such a goal has been visualized in various utopias and religious eschatologies through the ages. What he means is that the goal or end to be attained must be present in some measure at each stage on the way toward its attainment. The *means* realize the *end.* When the means used or proposed are contrary to their purpose or end, they can never lead to it, "for never does the end hallow the means, but the means may well disgrace the end."[90] If, then, the essence of religious socialism is true fellowship between men in every walk of life and in every phase of economic, social, and cultural activity, such fellowship must manifest itself in the daily lives of those who propose to promote this kind of society. This signifies that true fellowship must prevail in the very structure of society, here and now, even while the existing order is being restructured.

We might ask now, if man has the ontic potency of entering-into-relation with his fellowmen so that he can create real communal living, what stands in his way of realizing it and why does he find himself in crisis? To put it in terms of Buber's social structure, the question is, what has impoverished the present structure, what exactly needs to be restructured, and what means may be appropriate to this purpose? It should be pointed out that the restructuring of existing conditions and not the ultimate end of a perfect society is the goal of religious socialism. According to Buber's orientation, our salvation lies not in the consummation of the end but rather in our direction toward it. While we cannot turn back to our beginnings or to any prescientific and pretechnological age in our civilization, we can and must return to the only way we are destined to follow, not by setting up a plan, a doctrine or system of a "new" society, but by "renewing" the organic social drive inherent in us qua human beings.[91] But with all that, Buber's immediate purpose is to overcome the social crisis, and to that end there must be certain means contrived by man himself, even under the conditions of his poorly structured society. There must be a social technology, such that will counteract the kind of technology which has contributed to the crisis.

The Social and Political Principles

Buber regards the individualistic trend, which has dominated the modern world since the Age of Enlightenment and especially since the French Revolution, as the chief contributing factor in the process of emptying the social structure of its "communal content." His criticism of Rousseau, as the leading spirit of that age, is that he conceived the relationship between the people and the state in terms of individuals and not of small societies which are constituted independently of the state's planning and design. According to Rousseau, Buber says, the state cannot tolerate the kind of society which is made up of a variety of small and large associations. The right to free association was abolished by the French Revolution, because it considered it contrary to the absolute freedom of the state.[92]

With the growth of modern industrial capitalism, society became atomized into a conglomerate of individuals, who have as little responsibility for each other as one atom has for another. Thus "the State was prepared to tolerate only a pulverized, structureless society," in which man finds himself in solitude, homeless, seeing only his own self, but shuddering at his alienation.[93] To save himself from his loneliness, modern man has construed moral ideologies and life systems which glorify the individual but which are far removed from reality. "Modern individualism," Buber concludes, "has essentially an imaginary basis. This is its failing character, for imagination is insufficient for the actual mastery of the given situation."[94] Yet he believes that, despite all efforts to revive it, the age of individualism is now over. Even its idealized form as visualized by Kant lies in ruins. However, the social structure which has taken its place is not the kind that grows out of personal human relations, but rather a collectivism which has intensified the human crisis even more than individualism did. "Individualism sees man only in relationship to himself, but collectivism does not see *man* at all; it sees only 'society.' "[95] The collectivist spirit pervades all walks of life: in trade unions, political parties, professional and business associations as well as in academic institutions. In all of them man is departmentalized into useful elements serving the "group," the institution, or as it is called now, the establishment. "This applies not only to the totalitarian states, but also to the parties and party-like groups in the so-called democracies."[96]

What changes does Buber anticipate in the social structure that will meet the present crisis, and what forces will institute those changes? He recognizes two spheres in the social organism, which he designates as the social sphere and the political sphere, or the "social principle" and the "political principle." These are not to be identified with Society and State, respectively, for both the social forms and the state institutions are crystallizations of these principles.[97] The spheres differ in the way each forms its structural unity out of a multiplicity, or the whole out of its individual elements. In the social sphere, the primal relation of I-Thou governs the organic society, rendering man a free, independent member of that society. In the political sphere, the individuals are subordinated to the common purpose for which they are organized through a preconceived plan. Thus, under the social principle, the structure is formed and sustained by the free, spontaneous, primal act of entering-into-relation, which emanates from all those who constitute the social unity. Under the political principle, the structure is constituted and maintained by a force which issues from the established order and is imposed upon its individual members, even if it is contrary to their primal relation.

Considering human nature for what it is, Buber does not deny the need of the political principle in governing society for the protection of all its members against internal conflict, not to speak of outside danger. His concern is the extent to which this principle is used in each situation so that it does not become the dominant rule, overwhelming or coming close to annihilating the social principle. Where this occurs, society as such, that is, a free association of human beings, cannot survive. The dominance of the political over the social principle, Buber finds, is most pronounced in all forms of state dictatorships, of the "right" as well as of the "left," but it has also made itself felt increasingly in the democratic societies, and has reached a point of endangering their survival.

Evils of Mistrust and the Practice of Power

Buber does not regard the political principle an evil, except when it is misconstrued as a goal, that is, when the means, though contrary to the goal, is represented as reality and the goal is lost sight of. The political principle then harbors two main evils, one in the concept and practice of *power,* and the other in playing upon the feeling of *mistrust.* The second presents the greater danger, because in our day it has assumed an existential character. When persons or nations are regarded as functions of psychological or sociological drives beyond their own knowledge and control, their intentions are judged not by their deeds, but by their drives. Anyone who considers the drives hostile will not trust the intentions. This kind of mistrust is not of a man who intentionally tries to deceive for personal gain. With such a person one can negotiate in an attempt to show him the disadvantage of the deception to himself and come to a mutual trusting relationship. The mistrust which Buber designates as existential is of a person who is regarded as being compelled to deceive because he is the mouthpiece of a false ideology that renders him incapable of being forthright. Such, for example, is the mistrust between a communist and a capitalist, each considering the other as the spokesman of a perverse social system. Here there is no possibility of genuine dialogue: neither side listens to the other speaking, and neither side responds, as a person. And without dialogue there can be no communality, which is the basic act of the social principle. Then the political principle takes hold and forces the individuals, for their self-protection, to submit to the power of an organized body, such as a political party or state. With the growth of mistrust, individuals lose trust in themselves and in human existence altogether. This, says Buber, is the cause of modern man's social disease, which has become imbedded in contemporary culture through certain psychological and sociological theories, notably those of Sigmund Freud and Karl Marx, who gave it a rational foundation.[98]

The second evil of the political principle is power. According to Buber, power "is not man's private property [*Eigentum*]; it is lent to him so that he may fulfill his mandate as a governor."[99] It is not an intrinsic attribute of the human category but is attached to man for the performance of an assigned task, for which he bears responsibility toward a Being higher than himself. To prevent its misuse, it must be under ever renewed direction of the primary act of relation, that is, of the social principle. When man acts with his whole being, power is not of its essence, and since real society can be formed solely through such action, only the social principle can create and sustain the organic cells, the small communities and their larger associations. Nevertheless, there is no denying that power is a factor in the lives of small communities, and certainly in the lives of nations. Buber regards it as an obstacle to the realization of true communal life, even though he recognizes its necessity due to human limitations. If the social principle reigned supreme, that is, in a perfect society, power would be unnecessary both as a national and an international instrument. But Buber does not foresee such a perfect state of affairs. The social reality he speaks of harbors a tension between the two principles, and although politics is not the originator of this reality, it often protects it. The political sphere "belongs with the creaturely world"; its real evil is not in itself but in its use of power. Therefore, Buber's concern is not to abolish this sphere but to overcome its evil. "The political 'serpent' " he writes, "is not necessarily evil, it is itself only misled; it, too, ultimately wants to be redeemed."[100] He hopes to fulfill its redemption through an organic restructuring of the social order not according to the purity of either the social or political principle, but by subordinating the latter to the former.[101]

Neither a Utopian Nor an Anarchist

Is Buber a utopian socialist and anarchist? The question will be more to the point if we ask, Does he strive to establish a social order similar to one envisaged by different planners of Utopia, and if so, does he propose to fashion it on the principles of an anarchy and by anarchist means? What we are asking is whether Buber has a given Utopia in view, his own or borrowed, and whether it is of the anarchist type. Our forthright answer must be that he is neither a utopian nor an anarchist. Nevertheless, some misunderstanding may arise from his usage of these terms as well as from his view of a social structure which may appear to be falling within their orbit. To keep the distinction clear, a few general observations will suffice in our context.

The main feature of a Utopia is that it is a planned society according to a certain vision of a "perfect" order. Buber has no such plan; nor does he show any inclination toward one. He does speak of a utopian element in all forms of man's striving toward the social ideal. It is in the nature of a vision of social redemption in "perfect time." But he sets neither a specific time limit nor a certain kind of space for his social structure. He sees the utopian element in the striving as such, in the action here and now, without a preconceived plan or design. As he puts it, " 'Utopian' socialism fights for the highest possible degree of communal autonomy in a restructured society."[102] That is, socialism for him is an ongoing act of human fellowship in this place at this time, and not a dream of a "perfect place" which is nowhere *(utopos)*. In this sense, I would call Buber's socialism *topian* rather than *utopian*. His view of rightness in his social vision is akin to that of the prophet, of whom he says: "He sets no universally valid image of perfection, no pantopia or utopia, before men; . . . for realization he is directed to the *topos,* to this place, to this people, it being the people that must *begin."*[103]

As for anarchy, its chief characteristic is the absence of a government or state, and its aim is the immediate destruction of existing states, even before any other social form has emerged. If we take Mikhail Bakunin's word for it, "Abolition of the State and the Church should be the first and indispensable condition of the real enfranchisement of society. It will be only after this that society can and should begin its own reorganization." Out of this anarchic condition society will organize itself "by means of a free federation from below upward . . .[through] a social revolution [in which] . . . the action of individuals hardly count at all, whereas the spontaneous action of the masses is everything."[104] Buber does not advocate such a stateless society, nor does he propose to take the anarchist revolutionary path to socialism. When he speaks of "spontaneous action" in the restructuring of society, he means individuals or rather persons who are sensitive to reality *(die Realgesinnten),* coming from all groups, parties, peoples, who may not even know each other, but who nevertheless constitute one front for the creation of real society. It is the person that counts, not the inchoate mass, even in group

action. The revolutionary task of this front is not first to destroy
and then build, as it is for the anarchists, but to shape the new
society "in the womb of the old," collapsing one and then set
free what has thus taken shape.[105] The state, as such, is not
abolished either before or after "the revolution"; it is transformed with the transformation of man and his social order.

The State as an Acracy

Guided by his discussion of Pierre-Joseph Proudhon and Peter
Kropotkin, and noting the passages in which he speaks approv-
ingly of their views, we may designate Buber's concept of the
state as an *acracy*—a term he applies to the idea of state formed
by those two social thinkers. It means "non-dominance" *(a-
kratia)* rather than "non-government" *an-archia),* not the abolition of the state, but a curbing of its oppressive power.[106] Where
such power comes from and how it is to be counteracted is the
key problem in Buber's way of restructuring society. Since he
recognizes the need of some measure of power for the preserva-
tion of a given society in its internal and external relations, the
problem is to keep a proper ratio between the social and political
principles so that the former predominates while the latter is
being transformed into social nature. This is to take place within
the framework of the state. Small and large societies formed
around common needs and interests cannot themselves control
their inner conflicts; this can be done only by the state using
political means, that is, power. There is thus a critical element of
instability within the social organism that tends to disrupt its
unity and that can be kept in balance only by state power.

Political Surplus

When a social unit is threatened by an external crisis, such as
conflicts between nations, the state increases its power over the
internal situation in order to apply the full strength of its unifying
force to meet it. The state then tends to assume overwhelming
and oppressive powers and may become totalitarian. But even if
universal international peace were established, the internal social instability would not disappear, and the state would still
have to function as a stabilizing force. The important thing in this

relation between state and society is that, in Buber's view, society is created through interhuman relations without the use of power; that is, power comes into play only as a stabilizing factor or a deterrent against the element of conflict. Even in this negative sense, power is not a necessary evil. It becomes an evil, but not a necessary one, only when it asserts itself as the dominant arbiter of life. The state always possesses greater power than it needs for the control of social instability in any given situation. Buber calls this the "surplus" of the political principle or "political surplus." The danger arises when the political principle is taken to mean that public regimes may rightfully determine man's environment and disregard the human factor, as if the essence of man were his political conditions. In the modern world with its constant international crisis, the political principle is so dominant that the organic restructuring of society, such as might be attempted, is bound to suffer setbacks. According to Buber, society will be able to reconstruct itself if there is a positive change in "the prevailing anarchical relationships among the nations" toward full "cooperation in the control of raw materials, agreement on methods of manufacture of such materials, and regulation of the world market."[107] He sees in these economic factors the main source of international tension, leading also to a predominance of the political principle in internal affairs. Assuming, then, that the nations will be able to compose their rivalries over the control of raw materials and world markets and that society may reconstruct itself, how will the political principle, which will not cease even then, be kept within proper bounds?

In Buber's view, the state is not identical with the political principle but has a dual function of *administration* and *government,* the first realizing itself in the social sphere and the second in the political sphere. If the state could step increasingly into the role of administrator, it would transform the political power into social relations and thus release the social spontaneity of the people and their societies. The question, then, is not only how the state is to make use of its power, but also what kind of power it should possess so as not to become oppressive. Buber draws a very thin line of demarcation between these two powers, perhaps to allow the one to be converted into the other more readily; but in doing so he lets down the guards against the political principle. As he defines the twofold function of the state and elaborates on the capacities of each, he falls into the error of modern technology, which he has been trying to overcome. His definition of administration and government reads:

> We call Administration a capacity of making dispositions which is limited by available technical facilities, and recognized in theory and practice within those limits. When it oversteps its limits, it abolishes itself. We call Government a body which is not limited technically but only in a "constitutional" sense, which means that in the case of certain changes in a situation, the limits are shifted and sometimes even disappear.[108]

It appears that Buber is suggesting what all technocrats have assumed, that technical devices have a built-in safety valve which man may not overstep except at his own peril. At the same time he underestimates the capacity of government to expand its technical means even within its constitutional rights. He assumes on the administrative level that those who administer the economic and social establishments will go only as far as their technical apparatus applied in each area will permit. For if the administrator tries to exceed the capacity of his apparatus, the latter will break down and his administration will collapse. This has been the dream of all those who have planned a scientifically shaped society, run by technological machinery, automata, computers, and the like, which set their own limits and regulate themselves within those limits. This was Marx's hope for enabling man to achieve a stateless society, and Lenin's goal of converting the whole of Russia into one "vast people's workshop," administered "in accordance with the indications of these statistical bureaux."[109] B. F. Skinner has built these self-regulating valves in his engineered society in *Walden Two,* and Marshall McLuhan stakes the whole range of human communication on the automated machine. But this kind of administration, "within the limits of available technical facilities," raises the very problem which Buber himself has posed with regard to modern technology, namely, that technological devices have outdistanced the human capacity to administer them, and that man has become enslaved to the instruments he has fashioned. For administrative devices are also technical instruments, such as application forms with overwhelming statistical details, charts, and graphs that stagger the imagination, and a whole apparatus of statistical balances and counterbalances, as we witness today in all our governmental bureaus. This is part of the modern technological crisis, which Buber says is "man's lagging behind his works"; yet he puts much reliance on the experts of these works. In the realm of administration, too, he says, "It is necessary that experts direct how to carry out the desires and decisions of the union or association, and that those who are called upon to carry out the decisions fulfill them, each doing his share."[110] But expert advice may easily go beyond the sphere of administration into the realm of government politics. The expert is usually concerned with the question as to whether a proposed course of action is feasible technically, and when that is ascertained, he will claim in the name of scientific-technological efficacy a free hand to carry out his plan. This is what many biologists and behavioral engineers have been asserting in their respective fields, disregarding the warnings of some leading members of their own professions that their technologies must be submitted to governmental regulation. It means that technical limits, insofar as they lie within man's ability to master his tools, are fluid and may be shifted and extended at will. This may not be left to the experts in administrative procedure, but must come under government control. Nor is the task of seeing to it that everyone does his share a purely administrative one. There is nothing in any technical apparatus that may compel anyone participating in its operation to do his share. The element of personal advantage is more decisive than the proper impersonal functioning of the technical setup as a whole. And it is out of this personal element that conflicts arise and must be reconciled—a task, according to Buber's own position, relegated to the political rather than the social principle, that is, governmental rather than administrative.

Abolish Political Surplus

As said, Buber does not regard the political principle as the essence of man's communal life. This is to signify that, in principle, even though not in practical everyday affairs, man could restructure his society so that politics could be eliminated from his interhuman relations. Such a society, with its smaller societies and associations, would then constitute a true people. Since Buber differentiates between the social and political functions of the state, the ultimate goal would be to eliminate the political function by changing it into a social function, that is, by converting the government entirely into an administration. The spontaneous living together of groups would then be freed from the stifling control of the government and its institutions. Yet he does not want all political power to be thus converted, only the "political surplus," or that part of power which is over and above what is needed to control the internal and external tensions. Such a thin line of demarcation between one kind of power and another calls for constant vigilance and adjustment. Buber hopes that organizations and institutions of a political character will give way to communal forms of association, and that the governmental (the political) functions of the state will be applied to administrative or social purposes. In this process only the "political surplus" of the state, namely, that part of power which is not necessary for the control of social instability, will be eliminated, inasmuch as it can be dispensed with for purposes of administration. To put it in its negative aspect, "political surplus" is considered superfluous or a "surplus" because it is not applicable to administration, and to that extent cannot assume a social character. If it is not eliminated, it will turn into "pure" power or "power for power's sake" and become the instrument of an oppressive government.[111] This is the real danger of political surplus. How can it be averted or overcome?

Buber's ways and tools are not those of the revolutionary but of the educator. While he encourages the rebels and even associates himself with their cause, he has little confidence in their efficacy.[112] Instead, he advocates two paths of change, education toward communal living, and decentralization of political power. As to the first, he writes:

> Will society ever revolt against the "political surplus" and the accumulation of power? If such a thing were ever possible, only a society which had itself overcome its own internal conflicts would ever venture to embark upon such a revolution; and that is hardly to be expected so long as Society is what it is. . . . The way [to overcome it] is Education, the education of a generation with a truly social outlook and a truly social will.[113]

The second proposal, decentralization of government, is to prevent the accumulation of surplus power in the hands of an autocracy which may determine the lives of the entire nation and make everyone subservient to the state. In order to keep a workable relationship between the social and political principles, there ought to be a large measure of autonomy given to local and regional societies. The larger this autonomy, the greater the amount of social spontaneity. But here, too, the demarcation line between centralization and decentralization must remain fluid, to allow for adjustments as may be required in each particular situation under changing conditions. The choice is not between one and the other but rather a choice of areas in which the decentralization may be carried out to the greatest possible extent.

Role of Education

If we take another quick glance at the entire gamut of means which Buber proposes for a restructuring of society, we shall find that, in the main, he considers the political principle, as it manifests itself in a surplus of governmental power, as the chief obstacle. In order to overcome it, he recommends the conversion of Government into Administration, and a decentralization of its power to make decisions as far as possible and in as many areas as the given situation may allow. These are to be ongoing changes of the restructuring process, the first a "change in the *nature* of power," and the second a "change in the *apportionment* of power." On the other side, in order to enhance the social principle and give it the greatest possible self-expression, there must be a change in man's orientation toward life with his fellowmen, a release of his potency for true social living. That is to be accomplished through education. To this must be added another task, without which all other efforts would be in vain, and that is the rekindling of man's basic trust in Being as such. This, too, may be realized through education.

Who will carry out these changes—to apportion power, modify its nature, educate a new generation toward trust in being and for social living? Buber says, not an organization, institution, or government, which operates through the political principle, but "the men who appreciate the incomparable value of the social principle."[114] Such men, he believes, are everywhere. They are "the men of real conviction who are found in all groups" and all peoples, even the genuinely convinced members of a party, all those who carry on the battle against the antihuman in our society. These "truly human men" must start to talk with one another in genuine dialogue across the frontiers that separate them, "if the great peace is to appear and the devastated life of the earth renew itself."[115]

Once more we are compelled to ask the painful question, What instrumentality are these "truly human men" going to use in order to pursue their enterprise? If they do not organize locally, nationally, and internationally, and do not seek power, what influence can they possibly have on the actual course of events anywhere? Buber bestows on them spirit and direction, but not political power, for through the spirit, he holds, their influence can be very great and decisive, even though their victory may momentarily reside in failure. "The spirit can fail," as in the case of Plato and Isaiah (in different ways), but it is not "helpless in the face of history." Out of the crisis itself the awakening will come "in a late phase, to be sure, when men despair of power and its autonomous decisions, when power for power's sake grows bewildered and longs for direction."[116] These are Buber's words of hope and vision. But with all their optimism and confidence in man's renewal of the spirit, they leave us in a doubtful mood. In his efforts to cleanse interhuman relations of all mediating instruments, he proposes *to restructure society without any kind of instrumentality*. He may tolerate political power because society cannot do away with it altogether, but he sees no positive function in it, because basically he looks at it only as a function of government and implicity as an instrument of oppression. For him "Education is the great implement which is more or less under the control of society," and he pleads for "the complete overthrow of the political trend which nowadays dominates education throughout the world."[117] But education in itself is not really an implement, but only a setting in which the educator applies such implements as he may find effective for personal renewal. And if he is hindered by political powers, how is he going to "overthrow" them, unless he aligns himself with other powers which are favorable to his purpose?

The educator, Buber says, persuades, but does not compel. His task is to awaken, "to rescue one's real personal self from the fiery jaws of collectivism which devours all selfhood."[118] We may recall here Kant's plea on behalf of the philosopher-educator to be free to speak out publicly and to be heard by the king, but not to assume the latter's governing power. Buber thinks that thereby Kant showed disillusionment in the spirit, since he did not urge the philosopher to demand, but only "that he be heard" *(dass man ihn höre)*.[119] Be this as it may, Buber, too, does not want the philosopher or "social thinker" to seek power, such as a demand against the king would imply. Like the prophets of Israel, he holds, the social thinker neither possesses power nor should he aspire to it, but recognizing the political crisis, he counsels and prepares, educates and shows direction. This is the work of the spirit, not power. Actually, then, Buber the social thinker does not apply an implement called "education"; rather, he lets the spirit itself do the work, which, indeed, is the primary act of entering-into-relation, but not an implement or tool. For "the spirit of which I speak," he says, "is not one of the potentialities or functions of man but his concentrated *totality*."[120] An implement or instrument, however, must be a function of man or he will become a function of the instrument, and that is precisely the technological issue confronting modern man.

Through his technology of religious socialism, in its reliance on education, Buber has not resolved this issue, because he has not called into play an instrumentality that would control and direct the physicotechnological instruments. Education itself has succumbed to the electric media of modern technology. To counteract all these forces, even for the sake of restructuring society "towards the life men live together," man must create a kind of instrumentality that he can master and not be mastered by. Such an instrumentality is political power. Whether this power assumes the form of government, a political party, or some other institution, it must be of an ethical character. Ultimately, Buber invokes the ethical striving in man, as he puts his reliance on men of high moral motivation, "the great characters . . . who love their society. . . . Tomorrow they will be the architects of a new unity of mankind." These are the men, he says, who direct their way to God, who is the true king. But he leaves them powerless, because he maintains that "none but the powerless can speak the true King's will with regard to the state, and remind both the people and the government of their *common* responsibility towards this will."[121] He would not grant "the great characters" the important tool of the human will, which in everyday life (Buber's main concern) assumes the active form of political power. Can this power be truly an instrument of the ethical will? This leads us into the sphere of morality, which is another chapter in man's efforts to resolve his social crisis.

Moral Responsibility

The Moral Between in the World of It

Good and Evil

Is the world of everyday use and experience good or evil? Those who divide it into two compartments may say one is good and the other evil. Buber does not accept such a division. For him, "The primary word I-It is not evil—as matter is not evil."[122] This, however, does not obviate the fact that there is a real problem of good and evil in the world of It, which is a conflict between using fellowmen, on one hand, and entering-into-relation with them, on the other. Since man's function of using things reduces his power of relation, and since this function provides for his sustenance and equipment in all life situations on an ever-increasing scale of his cultural progress, is he not then doomed to succumb entirely to the world of It and thus fail to redeem himself as man? This problem is particularly pronounced in man's social institutions. If his social establishments are to help him cope with the ever growing complexities of everyday life—to alleviate or eliminate pain, disease, hunger, and other natural disasters—must not these establishments of necessity be concerned entirely with the things that will render man's existence on earth more comfortable, more livable, and physically more secure? Furthermore, can those who are charged with the affairs of the social establishments and with the increase of their effectiveness be at all concerned with man's mutual relations of I-Thou, which are unpredictable, not measurable, and not calculable for the purposes set by the establishments? It seems that if those purposes are to be realized, the leaders of the establishments—of the state, industrial, farm, and labor organizations, political and fraternal orders, educational institutions, even charitable agencies—must organize and use all their fellowmen to the utmost for the promotion of those ends. To the extent, then, that man increases the world of It, this world threatens to engulf him and eventually shut him out of the world of Thou completely. Is this fated, or can man be master of his destiny?

The intensity of this problem was brought to our attention a number of years ago by a television program on the outlook of the twenty-first century,[123] and by some leading scientist at an educational conference. The world-renowned biologist H. Bentley Glass, speaking at the convention of The American Association of School Administrators, in Atlantic City, N.J., predicted that by the year 2000,

> man will be free of hunger and infectious diseases; . . . defective parts of the body will be replaced, even prenatally. The frozen reproductive cells . . . will be used to create life. . . . "Here," he said, "is our 'brave new world' in full, with bottle babies in different kinds of solutions that condition their mental growth to suit a certain caste." But, he added, "this staggering power" over human evolution only "provokes another great crisis in human affairs—the crisis of values and goals."[124]

Such is the crisis to which Buber addresses himself. The critical point is whether man will learn to control his environment, even his heredity, for the sake of advancing himself as a human being, or become so overpowered by his own technological devices that he will become dehumanized. Buber does not advocate a turning back to a prescientific or pretechnological age, even if this were possible, but he urges man to stay in control of his instruments and not lose sight of his human destiny. For the world of It is not evil, nor is man in himself evil, except in the manner of his dealing with fellowmen and nature. Rather than turning back cultural progress, Buber advises, let man return to his primary potencies of relation with others in every aspect of life. Such a return will come about if everyone—leader and led, in and outside the establishment—will realize the meaning of good and evil, freedom and necessity, destiny and fate—the full import of himself as a person—and act accordingly.

The Way

"Man is not good, man is not evil," says Buber, "he is in an eminent sense good-and-evil."[125] Good is not a substance in man's being, but direction, a movement between two poles. Neither are the poles in themselves good or evil. What is good is the movement—man's decision to direct himself toward relation. Evil, then, is a refusal or failure to decide for this movement; it is the absence of direction. The polarity is a simultaneous "acceptance and refusal" of direction, until one prevails and overcomes the other.[126] In accordance with his twofold communication with fellowman as an It and a Thou, man is ontologically so constituted that he can remain in the world of It continually and thus treat his fellowman as an object of his experience and use; or he can decide, as often as he may gather strength to do so, to look at him as an exclusive being and move in the direction of relation with him as a Thou. Direction *is* the good; it is the way. Lack of direction is evil; it is not-a-way, but chaotic floundering.[127] Yet, while evil is a chaotic state, the way or good cannot be found without it. Man finds direction in his floundering by overcoming the chaotic state through decision.

> "Good" is the movement that reaches out in the direction of returning home [to the primary relation of I-Thou]. "Evil" is the whirl of man's possibility, moving about without direction; without it nothing happens, but through it everything fails if it does not assume direction and remains entangled in [possibility]. . . . Good and evil cannot be a pair of opposites like right and left or above and below.[128]

Good and evil are correlatives; their conjunctive "and" or the between is not to be overlooked. Good *and* evil work together, but in order for good to prevail, it must come forth even from evil.[129] Accordingly, Buber distinguishes three factors in the movement toward good: *(a)* overcoming evil, *(b)* decision, and *(c)* responsibility.

Movement toward the Good

(a) Overcoming Evil

To overcome evil is not to annihilate it, but to change its purpose, to find the way, to assume direction. When man uses fellowman for his own limited ends without regard to the human person, that is evil. But this does not mean that institutions which use men and things to promote the well-being of all men should be abolished simply because they use others for specific ends. Neither is there evil in the technological devices, except when man succumbs to their overwhelming power and allows them to dehumanize him. These devices are to be overcome by applying them to the goals of mankind as a whole, but not by annihilating them. What is evil in the use of technology is its application without direction; by giving it direction toward the human goal, it is turned into good.

(b) Decision

As was brought out in the preceding section, decision is a fundamental act of man's entering-into-relation with fellowman. One who refuses to enter-into-relation, or one who fails to decide for it, has allowed the evil inclination to gain the upper hand, although the two, refusal and failure, are not of the same degree. Buber illustrates the way of decision and its absence in his comments on Psalm 1. This psalm, he says, speaks of three types of men, the righteous, the wicked, and the sinners, weighing the latter two against the first. The righteous are those who decide to follow the way taught to man by God. The wicked are those who refuse to take the way, while the sinners are those who intend to follow but somehow *miss* it.[130]

The good is thus not the "good man"; it is "the way" which man, any man, righteous, sinner, or even wicked, can take. But how does one become aware of the way when he has found it or, for that matter, missed it? Buber accepts the traditional view that the way is God's way or the way of God, but differs from tradition on where the direction may come from.[131] We must remember his philosophical anthropology, which is grounded in man's double movement of distancing and relation. Good and evil proceed from the fact that these two movements represent aspects not only of man's relation to others, but also of himself as a human being. The distancing represents a *split* between man and the reality of others (nature, fellowman) as well as within himself. In this state he sees himself as an I split from Thou or his inborn Thou, or as a subject observing the other as his object; it means that he acts through part of himself and not through his being-as-a-whole. This split, if maintained persistently, is evil. Ontologically, evil proceeds not from man-as-a-whole, but from an abstracted Self, a semblance of himself, separated from his real *humanum*. If then this separated self and its object are taken as reality, says Buber, the first becomes a "phantom within" and the second a "demon" standing over it without: this is the source of evil. To overcome it is to decide for the second movement—for entering-into-relation with real beings: the relation is the good. The overcoming is thus a turning of evil into good. Man becomes aware of the way to the good as he becomes aware of the Thou in the act of relation, and this way is the way of God.[132]

Decision for the good, Buber further explains, does not come as a once-for-all deliberate evaluation of principles of good or evil, even though certain standards become manifest in the act of deciding. It comes as a flash in living confrontation, in unanticipated situations, as a continually renewed act of direction.[133] Coming from one's being-as-a-whole, decision is always an "existential decision" involving a risk and a commitment. The risk is in that man cannot step out of the world of It for any length of time and survive, and the commitment in that he cannot persist in this world only and fulfill himself as man. This holds true both in private and public life in all situations of personal and communal affairs.[134] Since the risk is so great, we surmise that there is something in man which prompts him to take it, and this something, says Buber, is *conscience* which is manifest in all acts of *responsibility*.

(c) Responsibility

Responsibility is the third and most important factor in the movement toward the good. In life we are addressed constantly by others and we are able to answer through our thoughts, speech, and actions. In most instances we do not listen. But when the address comes to us unexpectedly and we respond with our whole being, such response becomes responsibility, that is, "We practice responsibility for that realm of life alloted and entrusted to us to which we are able to respond" with proper action.[135] Each situation is unique. It is not something ordered, prearranged, or planned with foreknowledge, techniques, or programming. It is a concrete event and its signs and sounds cannot be reduced to systematic speaking. We become inwardly aware of the signs and we can respond or turn away. But responsibility shows itself only where there is genuine response. These concrete events, though unique, Buber emphasizes, are nothing extraordinary but simply the big and small personal everyday events of our lives. Their uniqueness consists in the fact that each situation is encountered for the first time and does not repeat itself in successive encounters. As we respond to a given situation we bring it into life—we make ourselves responsible for it, we guarantee it with our being. The experience of responsibility comes to us as "lived life" *(des gelebten Lebens)* of conscience and its correlative, guilt.

Guilt and Conscience

Buber considers guilt as the failure of man to respond to the summons of a being who confronts him; it means "not being there" to meet the other. This, he warns, must not be confused with guilt feeling. Rather, it is "existential guilt" that arises out of a lack of self-fulfillment, out of passing up the moment which presented itself for entering-into-relation. If one is "not there," that moment disappears like any other "changing presence" of being, and the one who has failed to respond cannot hold it and falls into a state of guilt, which has a superpersonal ontic character. Guilt is not *in* the person, but the person *stands in it* as in a between that has failed to consummate itself through relation, that is an empty between, a lack that envelops the guilty one "in the most real way."[136]

So much for the existential meaning of guilt. But what is one guilty of when he is "not there" to respond? What happens as a result of his "absence?" The answer lies in his category *humanum*. The order of mankind is realizable not through individuals in separation from one another, but through their mutual interactions, through everyone's participation in the totality of interhuman relations. Moreover, no one can fulfill himself except through his sharing in human destiny as a whole. One who fails to participate not only violates his own life functions, but also inflicts injury on the human order as such. Then only the person who has inflicted the injury may rectify it, and until he does it, he is in a state of guilt. His struggle to overcome it is his conscience.[137]

> Each one [Buber writes,] who has not fulfilled a task which he knows to be his own, each who did not remain faithful to his vocation which he had become certain of—each such person knows what it means to say that "his conscience smites him."[138]

Conscience, like guilt, is grounded in the primal movement of distancing. When one fails to respond and the other disappears, there comes a second call from the disappearance in the dis-

tance, demanding, "Where have you been?" "That," says
Buber, "is the call of conscience." It sounds as if it came from
myself, but actually it is the other who calls me. My response
now cannot be to the original appearance, even when the same
person is calling. That particular moment is gone; the situation
is no longer the same. I can respond to its new appearance in
another image if I am steadfast in my state of guilt, allowing my
conscience to elevate me to my human wholeness, for only by
being whole can one do good.[139]

According to Buber's philosophical anthropology, the factors
of responsibility, guilt, and conscience play a crucial role in
man's personal and public life. Responsibility, especially, is at
the root of one's total mode of behavior. It is the criterion of
freedom as distinguished from causal necessity, of destiny rather
than fate, and generally of man's self-fulfillment. In the following
two sections these factors will be considered in their communal
and personal manifestations, particularly in the politico-ethical
domain.

The Political and Religious Spheres

The Communal We

Buber's religious humanism is based on two interacting principles: communality and the centrality of the Absolute. According to the first, humanity in its primary sense is a communal
entity formed through the acts of interhuman relationships and
consisting of small and large communes unified in an overall
social entity. In this sense, communality may be conceived as a
We opposite a Thou, the same as an I is opposite a Thou.
However, such a We is not identifiable objectively as a collective, a crowd, or a group. Its objective existence comes into
fullness of being through the word pair I-Thou spoken between
many persons in common.[140]

The second principle is that the community as a whole has its
center in the relation with the Absolute. Just as all particular
lines of I-Thou intersect in the eternal Thou, so must the
communal line "be able to 'stand before the face of God' in all
reality as a We"[141]; or human society in its formation and
continued existence must direct itself to God. It means that
man's way to fellowman *ought to be* such that it leads to God,

and his way to God such that it goes through fellowman. This imperative underlies both the principle of communality and its center in the Absolute.[142]

The principle of communality further entails a political element, and since communality must direct itself to God, the question is whether religion and politics can work together toward the formation of the human order. Buber separates religion not from the state but from politics. The state and religion may harmonize insofar as both may be directed toward the messianic goal of establishing the Kingdom of God. But under existing social conditions, the political factor wields considerable power. Can it be reconciled with the religious idea?

Antinomy of Politics and Religion

Buber's view of religion and politics may be considered in the form of two concentric spheres having different orientations. The larger one, religion, is a way oriented toward a *goal,* the smaller one, politics, is a means oriented toward an *end.* The great goal of religion is man's destiny, not foreseen, planned, or calculated, but inherent in the human category of relation to God. It is man binding himself to God and following His way.[143] The small end of politics is not destined, but planned and calculated for man's temporal needs, which often deviate from the great goal or go contrary to it. It uses power to accomplish its end in any way possible. When religion is converted into politics, Buber warns, the goal becomes an end and the way a means, that is, man takes hold of the way and uses it as his possession instead of following it in response to the divine call. Thus religion becomes an instrument for the attainment of small ends rather than a striving toward the great goal. The achievement of limited ends, Buber admits, is undoubtedly necessary in our everyday affairs, but, he says, in our present age man faces a crisis which demands a fundamental restructuring of society, not just the achievement of limited ends in this or that situation. This entails a transformation not only of the social order but of man himself—a return to his primary act of relation with fellowman and God—which can be realized through the principle of communality, but not of politics.

As Buber sees it, religion can transform man, but politics is the business of untransformed man. Political means, like other technological instruments, whether mental or physical, can change external relations between men and their institutions, but not their inner, essential relationships. The latter can come only through religion as a complete turning.[144] Nevertheless, Buber does not altogether reject the work of the political leader who can establish institutions beneficial to human life, but he is uncertain whether this leader can be instrumental in the restructuring of society. To be sure, politics is part of public life and all human life is in the sphere of religion, but political means are entirely contrary to religious ways, the first applying coercion, the second using persuasion. If they are combined, the antinomy of goal and end cannot be resolved. "Only in the great *polis* of God," as Buber calls it, may the two be "blended into a life of world community, in an eternity wherein neither religion nor politics will any longer exist." Until then, he sees each of these spheres running its separate course with the "tragic contradictions between the unconditionality of spirit and the conditionality of a situation." Yet he assures us that "the situation will certainly be mastered . . . [in a] very roundabout not at all 'successful' step of the deity through history."[145]

Thus speaks Buber the non-*Politiker,* who advises that "one should . . . neither seek politics nor avoid it, one should be neither political nor nonpolitical on principle."[146] He sees the ever-present danger of politics becoming an oppressive force through ideological and centralized power in the hands of a party or government. Although he hopes that men "obedient to the spirit," even in the party and government, may be able to avoid this danger, he considers all political means as the "real evil" that stands in the way of man's goal—the Kingdom of God—and he urges all those working toward this goal not to use such means. Nevertheless, he feels that political power, if properly used, may help establish the kingdom of justice or an ethical social order.[147]

The Ethical Absolute

In Buber's social structure, political means are powers of the state, parties, and social agencies. If these bodies are to act with justice, they must use their powers in an ethical way sanctified by religious experience. Buber calls it the redemption of the political principle. But if this is to be practiced in actual everyday affairs, which is Buber's main concern, there must be an ethical norm to guide the state and the other agencies in their use of power. Where does such a norm originate and what is its redemptive force?

Ethics, according to Buber, is not a matter of moral will, feeling, or a fixed set of precepts, but lies deep in the very category of man as a being who enters-into-relation. Ethical norms can therefore not be derived from man's subjective faculties or from his reactions determined by objective factors. In the former, ethical conduct would be relative to aspects of psychology; in the latter, it would be imposed by outside natural or human forces and would thus preclude free individual action. The ethical norm which Buber seeks to establish must have its ground in absoluteness, and such a ground can come only through man's relation to the Absolute. Accordingly, this norm cannot be embodied in any code of laws or precepts, even when these are derived from original relational experiences, because the norm can arise only in the very act of that experience, as and when the situation calls for ethical decisions.[148] This is to say that man's decision for ethical conduct can be valid only as he enters-into-relation with the Absolute. It means, furthermore, that his decisions may not be anticipated or calculated for other possible situations. This is the only way the ethical may come within the sphere of religion and be sanctified by it. In this sphere one must ask himself what ethical action he should take in order to realize himself as man facing the Absolute. Thus the ethical and religious spheres merge in the spontaneous experience of his encounter with God. In this "concrete, personal situation" man faces the "ethical absolute" as the norm for "the factual moral decision of the individual, on one hand, and his factual relationship to the Absolute, on the other."[149]

If we now try to correlate this ethical absolute with the social principle, we are faced with the original problem of reconciling the individual with society in matters of decision: who decides for whom? Ultimately, in Buber's account of the ethical it is the individual who decides between right and wrong for himself, namely, whether a given action will enable him to realize his human destiny to the fullest. To be sure, his ethical decision must be grounded in communality and directed toward the Absolute, but his actual decision is nonetheless by and for himself. The interests of others that may come into play do not constitute a norm, because "right and wrong," in Buber's view, do not refer to what is best "for individuals and society," but to what man ought to be according to the intrinsic value of his *humanum.* This kind of ought only tells man to act in the right direction for himself, and if there are forces hampering his action, he must not participate in them. We must therefore conclude that political action, which is contrary to the religious principle, cannot come within the ethical sphere. Man cannot gauge politics by the norm of right and wrong, or, as Buber calls it, by the "ethical coordinates,"[150] because political action does not come through religious experience as such. We are thus left with two separate spheres but without a span to bridge the gap, which an ethical norm should provide. The basic issue then is whether such a norm can be found in tradition.

Validation of Tradition

Buber does not reject tradition, but he wants it subjected to new religious experiences on the part of each individual in each instance requiring an ethical decision. "Even when the individual calls an absolute criterion handed down by religious tradition his own," Buber asserts, "it must be reforged in the fire of truth of his personal essential relation to the Absolute if it is to win true validity."[151] To say that this validation is also communal because the personal relation is grounded in communality would be begging the question. For, while the primary relation is of a communal character, the acceptance of a norm through personal experience is an individual act. Buber's test of "true validity" is not in past religious experience but in ever-present relation. In other words, he tells us that there is an ethical absolute and that we know how it comes into existence in each situation, but we can never know what it might be until the situation arises. He does not recognize traditional validity because he regards the past, in general, as an It and therefore not valid unless it is "reforged" in a new I-Thou relation. But this is not the way tradition looks at itself. On the contrary, it considers itself an ever-living present which is of a nontemporal character. In Jewish teaching, in which Buber finds the primary source of his principle of dialogue, "there is no before and after in the Torah," meaning, there is no causal past, only a historical present. If the laws of tradition cannot be accepted in their nontemporal validity, there cannot be any ethical norm, for each momentary encounter with the Absolute turns into a past as soon as the relation ceases. All such past moments live on in tradition constituting a norm. A nontraditional norm is a *contradictio in adjecto*.

Buber is fully aware of this conflict between past and present, but he wavers between accepting and rejecting the validity of the past. His "ethical coordinates" fail him at the point of validation. He concedes that "without law, i.e., without any transmissible distinction between what is pleasing and displeasing to God there can be no historical continuity of divine rule on earth."[152] Yet he avers that divine law must be freely apprehended by each individual's own act. He sees tradition hampering the way of freedom, as he states:

> To the extent that one may adhere to a traditional bond, a law, a precept, one is permitted to seek support for his responsibility [in tradition]. . . . The more we "become free," the more is this support denied us, and our responsibility must become solitary in a personal way.[153]

If we hold with Buber that the ethical norm is obtained through man's relation with the Absolute in a given here and now, why can't we seek support in this experience when it is turned into tradition? If, as he claims, "becoming free" means breaking loose from the bond, then we are freeing ourselves from the relations which occurred in the past only to enter into new relations strictly our own. Even though such individual effort is desirable, how can anyone claim validity for his own experience here and now if he cannot accept as valid the experiences of past generations? Buber has no real answer to this question and relegates it to the realm of eternal mystery: "Here the eternal *dictum* is confronted by the eternal *contradictum*."[154]

On this last note, Buber's illustration from the event of Korah's rebellion against Moses (Numbers 16:17) is highly instructive. In that episode an established divine law had to be validated in the actual life of the people by political coercion rather than by religious persuasion. Buber regards this as "the tragedy of Moses." The lawgiver, he says, set out to build "the Kingdom of God on free will, on 'doing and hearing' without compulsion," but Korah's rebellion, which was a false application of that principle, compelled him to destroy the rebels in order to save "the Covenant between God and people."[155] Was this use of political means against "men of the Korah type," who try to replace divine law by their own willfulness, sanctioned by religion, as the Bible teaches on this and other occasions, or not? Buber justifies Moses' decision because it was a case of being zealous for God, but as to the actual means employed, he notes: "Indeed, there is something weird behind the legend of the earth which opened its mouth and swallowed up the rebellious host."[156]

The social crisis of modern man stems primarily from the deterioration of tradition, both in the religious and political spheres. If man has lost his way to God it is due to his inability to share the values of the past as normative precepts. Regard for tradition has all but vanished in our social-political life. A law enacted by a legislative body only yesterday may be flouted today by any individual or group of individuals who pit their willfulness against it under the slogan of sheer individual freedom. True, Buber points to this "deterioration of traditional bonds" and to the concomitant false exaltation of freedom, but he does not propose a renewal of those bonds. Rather, he holds that "to become free of a bond is destiny; . . . it means that a quite personal responsibility takes the place of one shared with many generations."[157] He points the way to God through a genuine communal We and at the same time singles out the individual relation as the only way to reach ethical-religious decisions. He does not call for a communal return. Although we cannot deny the importance of a personal return to the primary act of relation, the social crisis of today demands a return of the community as a whole, not just man as a whole, and with the full involvement of all its institutions, including the political ones. Furthermore, if a return to the human primary relation is the way out of the crisis, then there must be a return to something called tradition. This lies within the reach of the kingdom of man, even as he prepares for the Kingdom of God. In Judaism, from which Buber derives his concept of return (teshuva), the present and the past must be renewed together, as it is written: "Turn us, O Lord, toward you and we will return; renew our days as of old."[158]

In Buber's vision of the Kingdom of God, "Community does not have its meaning in itself; it is the place where the divine has not yet spent itself, the place of the coming theophany."[159] On the human side, he places the burden of this theophany not on actual communal living but on each man's return individually. "The empirical community," he advises,' "is a dynamic fact. It does not relieve man of his loneliness, but fills it, renders it positive. Thereby it deepens the consciousness of responsibility of the individual, the place of responsibility is man's becoming-lonely.''[160] But if the social principle is to become dominant and restructure society, it must assert itself in the empirical community; and if the religious *way* is to be consummated, it must pervade the political *means*. Their common denominator is the ethical norm. Buber's emphasis on the ethical absolute may be counted as his greatest contribution to modern man's socioreligious orientation. He has restored the essential connection between ethics and religion at a time when one or the other, or both, are put in question. Yet, he has not resolved the basic conflict between individual and community from the point of view of ethical conduct.

Strictly speaking, Buber's ethics cannot be designated as ''individualistic,'' for he rejects individualism as well as collectivism and opts for a third alternative, namely, communality.[161] But he individualizes it inasmuch as he places the burden of ethical decision on each individual in any given situation. The ethical norm as an act of decision is thus submerged in the religious experience which occurs anew at each moment of relation with the Absolute. Religion not only overshadows ethics, it actually eliminates it as an act of decision. "It is wrong," he says, "to treat the meaning of the act of decision . . . as only ethical; it is rather religious; it is the religious act."[162] On this level, finite individual man is raised to a state of an absolute free being who by his "personal and solitary" decision effectuates the ethical absolute. Its normative character may entail communal responsibility but not communal decision, and in this respect, Buber's ethical norm is individualistic. In the ethical sphere, his principle of dialogue is turned into a dialectic of communality in the womb of individuality.

3
Man's Relation to God

The Religious Issue: God and Reality

God-Is-Dead Theologoumena

The God-is-dead movement may have already passed its peak interest. Nevertheless, rather than treating it as an ephemeral fad, we ought to look into its underlying concepts which have dominated modern religious thinking for several generations. Buber does not deal with this movement directly, but its speculations are pertinent to the religious issues which he aims to resolve. Of prime consideration is the distinction, especially as Buber sees it, between religion and theology. "Religion," he says, "is essentially the act of holding fast to God."[163] It is not an intellectual act of ascertaining or proving God's existence, or a technological process of forming an image of Him, and not even an emotional expression of belief in God. It is the direct, intimate encounter between man as an independent being and the existing divine Being. This act, Buber points out, has weakened in our day, and to compensate for it man has tried to restore the relation through philosophical speculations about God's existence, nature, or essence. It is, he says, "the intellectual letting go of God," signifying that intellectually man cannot accept God as an object of perception, feeling, or imagination, and seeks to change Him into an object of thought or into a concept, such as the Unlimited, the Unknown, Spirit, or Being in general. All such designations are nothing but activities of our thinking faculty, of comparing concepts of finitude with a concept of an ultimate entity. The result is a metaphysical God, such as we may find in various theological speculations, but not the living God of religion.[164]

Man's tendency to philosophize about the Supreme Being is rooted in his impulse to control the powers beyond or to penetrate the hiddenness which confronts him in reality. If he cannot unveil it in direct relation, he either denies its reality or else forms metaphysical or psychological semblances of the divine, such that may fit into his particular mode of thought, feeling, or will. What troubles the philosophers of the God-is-dead persuasion is the idea of a transcendent deity which they cannot reconcile with the demand of the hour to make it relevant to modern man. Having lost faith in the possibility of immediate relation with a transcendent Being, they posit a something—a psychological I, a feeling of belief, or a subjectivized spirit—between themselves and the God idea which shuts them off from the divine presence: God is eclipsed from their view. This, according to Buber, constitutes the religious crisis of modern man. Seen as "the twilight of God" or "death of God," it becomes an issue in theology.

The philosophers and theologians of the God-is-dead movement seek God but cannot find Him. One declares Him dead, another nonexistent, a third is waiting for His resurrection, and a fourth espies Him in dying condition and murders Him. What they all have in common is that they miss God, or rather missed Him in their search, because they have lost direction as they move in a world which man himself has turned into chaos. Try as they may to repair the breach, they still cannot fit God into their world which they have structured out of physical, psychological, or some ideational elements. The two most representative and most influential thinkers of this movement in our time are Friedrich Nietzsche and Jean-Paul Sartre. To these we may add two very eloquent atheists of our own generation, William Hamilton and Thomas J. J. Altizer. Thus Nietzsche cannot create a new God out of the moral components which he has shattered; Sartre uses up every particle of freedom to constitute the human being and has none left for a God of freedom; Hamilton can spare no room for Him and finds Him superfluous in this world; and Altizer brings Him down with a heavy blow in order to reassure man's faith in salvation. The search for God, whether He is immanent or transcendent, in a world of chaos or in the experiences of man who has lost all faith, is a search in vain. But, one may ask, if we do not seek God as an active force in the world and in man's life, where else can we find Him and what meaning can He have for us in our mundane experiences?

The issue centers on the fatum of time which these philosophers have woven into their world fabric, leaving man suspended between the now and the never.

In order to attain an eternal now for man to live in, Nietzsche sets the entire cycle of time with everything it contains into an eternal recurrence[165]; Sartre sees man in each present situation as a perpetual founder of nothingness in a circle of selfness[166]; and Altizer looks to the End of all returns in a state beyond the Beginning.[167] None of them is able to cope with history as a factor in the here and now, because they cannot reconcile a continuous flow of natural time with the breaks that occur in every now in man's life. They cannot reconcile the being of time, as changeless fatum, with the becoming of man's changing experience. In essence, the past becomes a yoke for them, because it cannot be undone at man's will. Therefore, they regard God's revelations or manifestations in the past (insofar as they regard them at all) as irrelevant to the present, unless God Himself, not just the historical occurrence of His manifestations, is made an actual ingredient in each now of human experience. Thus God is made into a function of man's present existence, and, as such, He is no longer the living God of history. He may be cast into the oblivion of the past, killed and decomposed into moments of the present, or transformed into a supreme man of the future in eternal recurrence. Buber's reaction to this kind of theologoumena, particularly his direct response to Nietzsche and Sartre, will serve us as a fitting introduction to his own philosophy of man's relation to God in the reality of human experience.

On Nietzsche's Struggle with Nihilism

Time as a problem of a beginning and an end occupied Buber's attention from his youth. His two earliest encounters with it came when he read Kant's *Prolegomena* at the age of fifteen and Nietzsche's *Zarathustra* at seventeen.[168] Of the latter, he recalled in later years with some "lyrical weirdness," that "Nietzsche's *Zarathustra* wanted to enlighten me in my youth that God is dead. But, grand as it seemed, this could be recognized as Feuerbach's old confusion of a human representation of God with the real God."[169] Buber wrote this when he was fifty and had already freed himself of the spell which that work had cast on him when he first read it. Later, in his eighties, he again reminisced about the "rousing influence" of *Zarathustra,* which "carried me off into the realm of sublime intoxication, from which I was able to escape completely only after a long time, and find the road to a certainty of the real." "That the access to this road long remained closed to me goes back in no small measure to that enticement by 'Zarathustra.' "[170] What intrigued Buber in his youth was Nietzsche's doctrine of the "eternal recurrence of the same," that is, "as an endless succession of finite lapses that are the same in everything so that the end-phase of each lapse passes into its own beginning-phase." That, he thought, would answer his question how endless time can have both a beginning and an end. But in the light of further investigation this doctrine lost its spell and dissipated like the "mystic illusion" that it was. Instead, he was helped by Kant, who, he said, did not presume to solve the riddle of time's being, but pointed to our dependence on "time as the form of 'our' perception." In this sense, both we and time are in the timeless, in eternity, and that is "a totally different eternity than the circular one, which Zarathustra loves as 'Fate.' "[171] "Then I began to realize," he wrote further with reference to Kant's *Prolegomena,* "that there is the eternal, which is something entirely different from the infinite, just as it is something entirely different from the finite, and yet, that there can be a connection between me, man, and the eternal."[172]

Buber now sees the problem of time and the eternal, which was raised by Nietzsche, as the core of the anthropological question "What is man?," that is, the human problematic in relation to the world and the Absolute. Since Kant, he says, this problematic was placed by Nietzsche, as by no other modern philosopher, in the center of his world view, but at the same time he viewed man as part of nature, more specifically, as part of the animal kingdom, who is as yet to perfect himself as a certain species in conformity with his real nature. In other words, Nietzsche understood man in terms of an animal species of nature instead of a being sui generis which, according to Buber, is the essence of philosophical anthropology.[173] For Nietzsche, says Buber, the problem of man is thus a *"marginal* problem, the problem of a being that has fallen out of the core of nature to its outermost edge, at the dangerous end of natural being . . . where the dizzying abyss of Nothing begins."[174] This being is an aberration of the animal kingdom, the only one in that domain who is incomplete. He is a violent severance of the animal past and, by clinging to it, loses his purpose and meaning. And yet, in his present stage he is seen as the embryo of the future human species, for he can sublimate himself into a supreme man, the man of eternity.

Buber's main criticism of Nietzsche's view is that it places the human species in the general cycle of natural time without even assuring it the perfection it is supposed to strive for, since the time cycle in its eternal recurrence (assuming that by chance some men will reach this stage) will bring back the imperfect specimens together with the perfect. Nietzsche himself, says Buber, apparently had some misgivings about his goal if left to natural selection, for he advocated deliberate breeding to assure the successful issue of the highest specimens.[175] But most important is the character of his goal, namely, the attainment of an ever-surpassing will to power, which Buber regards as a false image of superiority or greatness. He says Nietzsche dresses up the concept of power in dithyrambic pathos. But stripped of this pathos, power is a means to an end, a capacity to realize a goal which the great man has set for himself, but not an object of desire in itself. Moreover, the goal must transcend the individual, even though it may also express his personal aim in life. The individual who fails to assume responsibility for the fulfillment of the goal and seeks only to attain or increase his power for its own sake—one who exhibits an insatiable will to power—shows weakness of character rather than strength.[176]

This new human being who is the embodiment of the will to power, Buber further notes, also becomes for Nietzsche the ultimate measure of all values. In creating this goal, Nietzsche tried to give meaning to human existence and thus save man from nihilism, which had pervaded European society at the time. He knew, says Buber, that absoluteness of value is rooted in our relationship to the Absolute, but he also understood that in the present epoch belief in God and in an essential moral order was no longer tenable. His cry "God is dead" was therefore meant as a historical turning point, not as an end point. He declared the Christian moral God untenable, but he searched for other possible gods who would serve as the measure of new values. Those gods, he thought, must come out of men—out of European men—who set a scale of life-affirming values of strong-weak, not of good-evil. Thus Nietzsche identified morals with what he called slave morality and divested the strong of all moral responsibility. This, says Buber, is substituting a new ambiguous scale of weak-strong for an old ambiguous scale of evil-good; such a goal will not save man from nihilism, which Nietzsche set out to accomplish. He concludes:

> Nietzsche himself wanted to overcome the nihilism which he himself had completed; in this he miscarried. . . . The "teaching of the supreme man" is not a teaching, and, . . . in contrast to the value-scale defined by the idea of the Good, the value-scale weak-strong is not a value-scale. . . . However, there is one thing we can learn from nihilism: a court of sheer morality will not lead us out of this situation into a transformed one.[177]

On Sartre's Professed Atheism

Sartre, like Nietzsche, having dispensed with God, is looking for someone else to give meaning to human existence. As Buber quotes him:

> "If I have done away with God the father," Sartre says literally, "someone is needed to invent values. . . . Life has no meaning *a priori;* it is up to you to give it meaning, and value is nothing else than this meaning which you choose."

"That," Buber adds, "is almost exactly what Nietzsche said, and it has not become any truer since then."[178] It means that with the disappearance of God there is no possibility of discovering absolute values and therefore man himself has to invent whatever values suit him individually. He has to create his world subjectively. Buber calls this kind of "creative freedom," wrested from an absent or silent God, "a demagogic phrase." "True human existence," he says, "means being sent and being commissioned." Creative freedom is established as the world is established, and may not be invented by man but only discovered by him. Sartre's statement that God is "silent" may be accepted as a correct observation of the present condition, but, says Buber, his conclusion that God is absent or nonexistent is drawn by the philosopher without trying to find out what part man played in the silence. Sartre, indeed, recognizes "the perseverance of the religious need in modern times," but instead of searching for its source in man's innermost existence, he advocates its abandonment: stop looking for God, forget God.[179]

Sartre's atheism, Buber says, is the logical outcome of his existential philosophy. God for him "is the quintessence of the other," who "looks at" me, as I look at him, as an object. Such an abstract divine Other can hardly be the ground for human freedom; therefore Sartre must negate him in order to establish that freedom.

Sartre claims that God's existence curtails man's autonomy by depriving him of the possibility of saying no to the God who is supposed to have invented Good and whose decision cannot be questioned. Buber, on the contrary, holds that man can say either yes or no to God's demand. "To God's sovereign address man gives an independent answer; even when he is silent it is an answer."[180] But why does not God address Himself to man in modern times? Is it because He is absent from man's world, as Sartre argues, or because man has withdrawn behind a wall and does not hear Him? This is the pivotal question of radical theology which Buber seeks to answer in dealing with the eclipse of God.

To End the Eclipse

As shown above, what disturbs the radical theologians is the "Wholly Other" whom they cannot accept as transcendent to man and the world, but whom they also cannot admit in their immanent totality. In Buber's manner of looking at it, the image of the radical "Other" casts a shadow against heaven and eclipses God from man's view. The image is produced by man himself out of his imagination and projected not to a real other, but to a semblance of otherness vested with quasi-reality. When man loses faith in the image he has thus created, the investiture loses meaning and he proclaims the "other" dead.

> This proclamation [Buber writes] in truth says nothing but that man has become incapable of apprehending and relating himself to a reality which is plainly independent of himself. He is, moreover, incapable of imaginatively perceiving and representing this reality in images, which in themselves do not approximate its contemplation.[181]

Buber would advise these theologians not to look for an apocalyptic "end of the world," but to work toward the end of the eclipse. Summing up his observations on "Religion and Reality," he notes: "Obscuring the light of heaven, the eclipse of God, is in fact the character of the cosmic hour in which we live." When we look at an eclipse of the sun we know that it is due not to something that occurs in the sun itself, but to something between it and our eyes. But when we speak of an eclipse of God we can only think of the human side that causes it, namely, our denial of the transcendence of God, who is always there, though at times He may be in concealment. We who deny Him or we who "slay" Him,

> continue to dwell in darkness, abandoned unto death. . . . Yet the true overagainst-us . . . lives untouched behind the wall of darkness. Man may ever-more abolish the name "God." . . . The one who is meant by this name lives in the light of His eternity.[182]

It is then in the encounter with this eternal Being who lives in concealment, yet is ever present to all those who go forth to meet Him, that Buber looks for the realization of man's destiny on earth.

Encounter with the Absolute Thou

Three Sets of Questions

When man decides to go forth toward his encounter with God, he steps into the between which he has established through his act of relation. This between is ontically the same as in interhuman relations. Indeed, Buber maintains that one cannot find his way to God except through his way to man; nor can one meet fellowman without relating himself to God.[183] However, in both relations one knows only his part of the way; of the other's part he can have only a lived experience in the occurrence of the encounter. To speak of something lying beyond this experience, Buber cautions, is to overlook our limits. To be sure, in relation with God there is divine grace from above; but it "concerns us only insofar as we go forth toward it and await its presence; it is not our object" of knowledge.[184]

Our concern with regard to the signs of the divine encounter may be stated in the following three sets of questions:

1. What is the difference in the two parts of the way between

man and man, on one hand, and between man and God, on the other? How does man overcome the contradictions of the world of things in the divine encounter, and what does he strive for in this encounter?

2. What is man's existence in the divine presence, and how does he become aware of it?

3. What is the meaning of the signs of the between (revelation) when man steps out of it into the world of It, and what is the reality of his representation of those signs?

Two Parts of the Way

Although in the divine encounter God is the Absolute Thou, there is no qualitative difference between man's relation with Him and with fellowman, except that in the first case man is a finite being participating in the infinite, while God the Infinite does not participate in the finite. In the second case, two finite beings participate in the meeting reciprocally. Nevertheless, in both cases the relation is one of partnership, as all primary relations must be. Another distinction is in the different roles played by each partner—the I and the Thou—in each type of relation before and after the encounter.

(a) Role of the Thou: When man goes forth to meet fellowman, he may not know the part of the way the other has gone toward him, but he knows who the other is before as well as after the meeting. That is, he knows him outside the relational event as an object (an It) in everyday affairs, since every finite Thou must become an It. But when man is on the way to his encounter with God, he not only does not know God's part of the way but also has no knowledge of Him as an object of cognition, affection, or even belief, before or after the meeting, as God cannot be turned into any kind of object.

(b) Role of the I: Man can enter-into-relation only as a being-as-a-whole, that is, he must first gather within himself all his cognitive, volitional, and affective experiences and conjoin them into a oneness in his own essence, which then becomes the I in the I-Thou relation. This ingathering into the I is what is meant by man-as-a-whole. Now when the partner in relation is fellowman, the ingathering is not achieved fully in its greatest intensity, for in relation with a finite being one touches the unconditioned and unlimited without reaching one's own fullness of being. On the other hand, when the partner is God, the in-

gathering must be complete before even the meeting can take place, for man's participation in the infinite cannot be of a partial character, as it is in the finite. Buber describes man's state of readiness for relation with the Absolute as "complete, reposing wholeness" which one may attain when the ingathering of all partial activities reaches a constancy, when one "is not agitated by anything of a particular or partial nature, that is, nothing in him encroaches upon the world." But, he warns, this state does not signify the abandonment of the I (without the I there can be no relation) or the negation of the sensate world (the I must have this world within his being in order to enter into relation), but rather the complete acceptance of the presentness in spontaneous experience *(Erlebnis),* and not in a conceptual or idealized form of empirical knowledge *(Erfahrung),* which only breaks the relation.[185]

God Cannot Be Turned into Any Kind of Object

This dictum, stated above at the end of paragraph *(a),* governs Buber's entire discourse on man's encounter with the Absolute Thou. A brief analysis of its intrinsic meaning will help us follow the various aspects of this encounter in all its manifestations. We may ask the simple question, Why, in Buber's view, can the Absolute Thou or God not become an object or It? The question has two phases: (1) Can God be a Thou as well as an It in Himself, and (2) can man know Him at times as a Thou and at other times as an It? The answer to both phases must be sought in the dialogical (I-Thou) principle of relation as such.

In the first place, God is neither a Thou nor an It, for He is incomprehensible, that is, cannot be described in perceptual terms or defined as a concept. If this be so, then why can man say to God "Thou" but not "It?" Or, what does Thou represent in the encounter that it cannot be replaced by It? This is because man *can* enter into I-Thou relationship with the Absolute, but *not* into I-It. The difference between the two kinds of relation is that the first is complete, inasmuch as man enters into it as an independent being-as-a-whole, meeting another independent being; neither one determines the other. The second relation is partial, as man enters into it with part of his being, through one or two of his faculties, meeting another in order to make him an object determined by his observation, use, or even theoretical study. The I-Thou relation, then, stands for wholeness, completeness, and independence of both partners in the meeting. The I-It stands for separation into parts, incompleteness, and dependence of one on the other.

What is important to bear in mind here is not the single terms in each of these relations, as if one being called "I" met another being called "Thou" or "It," as the case may be. As emphasized at the beginning of this study (Introduction, "The Primary Words"), these terms have a real existence only as word pairs, each pair designating a different kind of relation. In other words, we are dealing here with the reality of the relationship and not of each of the partners by itself; and we don't really know what either is by itself, only what we experience in the encounter, or *between* us and our partner, which is either I-Thou or I-It. This is especially the case in our meeting with the Absolute or God. We don't know him either as a Thou or an It; we know only the relation (the "between") in which we meet Him. Now man has the potency of entering in relationship with God only through his own being-as-a-whole, complete in himself and carrying in his wholeness all encounters he may have had with other, finite beings in his life experiences. When this complete wholeness is consummated, it bears the signs of having encountered God, or God's Presence is "there" in the meeting. For only in this highest encounter can man have a spontaneous experience as a complete being-as-a-whole and enter into a true I-Thou relation. In all other meetings, with things of nature and fellowmen, he enters only with part of his being and is thus fragmented to a greater or lesser degree, and his relationship is of an I-It character.

Now, even in his partial encounters man may reach a high degree of wholeness, that is, move toward an I-Thou relation, but he can never fully overcome his fragmentation. That is why, when he does reach an I-Thou state with finite beings, he is only relatively out of the I-It state and keeps swinging between the two states. But in the encounter with the Absolute there is no element of fragmentation, for if there were, the meeting would not be with the Absolute or God. This is the meaning of Buber's dictum that God cannot be turned into an It: in a state of fragmentation man cannot meet God, which is the same as saying that he cannot enter into an I-It relationship with Him.

Many questions come to mind in regard to this kind of dialogical relation, such as how it can be ascertained, how one kind of encounter may be differentiated from the other in actuality, and so forth. Earlier in this chapter these and other questions were enumerated in three sets, which will now be discussed in detail in the following pages.

Overcoming Contradictions

(a) *Discreteness and Continuity:* Although the world of things is not an illusion and may not be abandoned in the act of entering-into-relation with the Absolute, its contradictions must be overcome in this encounter. Basically, the contradictions of the ordered world arise when things are conceived both in their exclusiveness or discreteness and inclusiveness or continuity at the same time. On the other hand, in the world order both may be seen together in man's twofold movement of distancing and relation. The distinction between the two movements is that the first deals with "exclusion" (*Ausschliessung*) and the second with "exclusiveness" (*Ausschliesslichkeit*), or in the first the partner and all else are "excluded," while in the second they are all "exclusive" and yet included. It means that an excluded entity, an It, is separated from the I who observes it at a distance and seeks to use it in some manner. The connection between the two is a discrete one and must be bridged by a mediating cause. And not only the thing under observation, but also the other things in its surrounding—discrete entities which interact through causal mediation—are excluded. Such is not the case with an exclusive being, a Thou, who summons the I to enter into relation. Here the exclusiveness is the uniqueness of one being who is independent of an other and yet stands in immediate association with it through a continuous act of relation. Such a being does not demand the exclusion of all others around him but, on the contrary, wants them all included in the exclusive-inclusive event. This is how the contradition of discreteness and continuity of the world of things is overcome through the act of relation.

In man's relation with finite beings the contradiction is resolved only partially, because the movement of distancing constantly breaks into the movement of relation, turning the exclusive being into an excluded thing. The complete resolution of this contradiction can be achieved in man's encounter with the Absolute, in which the exclusiveness of the others is never abridged. Even though this encounter lasts only a fleeting moment, all that has been gathered into it from the world of experience is included continually, there being no separation, no distancing, no exclusion—only pure relation. When this moment ceases, the continuity is not broken, only suspended, and may be resumed "continually" upon man's "return." In this complete relation, Buber observes, the world is not to be placed side by side with God (in the manner of placing things side by side); neither is God to be placed in the world (as one thing is included in another), but all beings and things are comprehended in Him, "all is seen in God," and "that," he says, "is complete relation."[186]

This last observation may appear as a confession of pantheism or inverse Spinozism. Spinoza leads everything out of God and Buber seems to be leading everything into Him. Both speak almost the same language. Buber: "Seeing all in the Thou, . . . conceiving all the world along in the Thou, . . . comprehending everything in him [God]."[187] Spinoza: "All things are in God, and are conceived through God."[188] Buber's own remarks about Spinoza's position may help us resolve this difficulty. Spinoza, says Buber, tries to escape anthropomorphism, yet leads right back into it, as he establishes the relationship between man and God through the immanence of divine attributes of thought and extension, but leaving all the other attributes, infinite in number, unnamed and inoperative in the relation. Although Spinoza makes an ontological distinction between man and cosmos— man is thought and the cosmos is extension—his man cannot live in this cosmos nor can the latter be contained in man, but both must find their place side by side in the two infinite attributes of the divine Substance. Man does not meet God; he is *in* God. But neither does man meet the world. Both he and the world issue from the divine Substance, each running its separate course parallel with the other and returning to the Absolute in their separate ways. Buber, who does not share these metaphysical views, finds no satisfaction in this kind of relationship between man, the world, and God, because man here is not taken as a concrete living being but rather as a *mode* of a divine attribute or an abstraction. Nevertheless, he finds Spinoza's principle of *amor intellectualis dei* a valid relation between concrete living man and the Absolute, even though it is couched in intellectual language. For this kind of love, he says, is man's true spontaneous experience, and Spinoza, no doubt, must have lived it through himself. But Spinoza does not stop there. Upon investigating the essence of man's love for God, he asserts that it is the same as God's love for man, which, coming back to his metaphysics, is nothing but God loving himself, reflected in man's mind "regarded under the form of eternity." This, Buber maintains, is not in line with his own philosophical anthropology, but is rather a "sublime anthropomorphism" which Spinoza has been unable to escape despite his avowed anti-anthropomorphism.[189]

What is significant here, in comparing the two views, is that in trying to establish man's relation to God, Spinoza has to step out of his metaphysical system (which step Buber welcomes), but when he finds the relation and tries to fit it back into his system he loses man as a concrete being. God's love loving Himself does not establish true relation, which must be in the nature of exclusiveness of an I to a Thou. When Spinoza's man reaches out to God in love, he does not bring along the world in which he lives; the latter falls back into God independently. And when man reaches God he finds himself metaphysically in Him. On the other hand, when Buber's man goes forth to enter into relation with God, he brings with him all his particular relations with fellowman and nature, as he alone, without fellowman and the world, cannot enter into this relation. Buber's "seeing all in God" is not a metaphysical merging, but rather seeing all partial, finite relations in the complete relation with the Absolute. To him, God is indeed the *mysterium tremendum*. However, unlike Spinoza, he does not *define* Him, but tries to *find* Him in the act of pure relation.

(b) Infinite Space and the Nonspatial Infinite: When we ask "Where may God be found?" or try to come "near to God," we run into a contradiction of spatial relations as conceived in the ordered world. In our encounter with the Absolute we bring from the world of things a concept of infinite space in which we seek God as if He were an object of our distancing. A contradiction than arises between a spatial nearness and a spatially conceived infinite. But in our encounter with God, according to Buber, we come near to Him as to a nonspatial infinite in the concealment which is self-understandable and "which is nearer to me than my I." It means that God is not a concept arrived at inductively from spatial extension or deductively from human thought. He is not a datum, but the enduring Being "which can only be addressed, but not described."[190] Hence, the "where" in the question "Where may God be found?" has no meaning if conceived in terms of space separation, singularity, and ob-

jectification. Its legitimate meaning may only point to the between of the encounter, which is everywhere on the way to this encounter. In truth, Buber says, one does not find God by searching for Him as for an object in space, but rather by searching within oneself for one's wholeness of being and, when this is attained, by going forth on the way to the Center, awaiting the encounter, not searching for it.[191]

(c) Freedom and Dependence: If man's relation with God is a mutuality between two independent beings, how do we account for the former's creaturely dependence on the latter without violating human freedom? Buber tries to resolve this contradiction by drawing a distinction between a state of mind and an ontic human act. Here, as in other aspects of his philosophical anthropology, he wants to steer clear of relativistic psychology. If dependence on God is taken as a feeling, it can have meaning only when compared with a feeling of independence, or a feeling of freedom from God. The contradiction is then not in the divine encounter but between two feelings in the soul of man. A very pious person who is troubled by such a difficulty may try to subdue his feeling of freedom in order to actualize his unquestioned obedience to God. Having suppressed one feeling, he becomes unaware of the opposite feeling (dependence), because he has none to compare it with, and he may thus believe that he has experienced a *coincidentia oppositorum*. But all this is just a state of mind and not an act of entering the between as such.

In the reality of complete relation dependence and freedom do not contradict each other, because they are not concepts of cause and effect. Neither side determines the other; rather, both need each other for the establishment of mutuality. Dependence is thus seen as a need for mutuality, and freedom as the unconditioned act of its fulfillment. Now this may be so in man's relation with other finite beings where the need can be readily seen on both sides, but not in relation with the Absolute where it is evident on the side of man, but not of God. Instead of trying to circumvent this difficulty by theological speculations, Buber asserts that the need of mutuality exists on both sides also between man and God. For, he says, "how could there be man if God did not need him?" Both are partners in the highest intensity of the emerging I-Thou meeting, in the "becoming" of the existing God.[192] To obviate any implication of an evolving deity, Buber hastens to add that the emergence is not a "God becoming" in man or in the world (which, he says, is idle talk), but that the existing God becomes man's partner through the latter's act of meeting Him. Better still, not God becomes but the "between," which occurs in the encounter. Further, this partnership is not entirely of man's making, but comes also by the grace of God Who, in creating man, made for Himself "a partner in the dialogue of time and one who is capable of holding converse."[193] Man's role in this partnership is realized through prayer and sacrifice: Prayer (whatever one may pray for, but prays genuinely) shows his freedom in submission to God's will, and sacrifice shows his readiness to offer himself to God in order to actualize His will.[194]

Man's Striving in the Encounter

What may man hope for as he ventures toward his encounter with God? He is aware of the abyss that lies between himself, the finite being, and the Infinite One. What part can man have in the Infinite? Should he try to bridge the abyss by discovering God in himself, or himself in God, through an act of identification, or perhaps identify himself with the divine Being through absorption into an unidentifiable Oneness? The problem centers on God's transcendence and man's attempt to overreach it through his own efforts, mystic or metaphysical, or by divine grace, as the case may be. Buber follows neither alternative but offers a third way, namely, that man should accept transcendence as fundamental and yet venture to approach God through his own human potencies which will be aided by divine grace. He views this problem from the side of man's earthly living reality, and in this reality, he holds, "there is no oneness of being." He therefore rejects the mystic doctrine of unification as well as the metaphysic of identification.[195]

(a) *Mystic Unification:* We discussed earlier the difference between Buber and the mystics on the epistemological level. Here we shall touch on the psychological aspect of his argument. The claim to mystic unity without duality, Buber holds, is due to a confusion that a unification, which takes place *within the soul* of man on his way to the encounter, is a real unity of him with another *in the encounter itself.* In the first instance, the unification is of man's partial activities in his own being-as-a-whole, but when he brings this wholeness into the act of entering-into-relation, he may be in such a state of ecstacy that he becomes unaware of his exclusiveness and mistakes his inner unity as that of a merger with the other in the encounter. But in reality, the unity is a unitary relation, the wholeness of the between, and not a fusion of the two who meet in it. The mystic mistakes this psychological unawareness of exclusiveness as an actual absorption of one partner (the self) into the other (the Absolute).[196]

(b) The Doctrine of Identification: Unification, as we have seen, is conceived by the mystics as a dynamic process of God *becoming* man or man becoming God. Identification may be viewed as a static metaphysical schema in which God *is* man or man is God. In its ultimate state, man's Self is identified with the All or, as Buber illustrates from one of the Upanishads, the Self disappears before the All-being without self-awareness or self-recollection.[197] Contrary to this view, Buber maintains that in lived reality there is no oneness of being of an I unified with the boundless Thou. If these were identical, the relation, and hence lived reality, would be abolished. Neither can there be oneness of a pure thinking subject in lived reality, because thinking must have another to think of. Finally, there is no logical oneness in lived reality, no choosing between being and not-being, because real contradictions are resolved through the act of meeting and not through the abolition of an entity or its opposite in thought. Man's striving in his encounter with the Absolute is thus not for unification or identity with Him, but to be in His presence.

Man's Existence in the Presence

No Duality of Being and Appearance

The nature of man's existence in the divine Presence may be understood in terms of the encounter itself in which something happens to man when the meeting chances upon him and he suddenly finds himself in it. If, however, we try to analyze it conceptually, we face the antinomies of finite and infinite, necessity and freedom, relative and absolute. As concepts they are irreconcilable. We may posit a third element between each of these pairs, but will not fill the gap; we may separate them in two realms of thought, but will not bridge the gap.

Kant, Buber points out, adopted the second position, but did not come to grips with man's religious experience, because he posited a conceptual duality of being and appearance, instead of a living duality of being and being. Accordingly, man's existence in the presence of God is that of a rational being who has no special faculty of knowing God and who can at best deduce Him as "merely a relative supposition of being."[198] This is a deistic idea, but not a real Being in the theistic sense. For Buber, on the other hand, man's existence in the Presence is that of a finite being in relation to the Infinite One. The same duality of relation prevails in all spontaneous experiences of man with nature, with fellowman, and with God, but on different levels. In man's encounter with the animal world, the latency of Thou becomes actual only momentarily, hardly enabling him to realize its appearing and disappearing points. With fellowman it lasts longer, but in a movement of changing actuality and latency, as Thou and It. Only in encounter with the Absolute Thou is there pure actuality, never changing into latency. When man contemplates this pure encounter he may describe it in terms of It, but neither the Thou nor the relation will change as they do, or must, in his experience with nature and fellowman. In the latter two, latency and actuality swing back and forth with one's distancing and entering-into-relation, respectively. But in the all-embracing meeting of the I with the Absolute Thou, the presence of Thou is always actual, even when man withdraws from it. At his withdrawal he may speak of the divine Thou as He or It, but only in allegory. In pure relation, says Buber, "the unbroken truth of the world" dawns on man, and by speaking Thou to the Absolute he expresses truth in the mortal sense.[199] (see above, "God Cannot Be Turned into Any Kind of Object" section).

Knowledge of the Presence

According to Buber's philosophy of religious experience, God is incomprehensible, cannot be demonstrated or proved, or even presupposed as an object of belief, but He can be known through our immediate bond with Him.[200] Nevertheless, inquiring man (and not just the thinking mind) wants to know the signs of his entering-into-relation with God. To put the matter in dialogical form, he wants to know that the relation he has entered into is a genuine dialogue with God. Buber says he cannot explain this matter in terms of philosophical speculation, systematic or otherwise, but can only "point the way" and, at that, only the stretch of the way which man has to walk toward the meeting. The other part we know not, but it happens upon us in the meeting. If this is the case, how do we account for the exclusiveness of each partner outside the meeting? Or, to put it more pointedly, how do we account for the existence of the Presence as an independent reality if we know it only in the encounter and in no sense outside of it? Here Buber differentiates between knowledge within the relational event which he calls "boundless," and knowledge outside of it, which he calls "bounded." The first signifies a knowledge that is not confined within a spatiotemporal order, and the second, one that is thus confined.[201]

In the *incomplete* relationship with fellowman, knowledge of the other fluctuates between the boundless and the bounded. But in the *complete* relation with God it is altogether boundless; yet it embraces latency without turning into it (God never becomes bounded). That is, in the former, when latency prevails, the isolated moments of experience follow each other in space-time sequence, connected through causal mediators. In the latter, the same isolated moments (latency) are brought into the Center of relation with the Absolute and included in the actuality of the encounter which is not spatiotemporal or causal. But the knowledge that man has of the Thou prior to or after the encounter can be only of a bounded order, and since the Absolute Thou cannot be placed within such an order, he cannot be known outside the relation. Nonetheless, man knows the part of his way in preparation for the meeting, and it is this part that Buber investigates, hoping to find in it the signs that point to complete relation with the divine Presence.

The Finite Completed through Contact with the Infinite

Man's part of the way to God is through his limited contacts with nature and fellowman. Buber calls them portals to the Presence. In interhuman relationships the sphere of speech is preeminent, and since the relation to God is in the same sphere, man's way to Him is attained best through fellowman.[202] This may seem contrary to Buber's dialogical principle which calls for direct mutuality between two independent beings. Why should one have to go through other creatures in order to reach the Creator? If one's aim is to enter-into-relation, he should be able to do it alone as one exclusive being with another. Indeed, it would seem that the more one is isolated from everybody and everything finite, the better prepared he would be for the encounter with the Infinite. But this, says Buber, depends on what is meant here by isolation and preparation.

In all his writings on the principle of dialogue, Buber emphasizes that it is not a case of an I saying "Thou," but of man-as-a-whole speaking "I-Thou," and that the one who speaks "I-It" is not man-as-a-whole. His wholeness comes through the ingathering of all his finite experiences, and since he cannot address God except as Thou, his relation to Him is possible only in the highest degree of wholeness. In this act, man must isolate himself from using fellowman and things but not from relational contacts with them; on the contrary, without such contacts he cannot go forth on his way to God.[203] What he brings on his way is not his "self" alone—an abstract I—but all his finite relations of everyday experience, which constitute his preparation. In speaking the finite I-Thou, then, man also participates in the infinite, though not completely. Only in his meeting with the Absolute does he bring the fullness of all his finite experiences into the Center of the meeting where they complete themselves, i.e., where the relation is not accompanied by distancing. Thus, pure relation, Buber tells us, can come into being solely in the divine Presence. But what, in the final analysis, does he find in the category *humanum* that points to the presence? This question touches the very foundations of his ontology.

Ontological Argument for the Existence of the Presence

Buber does not present an ontological argument as such, as he does not propose to prove God's existence or His mutuality in meeting with man. But as an ontologist he does not escape this argument altogether. His principle of complete relation is lodged in his ontology, and this constitutes a form of the ontological argument. He differs from previous religious thinkers on this subject in three respects: (1) He deals with the question of God's presence in the encounter with man and not, as the others do, of God's existence, which for him can have no proof and needs none. (2) He seeks to establish the divine Presence on the basis of the prime reality of man's entering-into-relation and not by logical deduction. (3) He finds signs of the presence in the relation itself and not in postulated metaphysical principles. At the same time, his argument has several methodological features in common with other arguments of this nature. *First,* they all issue from the humanistic or anthropological viewpoint, that is, they take man as their starting point. *Second,* they posit perfection or completion as man's ultimate goal. *Third,* whatever perfection may mean in each case, they all maintain that man does not possess it; there is a certain lack in his being which he is trying to fill or complete. *Fourth,* they find something in man which points to perfection or completion outside of himself; that is, although perfection transcends him, there is something of it or like it immanent in him. *Fifth,* whatever that immanent something may be, it is not in man's psychic state, but in his ontic category of being. *Sixth,* what we may learn of the perfect being outside of man is only that it exists, but nothing of its nature or essence. In order to bring to light the specific character of Buber's indirect use of this method, I will contrast it with the well-known direct arguments of Augustine, Anselm, and Descartes.

Those three most distinguished exponents of the ontological argument seek to prove the existence of a most perfect being, each on his own grounds.[204] *Augustine* sees in man an imperfect will which cannot determine itself without God's help; man's striving for the realization of his will points to the ontic reality of a most perfect will, that is, God's will. *Anselm* finds man possessed of an imperfect reason and at the same time capable of grasping a most perfect reason; this capacity points to the existence of a perfect reason which is God. *Descartes* discovers in man an imperfect certitude that fills him with doubt except about his own existence, but this existence, being mixed with elements of doubt, can be assured and sustained only by a being in whom there is no particle of doubt, who is most certainly perfect, and that is God.

Buber does not argue for the existence of a most perfect being but for the existence of a most perfect relation, which man cannot attain except in his encounter with the Absolute. He rests his case not on logical deductions or metaphysical assumptions but on experienced imperfection in human communication. He does not proceed from logic and metaphysics to ontology, but from one ontological insight to another. To the extent that man's ontic acts of communication issue from his own potencies of relation with another finite being, there is a certain incompleteness in the relation. And yet, there is something in man that drives him toward complete self-realization. His ontic sense of Thou rebels against his limitations and will not be satisfied until it is in the full reality of presentness. It strives to discover "the most primary"—the primal source; it strives toward the eternal Thou. This striving, being of an ontic character, points to the divine Presence in a complete relation, in which alone it can be fulfilled.

According to Buber's ontology, man experiences his limitations in all three spheres of relation, namely, with nature, with fellowman, and with God. In his life with the world of things and with fellow human beings he finds a lack of completeness due to the fact that each Thou he encounters must be turned into an It, and also due to the "inner laws of our living with each other." To complete himself he must venture forth to the meeting with the eternal Thou, but even then he can only prepare his part of the way; the other part, which completes it, comes to him by the grace of the Eternal.[205] It should be noted that Buber, following Jewish tradition, does not posit divine grace as a substitute for man's own action. On the contrary, he says,

> The fact that we take human decision seriously does not impair our seriousness about grace. The former leads the soul on the way to the latter, which is attainable only through decision. In no sense is man given here complete power. Rather, what is decisive is the enjoined perspective of concrete action, which may not be curtailed in advance, yet must experience limitation as well as grace in the very process of acting.[206]

This limitation or incompleteness in man's ontic movement toward self-fulfillment points to the presence of a Thou who is absolute and who is "there" by grace to meet man in his striving. Thus, when Buber speaks of the eternal Thou as the one which "by its very being cannot become It, because by its being it cannot be set in measure and boundary,"[207] he does not mean to offer a proof of God's existence, but rather to show that only His presence can lead man to his own fulfillment in pure relation—in a meeting in which there is no I-It, only I-Thou.

The Signs of the Between: Revelation

Giver and Receiver of the Signs

Each time man enters into relation with the Absolute Thou something new occurs to him which he had not lived through before. That something Buber calls revelation. It was not there all the time for man to discover; nor is it an uncovering of the mystery of God, for it does not deal with the divine concealment, only with man's living experience in the face of it. Revelation is the dialogue between man and God as between partners in the same event. God chooses to address man, and man must decide whether he will give himself wholly in response or deny himself to it. "For revelation," Buber says, "is nothing else than the relation between giving and receiving, which means that it is also the relation between desiring to give and failing to receive."[208] The giver is the divine Being and the receiver is man, but the latter can receive only if he turns to the giver with his whole being. Both sides act out of free will. Man does not conjure up the Divine to come, and God does not compel man to accept the Presence.[209] Revelation waits for man to turn and answer, and when he answers he is met by God's redeeming grace. It is therefore not correct, according to Buber, to ask what is revealed. Man becomes aware of revelation as and when it takes place. He has no foreknowledge of it, nor can he decipher it through some hidden omens, conceptual analysis, or scientific formulation, because the revelation is the occurrence itself. It is not God's being that is revealed, but His relation to us and our relation to Him.[210] What is revealed is that the Divine and human meet in a between. Still, when man steps out of the relational event, he wonders about the "giving and receiving," the "address and response," and seeks some signs of their effects in his daily affairs, even though he may not be looking for omens or symbols of divine concealment. Where can he find those signs, what can he know of their giver, and how can he ascertain their meaning?

(a) *Where the Signs are Found:* The signs of revelation, Buber advises, may be found everywhere, in everything in the world with which man communicates. "What occurs to me addresses me,"[211] though I may not always be there to respond. When, for instance, one is addressed by fellowman in genuine speech, it is a sign that God calls on him to respond, and if he becomes inwardly aware of it the sign signifies revelation. If, on the other hand, he reacts to the other by using him as an object for personal gratification, the sign is absent. In true dialogue, Buber writes, "nothing can withhold itself from being a vessel of the word. The possibilities of dialogue are bound only by those of inner awareness."[212]

(b) Knowledge of the Giver of the Signs: Buber limits our knowledge only to the signs: we know nothing of the Concealed One.[213] In each particular dialogue I know the speaker in my inner awareness without naming him, but only during the moment of the encounter. The more I have lived through such moments, the closer I come to the awareness of the One Speaker, the Absolute Thou. Revelation is thus not a one-time appearance, but the eternal occurrence in all moments of life in which we encounter something which demands a response in mutuality. It is the same in small revelations as in the great historic ones.[214]

(c) Meaning of the Signs: The signs have their meaning in the revelation as such, for revelation, says Buber, *is* the meaning of everything. It does not point to anything outside itself, to a life beyond or, for that matter, to life itself. There is no life in itself apart from revelation; therefore, to ask for the meaning of life as such is an empty question. Revelation is the act of relation wherein man as a participant confirms everything in the world, including himself, with his life as a whole. The meaning is the acting, not, however, according to fixed precepts or traditions, but in each unique occurrence between one person and an other.

The Human Person: The Category Humanum

It may seem that Buber advocates an individualistic approach to the meaning of reality, but he disclaims it. His bearer of dialogue with God on the human side is not the individual, but the person. By the latter he means the one who, through his potencies of interhuman relations centered in the encounter with the Absolute, creates a "communality" among men, out of which grow communities, peoples, nations, and the universal community. It is in man's anthropological nature that he does not exist in isolation as an individual, but in communality as a person.[215] Indeed, the person does not grow out of the actual community, but is its formative element: the community first comes into being through the interaction of persons. When, therefore, we ask about the meaning of the signs for man, we must first answer the question, What is man to whom the signs may be revealed? Buber considers this matter basic to his philosophical anthropology, in contrast to Kant's question "What is man?," which, he says, was left unanswered by the philosopher. Kant, he reminds us, formulated four questions concerning the meaning of man's existence, namely: (1) What can I know? (2) What ought I to do? (3) What may I hope? and (4) What is man? Kant assigns each of the first three to a different branch of philosophy, but leaves the fourth to anthropology, which, he notes, actually embraces the other three.[216]

Buber agrees with the fourth assignment, but feels that Kant's anthropology did not carry it out.[217] For that, he says, we need a philosophical anthropology which sees man as a unique category of being who acts in a twofold movement of separation and entering-into-relation. He therefore reshapes the first three Kantian questions into one, putting the emphasis on the category *humanum,* namely, What category of being is man who can know, who ought to do, and who may hope? The three "whats" in Kant's original formulation can be answered only by the "what" of the category *humanum.* Once the latter is ascertained, the signs emerging from its ontic acts in relation to the Absolute assume the meaning of those very acts, as they are cognized as a partnership with God in creation, revelation, and redemption. However, this may answer what man knows and may hope for, but not the third question as to what he ought to do of his own free will. For if all the meanings follow from his ontic category by nature, what freedom does he have in determining his own action? In Buber's schema, the meaning of the latter comes from the first two, namely, revelation and redemption: man ought to do what he knows and hopes for. According to this anthropology (see above, "Movement toward the Good" section), the elements that give direction to the "ought" are man's "inclusive wholeness," or the ingathering of all his particular relations in himself, and his "responsibility" which comes through his response to others.

Man's Way to His Goal

What is the relationship between creation, revelation, and redemption with reference to man's goal toward self-fulfillment? When Buber speaks of man's partnership in creation, he does not mean in the "beginning of the world." That, he says, is a mystery which cannot be put into a proposition, such as "God created the world out of nothing" or the like.[218] Man's partnership with God was established in the very act of divine creation, in which man was given freedom to relate with his Creator as one independent being with an other. Such freedom remains a mystery that can be comprehended only in the fulfillment of its purpose, namely, that man shall be a partner with God in the redemption of himself and the world. He discovers it in revelation, which is nothing but the Divine calling him to work for redemption. We may readily comprehend how man is a partner with God in revelation and redemption, as both imply an ontic act on the human side, but we wonder how he takes part in creation, which is not of his making at all. Buber explains: man, having been created for dialogue with God, is aware of creation pulsing in him in each moment he enters into such dialogue. Or, "Creation—it chances upon us, it burns into us. . . . Creation—we participate in it, we meet the Creator, offer ourselves to him, as helpers and partners."[219] Furthermore, creation is also an ongoing act of bringing order out of chaos, direction out of lack of direction, good out of evil. Man, therefore, by his decision to go forth toward the divine encounter, that is, decision for direction, helps bring order out of chaos and turn evil into good, thus completing God's creation on earth. His part in it is the ultimate meaning of his dialogue with God which fulfills itself in the threefold way of creation, revelation, and redemption, as it is also the ultimate destiny of his self-fulfillment, that is, the fulfillment of the purpose for which he was created.

Although Buber differentiates three phases of man's self-fulfillment, he regards them all as acting themselves out together in what he calls the "threefold chord of world-time." They cannot be separated from one another without blunting the divine dialogue. Redemption cannot take place if man negates the created world of things, separates himself from other creatures, or fails to heed the call of revelation. "Creation," says Buber, "is not a hurdle on the road to God; it is the road itself. We are created together and for one another. The creatures are placed in my way so that through them and with them I, their fellow creature, may find the way to God."[220] Similarly, each man's return to God is redemption not of himself alone, but of the whole world of things and men, for without them he cannot return and cannot prepare himself for revelation. And without these two, without revelation and redemption, his world of creation, his cosmos, falls apart, splintered into chaos.[221]

The Absolute Person

Some forty years after *Ich und Du* was first published, Buber added a "Nachwort" to clarify his concepts in response to questions that had been addressed to him over the years. Of special interest here is what he had to say about the mutuality of man's relation with God. "There can be no proof of the existence of mutuality between God and man," he wrote, "as there can be no proof of the existence of God."[222] Man may only bear witness to this mutuality when he dares speak of it. But in speaking of it, Buber finds it necessary to say something further about God.

In the mutuality of relation, he points out, God is neither a principle nor an idea, but He may be designated as person, inasmuch as mutuality with us can exist only as between persons. In this respect, one may say "God *too* is a person."[223] The word "too," we must add, indicates that the "is" is not to be taken literally. The concept of person, more correctly "person-like" *(Personhaftigkeit)*, says Buber, cannot signify God's essence. If, however, one wishes to speak of God's attributes, in the manner of Spinoza, then Buber proposes in addition to the former's two attributes of spirit-like and nature-like, a third one, person-like, which, he says, is the only one that lends itself by its character to become known to us in immediacy. Now this concept, he cautions, implies relative, not absolute independence (man becomes an independent person not in himself but relative to others with whom he communicates) and may therefore not be properly attributed to God, the Absolute Thou. To avoid this difficulty, Buber designates God as the Absolute Person, i.e., "one that cannot be relativized," or, stated more specifically, "In his immediate relation to us, God enters as an absolute person. The contradiction," he adds, "must yield to higher discernment."[224] By designating God as person, he further notes, "I mean the one who—whatever else he may be—enters into an immediate relation to us humans, in creating, revealing, redeeming acts, and thereby enables us to enter into an immediate relation to him."[225]

Nothwithstanding his application of the word "person" to God, Buber may not be characterized as a philosophical "Personalist," as understood by the adherents of this school of thought. As described by Ralph T. Flewelling, one of the founders of this school, Personalism is a metaphysical world view centered in the concept of person as an independent, self-conscious, self-directing, and self-organizing entity, "both in finite individuals and in a supreme creative Intelligence which is the world-ground and source of all reality." Personality is here considered as the "supreme value" permeating all of reality, notably in its ethical character; "the cosmic order, being personal, is also ethical."[226] According to another leading spokesman of this movement, William Stern, author of *Person und Sache,* the fundamental presuppositions of philosophical personalism "are that *Weltanschauung,* science, and the conduct of life can be established only through a metaphysic, and that for our epoch and the succeeding one the basic metaphysical category must be that of 'person.' "[227]

Neither of these descriptions, which are typical of the personalist world view, fits Buber's religious world outlook. To begin with, Buber does not deal with metaphysical speculations about the essence or existence of man, nature, or God. He is not looking for a single concept to bring man, nature, and the divine Being under an all-embracing category varying in degree. His term "person" belongs in essence to the category *humanum* alone as the being who enters-into-relation with other beings. This particular category, he emphasizes, is not applicable to any other being in nature or beyond. When he uses "person" in reference to God, as shown above, it is not with regard to His essence, but rather to His relationship with man, as if to say God made Himself a person in order to meet man in dialogue; or in Buber's own words, "In order to be able to speak to man, God must become a person; but in order to be able to speak to him, God must make him, too, an actual person. This human person not only receives the word, but also answers."[228]

Representations of Revelation

What reality is there in man's expressions of his encounter with God? The eternal Thou, by its very Being, cannot be objectified; it cannot be represented as a form, perceptually or conceptually. Buber extends the commandment "Thou shalt not make unto thee an image" to mean "Thou canst not make an image."[229] Yet man is compelled to form images in order to translate the power he faced in revelation into a content of knowledge and precepts—into a theology, religious worship, ethical conduct. This tendency, which stems from man's double movement, Buber indicates, has its psychological and historical aspects.

Psychologically, man cannot feel secure with a revelation which he cannot express as a continuum in space and time. The drive toward revelation (the preparation for the encounter) leaves him in a psychic state of venture without assurance, of risk without guarantee, of ever going-forth-toward without a resting place. Man, as Buber phrases it, can glance up to God with his inclusive wholeness, but "that this glance of the being exists, wholly unillusory, . . . no other court in the world attests than that of faith."[230] However, faith is not a psychic capacity and cannot therefore satisfy man's psychic drive for security in his spatiotemporal existence; he then converts God into an object of belief. Similarly, the structural moment of revelation (the encounter itself) leaves man psychologically lonely. Even though he gathers within his being all things in the world in preparation for the encounter, he can enter it only by himself alone as a person and not as a member of a collective. He must speak Thou to the divine Being wholly by himself in his inclusive exclusiveness. In order to mitigate this aloneness, he seeks spatial extension in a community of believers; thus God becomes an object of a cult.

As long as man knows that these psychic factors help him to confirm the act of revelation in everyday life and that they must be continually revitalized through moments of pure relation, his continuum of the world of things, his cosmos, will be genuinely guaranteed. However, when he simply substitutes the objects of his belief and cult for the primary relation, his sense of security in a spatiotemporal world becomes illusory.

Historically, man's relation to God reflects both primary movements—individuation and connection or the contradictions of the world of I-It, on the one hand, and their reconciliation in the world of I-Thou, on the other. His true mission is to actualize the word of revelation in everyday life in whatever form he may be able to express it. When he turns to God, the word comes into being; when he extends his religious life in personal and communal forms, the word is still active, though in different forms; and when he turns again to God, the word is renewed in its being. That is, man actualizes the word in everyday life by converting it into images which tend to congeal into objects of belief and cult, but what he converts is not God but revelation, where he looks at the world in God and forms for himself God's countenance—a mixture of Thou and It, of the divine and the human.[231] What man turns into an object of belief or cult is the divine countenance; God is not in the cult, but near it whenever man is ready for the encounter. But when the countenance (whatever its religious image may be, for each religion forms its own countenance of God) becomes a substitute for the living God, it turns into a dead image, and the spirit is suppressed.

At certain historic moments, Buber says, there is a ripening of time and the human spirit is ready to break out and venture toward renewed relation with God. Such are the moments of great revelations, when the spirit is recast into new forms of God's countenance in the world. The person who responds to the call must step out of the community, which is sheltered only by the "temple-dome but not by the firmament," and go into loneliness. "The one who is sent forth in revelation takes along the image of God . . . in the eye of his spirit," not metaphorically, but in his very spiritual reality. What is activated then is not man's own power, nor God's passing through, but "a mixture of the Godly and the human," and the word becomes the *living word* again. The history of revelation, Buber concludes, continues its course, not just in the great universal revelations, but in all the small ones as well: all are eternal revelation. Even when man has distanced himself from God and the countenance has departed, the word continues to work until it breaks through again in the renewed return, and that is redemption. This course finds expression through the word which comes into being in the countenances of the living religions.

For Buber, man's relation to God is not an abstract philosophical speculation, not even a theological doctrine, but a personal experience of faith, which lies at the heart of all genuine relation with reality. In his own personal life, he tells us, this is what happened to him during the years 1912–1919:

> All the experiences of being that I had during [those years] became present to me in growing measure as *one* great experience of faith. . . . Since, however, I have received no message which might be passed on in such a manner, but have only had the experiences and attained the insights, my communication had to be a philosophical one.[232]

These experiences which Buber speaks of came to him through his Jewish faith, and it is in the sources of this faith that he found the insights which he transmitted in his philosophical writings. His philosophy of Judaism thus bears all the signs of his philosophy of communication in its primary forms. In part 2 of this study, we shall examine his teachings on Judaism, how they parallel the three areas of part 1, and how the Jewish faith exemplifies the dialogical principle in its experiences as a living religion.

PART II

Judaism:
A Living Experience of
Relation

Introduction

The Jew and His Jewishness

"Dialogue between Heaven and Earth"

The above title is the subject of one of Buber's "Speeches on Judaism" which he delivered "At the Turning," in 1951. In his preface he notes: "In these hours of destiny, the four speeches must be read as directed by a Jew to Jews. Yet what he says concerns present-day man in his humanity."[233] As a non-Christian, Buber cannot be expected to answer the perplexing questions of the modern Christian theologians, but as an "arch-Jew," as he calls himself, he is bound to seek a solution to man's predicament in the sources of Judaism, "from the Decalogue to Hasidism."[234] Israel's Holy Scriptures, he believes, reveal the Jewish view of existence: "The basic teaching which fills the Jewish Bible is that our life is a dialogue between above and below." As for Hasidism, "it is the fulfillment of Judaism."[235]

When Buber speaks of the Jewish religion or Judaism, he means the concrete reality of the relation between God and the Jewish people or, as he prefers, Israel, collectively and individually. His own experience of this relationship may be traced along his path to Hasidism, which began in his early boyhood during summer visits to the Hasidic Rebbe of Sadagora and lasted throughout his life.[236] He found in the teachings, sayings, and legends of the Hasidic zaddikim, and especially in their way of life, a spiritual force which to him was the religious reality of historical Israel. He saw in them not the dissent of a separatist sect, but a genuine return of Jewishness to its primary source. Through the Hasidic movement he sought to identify himself with the source rather than with the movement as such. For him the primary source of religion is the dialogical encounter between man and God. Although this is not confined to Judaism alone, he was "certain that no other human group has devoted such strength and fervor to this experience as have the Jews."[237] In modern times, he finds, Hasidism has manifested this religious fervor in an incomparable manner which has a bearing on the essence of humanity as a whole.[238] Before we deal with Buber's application of these principles to Judaism, we shall examine his view of the religious issue involved and his method of resolving it.

While Buber views the Absolute Thou as the center in which all lines of relation intersect, he regards man as the center of the problematic of this relation; that is, the problem is man's role in it. For when man prepares to enter-into-relation with the Absolute, he can know only his own part of the way, not God's. The latter comes to him by grace. Hence the religious issue for Buber is not a theological one, not what the *logos* reveals about *theos* or God the redeemer, but rather what religion teaches man who is to be redeemed. Furthermore, the dialogical relation between man and God, being a partnership between two mutually independent beings, poses the problem of relation between a finite being and an infinite one, as manifested in the acts of creation, revelation, and redemption, which religion attributes to the divine infinite Being. Accordingly, man can fulfill his part of the partnership only if he participates in these acts not merely for his own redemption but also for the redemption of the world.

We must also bear in mind that Buber does not view the religious issue in its metaphysical aspect, but rather as a problem in ontology. He does not seek to establish a theology which is nothing but a metaphysical system in terms of categories of thought in which God, man, and the world are reconciled as concepts of the understanding or pure reason. Instead, he deals with what he calls the *theologoumena* of religion or the manner of speaking about God *(theologein)* in relation to man, and not about "God the highest idea," or His divine essence or existence. "It is not of God, but of the meeting that we speak."[239] This meeting is essentially the same as in interhuman relations, except that in the former man strives for completion, which he cannot attain in the latter.[240]

When these *theologoumena* are applied to a historical religion, the question is whether the latter manifests this type of relation in the actual experience of men who profess to live by it. Buber's distinction between two types of faith is really a distinction between two types of men of faith, which resolves itself into the anthropological question "What is man?" Unlike Kant, Buber does not find complete relation in the interhuman sphere which the scientist-philosopher establishes independently of the relation to God; and unlike Nietzsche, he does not elevate the human sphere to the state of god-philosophers. He finds the possibility for completion through the man of faith exemplified in biblical sources: the prophet or prophet-messiah and, in Hasidic lore, the zaddik. His exposition of Judaism is a quest for man's self-realization, and we must look into it not for his verification of teachings, doctrines, or dogmas, but for his uncovering of spontaneous experiences of people who have lived and acted as Jews. We may not find in his interpretation of religious life the ultimate meaning of Judaism, only the meaning of its transmitted words. These words, which he interprets, are the religious experiences of the men who transmitted them.

The Method

Buber approaches the sources of historical religions by the method of selection. He is not the kind of researcher who gathers all available information for a presentation of the various trends in Judaism, but one who chooses from his sources those elements which exemplify his subject, namely, the man of faith. Furthermore, he scrutinizes his findings in the light of his own experience of the religious encounter. When he reads "the proclaimed revelation that reports the 'speaking' of God", and the claim made by others as to its meaning, he investigates "the legitimacy of this claim." "I must," he says, "whenever and however I read it, always myself be ready anew for meeting."[241] This is not an empirical method of weighing facts of observation or experimentation. Rather, it is the method of experience in which historical facts speak to one who comprehends them in a renewed act of relation. Summing up his approach to the sources of religion, Buber writes:

As far as the tradition of Judaism is concerned: a few of its great expressions, beginning with the biblical and ending with the Hasidic, together constitute the strongest witness for the primacy of the dialogical that is known to me. . . . I have not been able to accept either the Bible or Hasidism as a whole; in one and in the other I had to and I have to distinguish between that which had become evident to me out of my experience as truth and that which had not become evident to me in this manner.[242]

In selecting from the recorded sources of tradition, then, Buber holds that he himself must become witness to their truth through a direct act of meeting. This may suggest a subjectivist treatment of the sources, taking only what appeals to him individually and making himself the sole judge of their validity. However, this is so only to the extent that he postulates certain valuations of the text. For his act of entering into relation with the Absolute through the spoken word is an objective ontic reality of man, of every man, who experiences this relation. Buber regards himself as a filter of the material at hand, with all its tensions and contradictions from which he has chosen what he has chosen, according to his best insight into his own life with it.[243] However, while his criterion of selection is grounded in the factual, its objectivity rests in his ontology rather than in the historicity of the facts.

In keeping with his ontological view of speech as the essence of the relational event, Buber's exegesis of biblical text is mainly philological, with emphasis on the spoken word as the bearer of the message. "The Hebrew Bible," he states, "is essentially stamped and structured by the language of the message."[244] My purpose here is not to give a full account of Buber's methodology of Bible study but to indicate its ontological implications. Before we enter into this subject, two central elements of his method require closer examination, namely, "the category of *the uniqueness* of the fact [*Faktumseinzigkeit*] as a criterion of objectivity, and the "scientifically-intuitive [method], that is, searching as well as advancing toward the underlying *concreteness* of the record."[245]

"If one seeks methods without any definite problem in mind," said the scientist-mathematician David Hilbert, "his search is then mostly in vain."[246] Buber's overriding problem of biblical research is the redemption of the world according to the teachings of the faith of Israel. He traces the different forms of this faith through the ages, each reflecting a particular tendency, yet all expressing a unified trend of the Jewish Bible as a whole. In doing so, he points out, he is dealing with a history of faith and not with a history of religion. By the latter he means the development of symbols, rituals, practices, doctrines, and institutions; in the former all these are "submerged in the common life-relations of a community . . . with all its social, political and spiritual functions, the faith [which has] become flesh in a people."[247]

In Buber's science of religious relation, faith is the highest potency of establishing this relation. The history of faith, therefore, seeks to ascertain from the sources the basic concreteness of each record as a witness to the prime relational event which was experienced as faith. In the case of the Jewish people, Buber notes, there was a dual experience of this nature. One was that of a wandering people following their God, the leader, Who had taken them out of bondage and showed them how to distinguish the true way from the false one.[248] The knowledge of faith can only be a knowledge of the between, which comes into being in the act of relation. Such are the facts of the religious experience, and since they have come down to us through the words of the prophets, Buber's task is to investigate in each record the original intent of the word as it became flesh in the actual life of the people.

The other experience, related to the first, was the divine confrontation through individual prophet-messengers. The *nabi* or messenger is a man who experiences God's address to the people. Buber considers this prophetic experience as the true path of the Jewish faith toward redemption. Although he takes into account the folk experience, he emphasizes the personal relationship even when the people as a whole is involved. As he writes:

> That revelation "comes in community" . . . is not my view at all. Even when the community as such . . . seems to take part in an event of revelation transmitted in historical form, even when the report includes a divine address directed to a "You" (plural), I can understand as the core of the happening discernible by me only as a central human person's coming into contact with transcendence.[249]

This view of the role of the individual in the life of the community creates a tension in Buber's thinking not only in matters of religion but also in his socio-political and ethical philosophy. As may be seen from his teaching on the restructuring of society, he has not been able to overcome this tension, or perhaps never intended to, as his "historical bias" in interpreting the formation of tradition leans toward the individual rather than the community.[250] He treats the history of faith, in the case of Moses as well as the other prophet-messengers, as "the homogeneous image of a man and his work,"[251] in which he seeks a confirmation of his hypotheses. "What really happened" in fact, he points out, cannot be determined by sifting the layers of tradition, for the real happening is not so much in the events themselves as in "the manner in which the participating people experienced those events," that is, as an encounter "between this people and a vast historical happening that overwhelmed it."[252] Thus, what Buber investigates in the history of faith is the between which came into existence when the people, along with its prophet-messengers, met the divine power that shaped its destiny. The reality of this between constitutes the facts of this history, as it also constitutes the facts of every present encounter with God. Each meeting is unique by its very nature as an act of entering-into-relation. Therefore, Buber uses the "category of uniqueness of the fact" as a criterion of objectivity of the historical account. His task now is to find in the biblical record the experience of an encounter which was actually expressed by the people at the time of its occurence and not as it was imagined later by those who recorded it. He calls it a "critique of tradition . . . [which] approximates us to the original meeting."[253]

From his ontological viewpoint, then, Buber cannot investigate the history of Israel's faith as such, only the evidence that certain acts of meeting with God took place. He cannot reconstruct from the record the exact events which manifested themselves in the encounter; he can only derive from it some indication that the encounter occurred. Since he maintains that "the historical relationship between YHVH and Israel has to find its expression through the figure of speech used,"[254] his "critique of tradition" is directed to the verification of the evidence found only in records of the spoken word.

Buber places more credence in the historical saga than in official chronicles, because he considers the former as spontaneous and untarnished in "the predominant method of preserving the memory of what happens."[255] This, too, is in keeping with his science of religious relation in which the spoken word is the essence of meeting. He finds in the sagas, especially those expressed in poetic form, the true kernel of the spokenness of man's encounter with the Divine throughout the biblical text. "Everything in Scripture," he says, "is genuine spokenness."

"In every member of its body the Bible is a message."[256] He sees its objective reality in the narratives of imagery, its rhythm, word formation, and parallelism, and in the repetitive phonetic-rhythmic or paronomastic methods of the Bible.[257] These forms are the expression of what he calls (borrowing a phrase from Jacob Grimm) "objective enthusiasm" on the part of the narrator who "saw" the "historical situation of his community" through the stirrings of his entire being, not just in imagination or as an interpretation. "Even the subsequent comprehension of the flashing lightening-like visions within the consecutive report of the saga is not arbitrary in character. An organic and organically creative memory is here at work."[258] And when he investigates the underlying concreteness of this record he comes upon its objective reality through a "scientific intuition," perhaps in the same manner as the original narrator came upon it through his "objective enthusiasm."[259]

It is noteworthy that Buber's method of biblical interpretation hews very close to the Pharisaic line of Talmudic-Midrashic hermeneutics. If we relate method to purpose, as we must in order to render the method meaningful, both Buber and the Pharisees place their respective methods in the service of God. Both aim at the redemption of man in this world; both are concerned with the interpretation of the Torah so that man may live by it here and now on earth.[260] In the *Vorwort* to his *Schriften zur Bibel* Buber points out that he wrote his biblical essays some twenty years after he had already published his major works on philosophy and Hasidism. "This told me in a particularly emphatic manner, . . ." he noted, "that I had first to mature in the service of the Bible." And from this he also learned, as he later admonished his young listeners, to read and interpret the Bible "as a service of knowing the soul of the original Hebrew language, but not as a work of literature."[261] This is entirely in the spirit of Talmudic-Midrashic interpretation of Scripture. There is much affinity between the latter and Buber's method, but I shall indicate here only two main characteristics which they have in common, namely, that the living, spoken word of the biblical text is the dominant factor in determining basic meanings, and that the rules of interpretation follow the same general patterns.

Buber combines many features of the two great Talmudic interpretations of the Bible, the *Otiot d'Rabbi Akiba* and the *Shelosh Esreh Midot d'Rabbi Yishmael*. One is Akiba's free, intuitive exegesis of every extra or double word as implying a fundamental teaching and the other is Yishmael's use of parallel words or passages as signifying the same general idea in different parts of the Torah. What Buber really claims with reference to Pharisaic hermeneutics is that the modern scholar has as much right to adapt the living core of biblical, and for that matter Talmudic, teachings to the needs of his time as the ancient Talmudic scholars had in theirs. In this respect he follows in the footsteps of another modern scholar, Eisik Hirsch Weiss of Vienna, who revived the original intent of the Talmudic dictum of "Sinaitic tradition" *(kabbala mi-Sinai)* and applied it intuitively as an interpretive method of both Scripture and Talmud. Unlike the dogmatists, Weiss does not interpret the doctrine of "Sinaitic tradition" to mean that it represents fixed laws which have come down from Sinai in detailed explication in the form of oral transmissions for all generations to follow literally unto eternity.[262] Similarly, Buber considers the Pharisaic exegesis of the Torah text as free intuitive interpretations. He says they "put the Torah [*die Weisung*] in the living tradition, which modifies it as it interprets it."

> They want reality, not just any reality, but reality out of the word; they want life, not just any life, but life in the Presence; they want the people, God's people, acting from God, living with God. . . . The Pharisee is the man who is concerned with nothing but that the word assume an image in all things, the man who affirms the world as God's world actively, not just with a few of his life-expressions, but with all of them.[263]

And while Buber does not propose "to revive Pharisaism" in our time, he considers himself as its true spiritual heir, more legitimately, he claims, than the rabbinic fundamentalists.[264] He sees himself as their true disciple, principally in his exposition of the messianic idea, which to him is the essence of the faith of Israel. The investigation of this idea as the Jewish expression of the act of redemption is the chief concern of his studies in Judaism.[265]

The Problematic of the Jewish Soul

As we have seen, Buber's method of investigating the history of the Jewish faith is closely connected with his ontological concept of dialogue. When he grappled with the question of the

Jew and his Jewishness in his "Speeches on Judaism" in the decade 1909–1919[266] prior to his publication of *I and Thou*, he discovered in the Jewish soul the rudiments of the dialogical principle. He saw the Jew facing what he called "the personal Jewish question" of finding wholeness in his inner self in order to be able to reach out toward a proper relationship with the outside world and with reality as such. To be sure, the principle of dialogue deals with the problem of man, in general, but Buber first recognized it as he was searching the way of his people in which he sensed the ebb and flow of this problem in its greatest intensity. For the dialogical way is primarily a matter of unification of the human self that enables it to enter into relation with others and to reach out for redemption—man's highest goal. As Buber delved into the problematic of the Jewish soul, he saw in it the very problem of man's striving toward his goal—his self-realization as a human being.[267]

The Return

Buber started addressing himself to mankind through his speeches on Judaism in his mid-twenties, after he had undergone a complete turning in his spiritual development and had freed himself from the influences of German universalism, rationalism, and mysticism.[268] He then began to look for the universal in the particular by placing the individual Jew and the Jewish people at the center of his world view, not, however, in a narrow, particularistic sense but in a way of guiding them, and through them all mankind, toward redemption. In this respect, he conceived of the Jewish people as a paradigm for mankind.

> It is as if this small community had been put up as an example, a paradigm for humanity: because the process I am talking about [the unification of duality] fulfills itself more purely, more strongly, more clearly in this community than in any other human group.[269]

However,

> the Jew is not a being of a different kind, . . . only it is so . . . that the mystery and primal destiny of duality step forth here, in Judaism, more strongly, more purely, more demanding than in any other community, that the task of overcoming it is here the greatest, and hence its fulfillment occurs as protoforming,

as directive for mankind. . . . The cause of Judaism and the cause of humanity are one.[270]

This view of the Jew and the Jewish people *sub specie aeternitatis*[271] harbors many tensions, contradictions and, most important, practical problems, which brought Buber into sharp disagreement with other leading interpreters of Judaism, traditional as well as modern, religious or national. For in practical, everyday life, the Jew and his people must contend, through their very Jewishness, with the contingencies of life within their fold and in the world around them. How does the primal force of unification, which demands of the Jew his utmost fervor and perseverance, preserve him and his people in the vicissitudes of mundane affairs? Buber was not unaware of this question from the start. His aim, though, was not to expound a theory of Judaism as a universal philosophical system, a theology, or nationalism, but to meet the realities of Jewish existence in the diaspora, especially in the Western countries, as he saw them. He asked about "the meaning of Judaism for Jews" not in the abstract, but in the concreteness of their inner life under existing conditions. Nor did he describe its meaning just in terms of outside pressures, but primarily in its internal situation. "I do not ask," he said in his very first speech on Judaism, "about the external forms of life but about its inner reality. Judaism has as much meaning for the Jews as it has inner reality."[272] He wanted to direct the Jew on the way to self-fulfillment here and now, in this life on earth. But while he addressed himself to Jewish life in modern times, he raised his sight toward the self-fulfillment of all men, for the problem of unifying the primal duality in the human soul is common to them all. Moreover, Buber's own *return* to his people at the time of his turning toward the life of relation signalled to him the possibility, even the necessity, of the return of every Jew unto his fold in an innermost manner. This meant a turning toward the unconditioned and, in like manner, a return of all men to a relation between man and man, and, through it, between man and God.

Social Thinker and Teacher

We shall understand the true character of Buber's addresses to his people if we see him in his role with regard to his listeners, and that is as a speaker in dialogue. He did not present himself as a theologian or ethical theorist, but as a Jew who had experienced his Jewishness and wanted to share it with his fellow Jews.[273] While he regarded this experience essentially in the nature of prophetic Judaism, he did not come to his people as a prophet, but as a social thinker; and while he extolled the qualities of true leadership, he did not consider himself a leader, but rather a teacher. In these two capacities, then, as social thinker and teacher, he directed himself toward the problems of the modern Jew.

In accordance with his general social philosophy, Buber thinks that the essence of Jewish communal life arises through the individual striving for the unification of the duality in his soul. This has been particularly a problem for the modern Jew since the days of his enlightenment and emancipation. Although Buber tries to resolve it through a restructuring of society and a renewal of the Jewish community, he nevertheless places the burden on each individual Jew, and while he advises him not to try it in isolation, he calls on the "solitary ones" capable of forming "directness between men" "who are the seeds of true community," to become the bearers of the renewal. With this emphasis on the individual, he sets out to establish the inner meaning of the soul of the Jew qua his Jewishness.

Buber assumed the role of teacher gradually, as he developed his own ideas of education and became fortified in his conviction, as he put it in later years, that the teacher is to give direction toward the way, "but not the manner in which one must strive for this direction: that each must discover and acquire for himself." "This great work" is to be performed by each individual and this, he says, is not much to ask, for "how then except through such expectations could we learn how much the individual is capable of?"[274] But how is this capability to be fostered and brought to fruition?

In order to attain a given end, Buber explains, the leader of a group or people will often make decisions for all of its members and drive them to action, even using force when necessary. However, the true leader, he points out, shows responsibility toward the goal of the unconditioned, that is, follows a teaching that guides him and his people toward their goal. Such a combination of leader-teacher is very rarely found in one person. More often, especially in modern times, the two functions are divided between different individuals, and the tendency today is to get rid of the teacher in public affairs. This is deplorable, says

Buber. "Certainly the people that has no leader is unfortunate; but thrice unfortunate is the people whose leader has no teacher."[275] As for himself, he chose to serve his people in the teacher's role.

The teacher does not decide for the people or for any of its members, and certainly does not use force to promote his teachings. He admonishes, persuades, calls the individual to responsibility, and generally helps him to release his inner forces, notably the "instinct of communion," which is a longing for the world to be present in him as a person. The true teacher is one who has himself experienced an inner turning toward this goal. He is like the prophet of old. "The inner turning of the prophet is an actual rebirth, and the educator, who brings the precious ore in the soul of his pupil to light and frees it from dross, affords him a second birth, birth into a loftier life."[276] The educator starts "by pointing to the relation of the individual to his own self."[277] Hence the educator's first step is to bring the modern Jew to a self-awareness of his Jewishness; and this is how Buber began his teaching of Judaism.

Three Phases of Development

Although Buber does not engage in systematic philosophy or theology, he nevertheless treats the subject of the Jew and his Jewishness within a philosophic frame of reference. He translates, as he says, the compound *(Zusammenhang)* of his "decisive experiences into human thought-values" and, having "received no tidings which could be transmitted as such," but only insights, his "communication had to be a philosophical one."[278] His general philosophy grew out of his contemplations on Judaism in successive stages, the general, as a rule, following the Jewish works. We may thus distinguish three phases in Buber's philosophy of Judaism which run parallel to his general philosophy, as follows: (1) as *substance* in the act of realization, (2) as *relation* in the encounter with the Absolute, and (3) as essence of the messianic goal. The first phase is developed in a series of "Speeches on Judaism" from 1909 to 1911, and given a philosophical ground in a theory of realization in his book *Daniel* (1913), and in another set of "Speeches on Judaism" (1912–1914), in which he expounds his philosophy of religion, religiosity, and mythos. The second phase is developed in two other

"Speeches on Judaism"—"The Holy Way" and "Heruth: On Youth and Religion" (1918–1919)—and in his early writings on Hasidism, which crystallized in the dialogical principle of relation in his essay *Ich und Du* (1923). The third phase continues along the lines of this principle as expanded in his studies of the Bible and his later "Speeches on Judaism" (1939–1951),[279] which were given religious philosophical expression chiefly in his books *Kingship of God, Eclipse of God,* and *Two Types of Faith.* This is not meant to imply that the three phases rest on mutually exclusive grounds. Quite the contrary, all of their grounds are manifest in each phase, only in different stages of development, the last one representing their fullest formulation.

4

Substance in Self-realization

Individual Self-realization

The Jews in Western and Eastern Europe

In his first three speeches on Judaism, Buber addresses himself to the individual Jew in Western Europe, rather than to the Jewish people as a whole. He points out that Jewish civic emancipation and the general enlightenment of the eighteenth and nineteenth centuries which released the creative forces of the individual also broke up the old Jewish body politic and thrust its members out into the outer world that had just been opened to them. This development came so suddenly that the Jew could not absorb the outer culture and make it part of his inner communal way of life, as was the case in Eastern Europe. There, enlightenment in the form of Haskalah penetrated gradually and slowly, without breaking up the inner structure; at the same time an inner liberation in the form of Hasidism further cemented Jewish communal living. But in Western Europe the outer liberation overwhelmed the Jew, cracked the wall of his communal structure and put great obstacles in the way of his self-renewal as a Jew. He could awaken to his Jewishness only if he became conscious of those obstacles and sought a way of removing them. One power of such awakening, operating on the communal level, was Zionism, and the other, on the individual level, was a recognition of the meaning of his Jewishness. Buber, himself, after he had wandered off into the emancipated world of German culture, was brought back to his own fold by embracing the Zionist cause. He then tried to blend the two powers, the communal and the individual, or the Eastern and Western, into

144

one force for the renewal of Judaism in his own time. "When West and East interpenetrate," he wrote, "there arises a new productivity—a specifically Jewish productivity—which forms an image of a Jewish mode, a Jewish outlook, and Jewish values."[280]

To bring the individual Jew to a self-awareness of his Jewishness, Buber offered him what he considered to be the *substance* of Judaism and the meaning of its *realization*. The basic idea of this approach is that every Jew carries within him the substance of Jewishness which lies dormant in his very blood and awaits the conscious act of realization. In this phase of Buber's philosophy of Judaism, the aim is to bring Judaism into the innermost of each individual Jew rather than to lead him outside of his estranged self to the Jewish fold. For the estranged individual has no image of a people with whom he can identify himself, unless it is presented to him as something indwelling in his own personal being, and that is the substance of his Jewishness. By becoming conscious of this substance the individuals will weld themselves together into a renewed people through which they will strive for their self-realization and for that of humanity as well. The emphasis here, it must be noted, is on the redemption of the individual, not the people as an entity in itself. An appeal is thus made to the Western Jew who had sought to identify himself with humanity in general, to see his Jewishness essentially the same as his human self, differing only in degree of intensity; to recognize that he cannot realize his own humanity except through the realization of his Jewishness. This is the theme of Buber's first three addresses, namely, "Judaism and the Jew," "Judaism and Mankind," and "The Renewal of Judaism," which we shall now consider in broad outline.

The Jewish Question

Not finding any fulfillment of Jewishness as autonomous reality, either as a religion or as a nation in contemporary Western Jewish life, except as a recollection and perhaps a hope, Buber poses the Jewish question in the following manner: "What is it, then, that makes a man's people an autonomous reality in his soul and in his life? What makes him feel the people not just about him, but in him?"[281] The feeling of belonging to a people, Buber explains, has its origin in man's constant experiences of homeland, language, and custom, which he has in common with others outside his family and close circle of friends. While this contingent level of belonging may satisfy many persons, there are also those who strive for permanence, that is, not just for constant forms of experience, but for constant existence which is the bearer of all experience. In this kind of striving, the individual I discovers in his relationship with his community his own spiritual permanence, "an enduring substance," extending beyond his own life-span—an immortal life. The individual feels this most strongly when he discovers the succession of past generations, of parents, grandparents, ancestors, whose confluence of blood has brought his life into existence. In this immortality of generations, the individual feels a communality of blood in his I's duration in an endless past, and he thus discovers that the blood is the core of his I and determines his thoughts and his will. His world now assumes a twofold character, each on a different level, one of his *surroundings,* which are the world of his impressions and influences, and another of his *blood,* which is the world of his substance receiving those impressions and influences.

Man's self-identification on the second level, that is, as substance, is no longer with those with whom he shares the external elements of homeland, language, and custom, but with the community of those with whom he shares his inner experiences of a common substance. His people now represents not his outside world, but his inner soul—a community of all those who were, are, and will be, all forming one unity. This subjective side of belonging to one's people becomes objectified when the inner substance of blood relation and the outer surroundings of homeland, language, and custom are combined into one living reality. However, such conditions do not prevail in the relations of the Western Jew to his own folk, because he lives predominantly in the outer world of another folk, while his inner world is only a faint memory of ancestral descent. If his world of substance is to become a reality, he must relate himself to it not only as the past, but also in the fullness of its present existence and in its hope for the future.

We need not now debate Buber's view on the ultimate source of folk-belonging in its inner and outer aspects, a view which he himself later changed or modified. What concerns us here is his approach to an existing situation in Jewish life, notably in the West, which was overwhelmingly, if not exclusively, determined from the outside. Here Buber does not propose a territorial solution to the Jewish question. Rather, he recommends that the

Jew in the diaspora must live in two worlds, but he wants him to be his own master in his twofold existence.

> We want and ought to be aware of the fact that we are a mixture of cultures in a more pregnant sense than any other people. However, we don't want to be the slaves of this mixture but its masters. The choice means a decision about supremacy, about what ought to be dominating or dominated in us. This is what I would call the personal Jewish question, the root of all Jewish questions, the question that we must find in ourselves, clear up in ourselves, and determine within ourselves.[282]

How does Buber, in this early phase of his thoughts on Judaism, answer this question? How does he propose to awaken the individual to a consciousness of his Jewishness and to induce him to act toward its renewal?

The Duality of the Jewish Soul

When the Jew looks into his own soul, Buber says, he finds in it a prime duality of extremes, of the highest and lowest human traits and aspirations, which contend against each other and drive him from pole to pole, "from crossroad to crossroad." This is the substance of his Jewishness. Now, when he looks into the soul of man in general, he finds the same polarity of contradictions, the same wandering restlessness of an inner duality, seeking its resolution in an inner unity. However, since the Jew throughout his history as a people has experienced this dualization more strongly than any other people, he has also produced the greatest spiritual forces of striving toward unity, a striving which has spurred his creative powers to produce the idea of God's unity, universal justice, and universal love—the idea of redemption. While the duality in the soul of the Jew is of the substance of his Jewishness, it is basically of the same nature as the duality in man in general. Therefore, the Jewish question as a problem of redeeming the Jew from within becomes a general question of redeeming mankind as a whole.

Now what does Buber advise the individual Jew in this regard? He tells him that his self-realization means the unification of his inner duality which can be attained through his identification with his people, whose problem is, in substance, his own personal problem. But if this concerns the Jew and his own people specifically, why, we may ask, must it seek its solution by extending itself into a problem of mankind as a whole? As noted, Buber addresses himself to the Western cosmopolitan Jew who does not see in his own people a vehicle for his personal salvation, as he does not see any reason for his people's existence as such. As for his personal redemption, he would rather identify himself with the goal of humanity in general. Buber, therefore, wants to show his cosmopolitan Jew that he would be working toward the same universal goal by identifying himself with the Jewish people, because this people, more than any other, is best suited to lead him toward it. Judaism, says Buber, cannot give mankind new things or new content, because it is not strong enough for that. It can give only new *unity* for humanity's content, new possibility for synthesis, perhaps one embracing all past syntheses.

In order to grasp the full import of this advice, we must understand what Buber means here by "the highest and lowest human traits and aspirations," which he finds so strongly represented in the Jew. Once more it should be noted that he directs his advice to the Westernized Jew who has severed his ties with his people and seeks his redemption as an *individual* in some hazy notion of cosmopolitanism. Buber considers this extreme individualism as the lowest trait in the Jew, because it strains his inner duality to a breaking point and is therefore bound to lead to his self-effacement and destruction. The opposite of this trait, or the highest, is a strong tendency on the part of the Jew toward a unification of his inner duality, which may be attained only through his identification with his own community. When Buber founded, in 1916, the magazine *Der Jude,* he set as its motto the return of the Jew to his own people. Writing in the first issue (April 1916, p. 3), he recalls that in 1832, Gabriel Riesser, a sharp opponent of Jewish nationhood, started a publication under the name *Der Jude* for the purpose of gaining equal civil rights for Jews as individuals. Now, says Buber, "we are calling our paper by the same name, but we do not mean 'der Jude' as individual but as the bearer of his peoplehood." This is how Jews will gain their freedom and also "fulfill their obligation to humanity."

Role of the Jewish People

Every people has a function to perform in the redemption of mankind. A people that lives on its own soil, speaks its own language, and breathes the atmosphere of its own culture expresses the universal goal naturally in every aspect of its life as a group. Its particular existence as a people is, therefore, never questioned by its members or by the outside world. This is not the case with the Jewish people in the West, whose separate existence in the diaspora is put in question not only from without, but also from within. This is due to the fact that the Western Jew has lost his original language, land, and culture through which he might express his universal goal. Nonetheless, he too has a specific function to perform on behalf of humanity, only it is not recognized by him as a Jew or by his non-Jewish neighbor. This function will become evident to both, if the Jew will become conscious, and make others aware, of the unique quality of his people to serve mankind in its quest for redemption. The individual Jew will then be aroused to seek identification with his own people, because he will find in it a reason for its existence as a people, namely, its mission to set an example of the universal goal of redemption.

The role that Buber assigns here to the Jewish people on behalf of mankind has been a dominant motif in his philosophy of Judaism as it passed through several stages.[283] As we shall see later, it was also at the core of his Zionist idea, which set him apart from the mainstream of the Zionist movement. In this outlook, the Jewish people serves as an intermediary between individual man and humanity as a whole, originally intended to serve the individual Jew but basically directed toward man in general. The people is thus not an end in itself, and its own redemption is not its primary goal. This makes its function unique among the nations of the world, but this uniqueness, Buber holds, is what makes it the most appropriate vehicle for humanity's redemption.

Buber could not remove the apologetic element from this particular philosophy of Judaism, despite his efforts to do so. All those who seek to explain to themselves and to others why the Jewish people must exist as a people are in essence apologizing for its existence. The so-called abnormality of its life in the diaspora does not warrant putting its existence in question. For what is normal or abnormal about it is ultimately a matter of conceptual interpretation of what constitutes a people or nation, whereas the Jewish people exists, as Buber himself has emphasized, as an actual people, whether or not we can define it. There is therefore no need to establish an external reason for any of its members to identify themselves with it, no matter how lofty and universal such a reason may be. On the contrary, the very fact of its actual existence is sufficient reason for a Jew to consider himself part of it, as *his own* existence is *in it,* even when his ties are very tenuous.

Renewal of Three Basic Tendencies

The universal goal of mankind as a whole also dominates Buber's concept of the renewal of Judaism, as he calls on the individual to renew the substance of Jewishness in his soul, and that is "the renewal of humanity" in it. This renewal is not meant to be a gradual development of new forms out of old precepts so as to accommodate traditional Judaism to the ways of modern life, as advocated, for example by Moritz Lazarus. Nor is it meant as a rebuilding of a Jewish nationality in its ancient homeland in a new form of a cultural center to serve as a spiritual force for world Jewry, as taught by Ahad Haam. By renewal, Buber means a revolution in the life of each Jew, a complete return to the fundamental spiritual process called Jewishness, which has manifested itself in three main ideas or tendencies, namely, the ideas of *unity, deed,* and *the future,* all directed toward humanity's final goal.

> Thus [he says], if we adhere to the innermost life of original Jewishness [*des Urjudentums*], strive for unity in our soul, purify the people, we will be contributing toward setting it free, that is, toward making Judaism free again for its work in humanity.[284]

This purifying and freeing of the people is not a religious, national, or cultural purification, as understood by the religious and cultural nationalists mentioned above, but a freeing of its inner forces—the ideas of unity, deed, and the future—in a word, individual self-realization. As Buber describes them, "these ideas actually struggle for themselves, for their own liberation from the straits of the folk-drives, for their self-assertion and fulfillment."[285] What is the nature of this struggle and how is the liberation to be attained?

Buber finds that the three ideas or tendencies are embedded in the Jewish folk character and are manifested in two directions, one as the relative, conditioned everyday life of acquisition of worldly possessions, and the other as the striving for absolute, unconditioned spiritual life. Moving in the second direction, the idea of *unity* is to see the whole before the parts, the community rather than man, the universal concept before the particular object. In its absoluteness, this tendency is found in the Jew's yearning to save himself from the dualization in his soul. The idea of *deed* is grounded in the Jewish folk character in that the Jew is inclined more toward the moving than the sensory forms of life. He finds more substance and personality in action than in perception. That is why, from the very start, the center of Jewish religiosity is deed, not belief. Buber regards this to be a characteristic of the Oriental person in general, but finds it most pronounced in the Jew. The idea of *the future* is one that seeks to rise above the contingencies of everyday life and to strive for the absolute reign of justice and love, or the messianic days. It is found in the Jewish folk character, in that the Jewish sense of time is more developed than that of space, and the feeling for sound, music, and movement more than for plastic form and color.

> Messianism [Buber writes] is the deepest original idea of Judaism. . . . In the realm of the future, where only playful, faltering, unstable dreams may hazard, the Jew has ventured to build a house for humanity, the house of true life.[286]

This is not just a wish that may or may not come true. The Jew feels it as a certainty, one that must come in the end of days, in the absolute future, as it is guaranteed by every moment, by the blood of generations, by God Himself.

The realization of the three ideas in personal life is the goal of the people and of every one of its members. But the people's drive for success in everyday matters, in economic and political affairs, militates against it. Such is the inner struggle between the relative and the absolute, the temporary and the future, the desire and the deed. Reviewing the highlights of Jewish history in which the relative was dominant, Buber also points to certain periods when the absolute asserted itself in the life of the people and in the works of its great men—in the prophets, the Essenes, early Christianity *(Urchristentum)*,[287] and early Hasidism. Through the great men of these periods, the spirit of Judaism created and cultivated its strivings toward the realization of the unconditioned ideas of unity, deed, and the future. But in time, these ideas were turned into lifeless rituals and ceremonies,

controlled by priestly proscriptions and rabbinic legalistic regulations. Such a lifeless state of affairs, Buber tells his hearers,
exists in the Jewish community today, and he admonishes them
to act for the reawakening of their Jewishness, to purify the
people so that it may work toward the fulfillment of their
spiritual tendencies. This is the task of every Jew in his personal
life, as he becomes conscious of the substance of his Jewishness
and creates a "synthesis of the three ideas of Judaism in a
world-feeling of the coming man." Buber does not chart any
particular way of doing it, as no one can say or even surmise how
the future will arise. But, he says, "You can and you must find a
new appearance, a new form, a new fulfillment, welded into a
new world-feeling." We know it will come, though we don't
know how. "We can only be prepared. . . . And to be prepared
means: to prepare."[288]

Daniel

The ideas about the substance of Judaism which Buber carved
out of the Jewish folk character and which, he thought, could be
realized through their renewal in the consciousness of every
Jew, found their universal philosophical formulation in his book
Daniel, published soon after his first "Three Speeches on
Judaism," in 1913. Significantly, he gave this book the subtitle
Conversations about Realization.[289] Its basic principle is derived from the first two ideas, namely, unity and deed. Realization is the work of the soul insofar as it acts toward its own
unification or unity, which is reality. In *Daniel* this principle
assumes an epistemological character, in that the unity is
realized as an act of knowing. The human soul, like everything
else in nature, is a living duality in infinite possibilities, or more
specifically a polarity, such as being and not-being, good and
evil, positive and negative. This is the subjective side of the
world as man experiences it. Between these two poles there is a
stream of antagonisms, contradictions, contending with each
other in all things in the world. Man knows this polarity through
the polarity in his soul: the world is experienced truly as a
duality. But he who masters this duality in his own soul knows
the world as unity at every moment that he acts with his united
being. Man does not produce the reality of the world of things
but, rather, lives it in his soul, which is realization or rendering
the world real as a unity. This unity *is* reality. This is not to be

conceived as a fusion or identification of the soul with the world, which Buber rejected even then, but merely as an act of unification of the multiple possibilities in the world, thus making them actual. It is a directional act of the soul from the possible toward the actual, which Buber designates as man's "inborn direction." It "is the primal tension of the human soul which moves at times out of the infinity of the possible to choose this and nothing else and to realize it in action."[290] This act makes the world real and, to that extent, meaningful.

Buber considers this act as the particular mode of expression of the Oriental religions, namely, "the Chinese teaching of the Tao, the Indian teaching of liberation, the Jewish and early Christian teaching of the Kingdom of God."[291] They all teach *the way,* but it is most strongly manifested in the Jewish folk character and in its teachings.[292] Buber developed these views in his essay "The Teaching of Tao," written about the same time (1910) as his first speeches on Judaism and in the same spirit. Thus, when he calls on the individual Jew to strive for renewal through the absolute ideas of unity, deed, and the future, he means for him to live "the genuine life of the completed man," the same manner of life in which the "Tao realizes itself." According to "the teaching," "realization means nothing other than unity," that is, the unified man who fulfills his destiny "as purposeful undividedness." "The unity of the world is only the reflection of this unity; for the world is nothing alien, but one with unified man."[293] In Jewish teaching about inner duality, as distinguished from the Indian which deals with outer duality, the way is the messianic goal of redemption. "As the idea of inner duality is Jewish, so is the idea of redemption from it," that is, freeing the soul from its duality through a transformation and return to its primal unifying forces. "From this the messianic ideal of Judaism took its humaneness [*Menschlichkeit*]."[294] Thus Buber's teachings about the Jewish ideas of unity, deed, and the future found their full expression in his early philosophy of realization.[295]

Jewish Religiosity and Mythos

In his philosophy of realization, as expounded in the first three "Speeches on Judaism," in *Daniel,* and in "The Teaching of Tao," the religious aspect is hardly noticeable, that is, the center of attention is man, not God or even man's direction to God. The inborn direction spoken of in *Daniel* particularly is with reference to man's inner self. In the second set of three speeches— "The Spirit of the Orient and Judaism," "Jewish Religiosity," and "The Mythos of the Jews" (1912–1914)—Buber further develops the idea of substance of Judaism as that of religiosity and mythos. While in the first set he dwells on the realization of man and his world, in the second his theme is what he calls "the realization of God through man."[296] It should be emphasized, as Buber later explained, that by "the realization of God" he does not mean to imply the idea of a becoming God as a metaphysical concept, an ethical idea, or any other form projected by the human mind, but the realization of God's appearance, the *theophany,* in man's religious experience as a "phenomenon of religious reality." In such divine appearance man is the active participant and, in this respect, a contributor toward the realization of the theophany.[297] Here, too, the goal is unity of duality. As the most representative bearer of the Oriental religious spirit, the Jew has the inner power of striving for the unity of the divine in the world. It is the call to return that was pronounced by the prophets and by the early Christians, and expressed in the fervor of a Hasid's prayer. Buber considers realization under the concept of sin, and the return as an act of decision to free oneself from sin, which is a lack of decision. Hence, decision is return, and return is renewal.

> When in the midst of "sin," in the lack of decision, the will to decision awakens and bursts the crust of accustomed life, the primal power breaks through and storms toward heaven. With him who returns, creation recurs anew; in the renewal, the durability of the world is renewed.[298]

The ideas of return and renewal now assume a new dimension in Buber's philosophy of Judaism, as he sees the possibility of their fulfillment only when Judaism is reunited with the land of its forefathers, Eretz Israel. The dispersion which followed the destruction of the Second Temple and, especially, the revolt of Bar Kokhba, broke the creative spirit of Judaism by divesting it of its roots in the land and in the religious climate of the Orient. The Jews became Westernized, though only by adaptation, and thereby subdued their intrinsic striving for the real life, which Western civilization negates and is itself devoid of. The West,

Buber says, cannot find genuine life in or through its own civilization. It has the most developed knowledge, but cannot find *meaning;* it has the most stringent training, but cannot find *the way;* it has the richest art, but cannot find *the sign;* and it has the innermost belief, but cannot find *God.* Not that it lacks unity of thought, symbolic functions, or the capacity to construct; rather, "it lacks the exclusiveness of the lore of genuine life, it misses the inborn certainty of the One."[299] In contrast, the teachings of the Orient posit true life as a fundamental principle which is not derived from metaphysical speculation, and this has made them creative. For them, there is no meaning or truth of a unified world except in genuine living. This, says Buber, is *the way;* and whoever goes this way follows in God's footsteps.

To the extent, then, that the Jew has become Westernized he has lost the way of his own teachings. He must now return to the way, which he can best attain by severing his ties with the West and by resuming his old connections with his ancestral land in the East. This, it must be noted, is the fundamental goal of Buber's Zionism, which will be considered later. The thing to bear in mind, however, is that his view of the Jewish settlement in Eretz Israel is not an end in itself (for "the so-called 'solution of the Jewish question' " in a Jewish national territory), but for the renewal of Jewish religiosity, which is "for Judaism the only subject of unconditioned actuality, the driving power of its destiny, the direction of its redemption, the force that, if rekindled, will give it new life, but if completely extinguished will deliver it to death."[300]

Three Layers in the Act of Decision

The act of decision in Jewish teaching, says Buber, is not just ethical, but primarily religious. "It is the religious act; for it is the realization of God through man." It is Judaism's fundamental *religiosity,* the one that realizes "divine freedom and the unconditioned on earth." It has manifested itself in Jewish religious life in three layers, through imitation of God, through enhancing His reality, and through bringing the divine Presence into the conditioned life on earth.

In the first layer, to imitate God means to *become like* Him, not to *be* God. Buber interprets the verse in Leviticus 20:26, "You shall be holy unto me, for I the Lord am holy," and its commentary in *Sifra* (Holiness, 184), to mean: " 'As I am separated'—that is, not determined by anything, removed from all that is conditioned, acting out of myself—'so you shall be separated.' " Also, the statement in *Sifra,* "As God is one and unique, so your service be one," means that man's goal is God, to imitate Him in His oneness, and this means to master one's own duality and become one. In the second layer, God's reality is enhanced through man's act of decision. Buber cites Simeon bar Yohai's commentary on Isaiah 43:10, "You are my witnesses," as signifying "When you are my witnesses I am the Lord, and when you are not my witnesses I am not the Lord." Similarly, the verse "Render strength unto God" (Psalm 68:35) is interpreted to mean that the righteous increase the power of the rule of Heaven above, and the rabbinic saying "Man is God's partner in the eternal work of creation" signifies that every human act of decision flows into the sea of divine power.[301] In the third layer, which became manifest first in the Kabbalah, the realization of God rises to the idea of man's influence on God's Presence on earth. God's Shekhina (Presence) decended into the world of the conditioned and, like Israel, wanders dispersed in the realm of things; like Israel, it wants to be redeemed, it wants to be reunited with the divine Being. But the only ones who can act toward this redemption are those who have themselves risen through the act of returning from the conditioned to the unconditioned. Of them Hasidic lore says, "Those who return redeem God."

What the three layers have in common is "the view of the absolute value of human deed." Man's deed has something of the Infinite, not in its content, but in the manner of its performance. Every act is sanctified by doing it in holiness and with unconditioned intention. Ultimately, this is Buber's meaning of realization of the substance of Judaism: an act performed out of a "basic feeling" that comes as a demand from above.

> The unconditioned [he writes] is the specific religious intrinsic worth [*Gehalt*] of Judaism. Jewish religiosity is built not on a doctrine of belief and not on an ethical precept, but on a basic feeling which gives the human being its meaning, on the basic feeling that it needs to be done.[302]

When the religiosity is acted out in communal life, the "basic feeling" on the part of the individual becomes a *demand*, and there ensues a struggle over its fulfillment—a struggle between two leading types of men, the one who demands the truth of the unconditioned, and the other who is ready to compromise for the sake of holding power with the people. Buber considers them as "the eternal types in the history of Judaism," namely, the prophet and the priest. Their differences became apparent at the very inception of the Jewish people at Siani, when Aaron compromised with the people and made them the Golden Calf, while Moses demanded the full truth of the deed as he had heard it from the divine Voice and ordered the destruction of the transgressors. "In the destruction of the half-truth and the insufficient, the proclaimed God reveals Himself as the consuming fire of the unconditioned."[303]

Religiosity and Religion

The line here is drawn for all time between what Buber designates as "religiosity" and "religion." The first, which was promulgated by Moses as the deed of the unconditioned, was turned into the second, that is, into a religion of formal laws, rituals, and ceremonies. These are necessary for the life of the community, Buber grants, but when they become restrictive, formalized regulations controlled by organized "official Judaism," they tend to deaden the spirit of religiosity, which is "the ever newly becoming, ever newly self-expressing and forming—the astounded, prayerful feeling of man," striving for true life. "Thus religiosity is the creative principle, religion the organizing one."[304] The struggle between the two has been the hallmark of Jewish tradition. At times, religiosity breaks out of the confines of organized regulation and elevates religion to a higher life; at other times it fades out after a brief revival; but it is always there, acting in the depth of the folk spirit. Buber sees this process repeating itself in three decisive movements in Jewish history: in the age of the prophets who struggled against the formalized sacrificial cult promulgated by the priestly caste, in the time of the Essenes and early Christians, who tried to revive the act of intention in the face of opposition from organized Judaism, and in the Kabbalistic-Hasidic teachings, which sought to break through the accumulated weight of narrow rabbinic legalism.

The three movements, Buber points out, never succeeded in gaining an adequate form or sway in Judaism, even though their aim was not to abrogate the rites and ceremonies, but to renew them through the deed of true living. Official Judaism, he maintains, was always able to have the upper hand in the contest and to suppress these movements after their brief flourishing. But Buber does not consider their lack of success in gaining power as a real failure. This is the very nature of the struggle: religiosity does not seek to gain power, for its effectiveness is not in power over the people, but in the innermost intention, in the "basic feeling" that each individual has for the deed that "needs to be done." Religiosity is not to be taken as reverie, enthusiasm, or an intellectual game. Its aim is to mold the unconditioned into the stuff of everyday life on earth. It never assumes a definite form, for it always strives to be not a content to be discovered and appropriated, but an ever-creative force spurring man toward his goal of turning chaos into a world order. As expressed in the three movements, religiosity is the eternal call to the renewal of Judaism. Everyone is capable of responding to this call, if he takes his place "in the natural domain of living together with fellow men, . . . for through him God does not want to be believed in, debated, and defined, but realized."[305]

The idea of action without aiming at success, or of a goal that does not lead to success, is a theme that runs through Buber's philosophy of Judaism in all its phases and, for that matter, in his outlook on man's destiny in general. He distinguishes "purpose" (Zweck) from "goal" (Ziel) as contrary concepts, the first aiming at the accomplishment of limited, conditioned tasks, whereas the second is man's overriding aim at redemption—a striving for the future to bring the Infinite into the finite, or as he conceived it later, for the finite to meet the Infinite as mutually independent partners in the act of redemption.[306] The leading men of the three movements who worked toward this goal may have failed at certain moments in history, but their deeds and their very lives continue to influence the destiny of the people. At the same time, Buber attributes their failure not to their weaknesses, but to opposition from "official Judaism."

The Mythos of Divine Action

The same kind of opposition, Buber finds, is encountered by what he considers to be the Jewish mythos. "The history of the development of the Jewish religion," he holds, "is in truth the history of the struggle between the natural formation of the mythico-monotheistic folk religion and the intellectual formation of the rational-monotheistic rabbinic religion.''[307] It goes back, he says, to the official priestly biblical canon which sought to eliminate every vestige of myth from the extant sources. It still continues to this day in scholarly research of postbiblical lore, where mythos is regarded as a negative phenomenon in religious literature that beclouds true monotheism. The issue, as he sees it, centers on the meaning of myth, in general, and on the concept of Jewish myth, in particular.

Taking his clue from Plato, Buber designates as myth ''an account of divine occurrence as sensate reality. Hence one cannot call it myth if the divine occurrence is accounted for as coming from a transcendent source or as an experience of the soul,'' as, for example, in a theological exposition or in a report of an ecstatic vision.[308] However, if God appears in sensate reality, He is a multiple being even when conceived as a monotheistic unification of a multitude of divine forces. Here the Jewish tendency toward perfect unity changes the myth into a new form. ''The cosmic, national YHVH is extended as the God of the All, the God of mankind, the God of the soul.'' He is not Himself a sensate reality whose action or passion is manifest in a sensible substance of godhood, which is the mythos of polytheism. The Jewish mythos goes beyond this concept. Its meaning is ''that we must give the name myth to every story of a sensibly actual occurrence which is perceived and presented as a divine, an absolute, occurrence.''[309] That is, Jewish myth does not describe God Himself as sensate reality, but sensate events as having a divine source. In this connotation of the word ''mythos,'' there is really no difference between Buber's view of God's role in the world and that of rabbinic Judaism. Both see His role manifest through His works. Nevertheless, the two views diverge along major lines.

Buber's Differences with Rabbinic Judaism

While Buber may argue that the ''terribly rationalized Jewish monotheism'' woefully misunderstands the meaning of mythos, his argument does not hold when he directs it against the traditional rabbinic view. The latter accepts fully the idea that ''sensate reality is divine, but it must be *realized* in its divinity through one who experiences it in genuine living,'' as Buber puts it.[310] What rabbinic Judaism contends against is the anthropomorphism of God, which Buber, too, rejects. The real struggle of rabbinic monotheism against myth is not against those who see God's Presence manifest in nature and history, but against those who see nature as a manifestation of the divine *substance,* as a plurality of sensibly experienced gods, or even as one God splintered into endless sensate experiences. The rabbinic view is that God is an absolute, transcendent Being, The Holy One, Blessed Be He, "holy" meaning unique and unlike anything in the world of man or nature. In a later stage Buber also adopted this view,[311] but in his early phase he was still wavering between a transcendent and an immanent God, leaning toward the Kabbalistic-mystic visions of the divine appearance on earth, which are of a substantive nature, often considered as the substance of God Himself.

Similarly, Buber's argument that rabbinic Judaism has stifled or submerged the creative act of religiosity by elevating rites, ceremonies, and the fulfillment of the commandments above religious intention is a narrowing down of Rabbinism to a restricted formalism which was never the case in Jewish history, even when it was overladen with the minutiae of daily observances. Rabbinic Judaism regards these observances as fundamentally communal and, therefore, considers all laws, without exception, as preservative forces of the community of Israel, guarding against any transgressors lest they "break the fence" of communality. Indeed, Buber does not deny this, but he wants a fluid law to be confirmed in each situation by the individual himself, as and when he is motivated by his striving for the unconditioned. But this is exactly what "official Judaism," as Buber calls it, the Pharisees and, later, the Rabbis opposed in the movements of the Essenes, the early Christians, and early Hasidim, namely, their individualistic trend that would permit anyone to step out of the community and establish his own teaching. They opposed the very thing that Buber erroneously prizes in Hasidism, for example, that "everyone should become a Torah, a law through genuine living."[312] To be sure, the Hasidim foster genuine living according to the Torah in action as well as in intention, but not that each become *a* law unto himself. Hasidism does not follow the path suggested by Buber. It advocates that each one become *the* Torah, not *a* Torah, in his personal conduct, and that is why it has survived as a movement and exerted great influence on the Jewish community as a whole.

I will return to Buber's views on Hasidism and nationalism in the third phase of his teachings. Here it should be noted that his idea of striving toward a goal without success is what separates him in the main from the traditional and nationalist exponents of Judaism in modern times. According to him, one who strives toward a goal has no formed plan or even premonition of what action to take that might lead him to it. His act is a decision of his inner self out of the "basic feeling that it needs to be done." Buber calls it the act of religiosity which is free and creative, in contradistinction to the act of religion which is prescribed for a given purpose and carried out as a divine command under the aegis of the organized community. However, rabbinic Judaism does not draw this kind of distinction, whether in principle or in practice. It considers every deed as having its particular purpose and, at the same time, leading to the goal of man's realization of the Divine on earth.

Neither does rabbinic Judaism share with Buber his concept of divine realization. The latter speaks of "the realization of God through man." Even after he has elucidated it to mean the realization of God's theophany, he still speaks in terms of a divine substance which permeates all changeable things in the world, as the theophany changes.[313] Rabbinic Judaism eschews all such references which may have the slightest implication of a changing God, even in the form of a changing theophany. *Sifra on Leviticus* (Holiness, 174), from which Buber derives his principle of action toward the unconditioned, has a pertinent commentary on the verse "You shall be holy for I the Lord your God am holy" (Lev. 19:2), which reflects the rabbinic view: "The words 'for I am holy' teach us to mean that 'I endure in my holiness, whether you sanctify me or do not sanctify me.' " If God's holiness is a theophany, it endures as God endures, and not as man may make it so. What Buber teaches about "the realization of God through man" by imitating Him, enhancing His power, and influencing His destiny on earth, can have meaning in rabbinic Judaism only as man's realization of God's will on earth.

5

Relation with the Divine Presence

Jewish Reality in God's Presence

The second phase of Buber's philosophy of Judaism took shape in the years 1916 to 1918, during which he delivered two more speeches on the subject, subsequently issued in 1923 in a "collected edition" which included the first six and an introduction clarifying his views of the entire series.[314] Later Buber recalled this period as "the decisive years for the way of my thinking, 1916 to 1920."[315] During this time he also projected his major philosophical essay *I and Thou,* which he had sketched in 1916 and first drafted in 1919. In the latter year he came to realize that the Jewish teachings are "based entirely on the double-directed relation of Man-I and God-Thou, on mutuality, on encounter [*Begegnung*]."[316] He was then driven, as he said, "by an inner necessity . . . to bear witness to it."[317] The essay was completed in the spring of 1922 and published the following year. We can see from this testimony that Buber's principle of dialogical relation was derived primarily from his insights into Jewish lore, notably the Hasidic tradition. Other influences that played a part in its development and elucidation came through his contacts with Protestant and Catholic theologians and other thinkers after the publication of *I and Thou*.[318]

The second phase, like the first, deals with the renewal of Judaism as the people's primary task. The two phases differ in their approaches to religious experience, the first viewing it as the subjective redemption of man and his world, and the second as an encounter between man and the Absolute. Both are characterized by man's deed, but in the first it is an act of unification of his own duality, or reality is the unity of a duality in one and the same being, whereas in the second it is an act of

162

relation between mutually independent beings. I have dealt with Buber's concept of man's encounter with the Absolute in part I, above.[319] Our concern here is to show how it applies to his ideas of the renewal of Jewish life as a community.

The I-Thou Relation in the Jewish Way to God

From Buber's principle of dialogue we learn that man, as a finite being, can meet God, the Infinite, insofar as he (man) enters into relations with other finite beings, since all those relations intersect in the eternal Thou. As Buber puts it, if "one wants to speak with God without speaking with man, his word goes astray."[320] The same holds true of man's relation with other beings in nature, but his interhuman relation is best suited for the divine encounter, because both are expressed through speech. In reality, then, a meeting with God is attainable through communal life, in which man reaches his highest self-expression as a human being.

As Buber develops these concepts in his second philosophical phase, he now sees man's self-realization not as an inward turning into one's "self," but as an outward act of entering-into-relation with others; thus the goal of one's striving toward the Absolute assumes a different character. The goal is still God, but not so much to imitate His oneness as to live in His Presence. Man's effort to overcome his inner duality now becomes a preparation for his entering-into-relation with God, since only man-as-a-whole in the highest possible degree may look to this kind of meeting. What is thus realized is not God in things, but His presence between things, and the reality that is being realized is not a substance which *is,* but a relation which *becomes* through the very act of entering into it. Buber finds this "tendency of realization" most strongly represented in Judaism; it "means true human life in the face of God." To the Jew, he says, God is not an idea either of pure reason or practical postulates, but the Being that is present in "the mystery of immediacy." The locus of the presentness is not individual man, but life between man and man—in the community. "The true place of realization," he writes, "is the community, and true community is the one in which the Divine realizes itself between men."[321]

According to Buber, the Jewish teaching of realization is not a theory, not a formulation in words of reasoning, but the word being actualized in speech; it realizes itself as such. The key to it is *deed,* which is not the truth of an idea, image, philosopheme, or a work of art, but the *truth of deed,* the formation of "the community on earth." It is also the truth of *unity* and of *the future,* for Judaism strives for the unity and redemption of all life on earth.[322] There is no spiritual world divided into spheres of works and grace, no separation between the Kingdom of God and the kingdom of man. God's kingdom is the becoming of man's kingdom, not the "other world," but the "coming world," the coming community through man's will and God's grace welded together in the act of relation. This teaching of realization or, as Buber now calls it, fulfillment signifies "the mystery of the covenant between man and God," as presented in the biblical covenants with man, with Abraham, and with the Jewish people—covenants based not on what is—on being, but on what will be—on becoming. The mystery is in the deed: "We shall do and we shall hear." We hear the word of God through our doing, through our deed of becoming a true community.

The Western nations, Buber says, have adopted some of the Jewish teaching through early Christianity, but not its most essential aspect, namely, the teaching of fulfillment. They have perpetuated a dualism of truth and reality, idea and fact, morality and politics, which militates against this teaching. And the Jewish people, which has lived among these nations, has had to accommodate itself to their mode of life and thought, so that its messianic fervor has been submerged in the struggle for adjustment. The question now is, What shall Israel do to redeem itself from the ghostly unreality of its present condition and to renew its striving for the goal?[323] Buber reviews three possible ways, which he designates as Humanitarianism, Dogmatic Nationalism, and Dogmatic Law. The first advises the Jews to give up their separate identity and throw their lot in with the revolutionary movements of humanity as a whole. To this Buber replies that experience has shown its futility as far as the Jews are concerned. The Jews must be able to take their fight for freedom into their own hands and build on their own soil, free of foreign domination. The second way advocates the latter course, but is dogmatic in applying the current Western idea of nationalism as a supreme end in itself, to make the Jewish state sovereign without regard to its fundamental striving. The third way claims that the goal may be attained only by strict observance of the laws of Torah and Talmud without deviation, change, or innovation. Buber rejects these last two ways because of their dogmatic restrictions against the people's creative spirit. Instead, he proposes "the way that leads through Zion to the renewal of the human community,"[324] emanating from a prime religious act and embracing the human aspect of the Jew, his free national regeneration, and the renewal of the teachings of the Torah. When the Jewish people reunites with its land, it will work toward rebuilding its true communal life, which must go hand in hand with the renewal of man as a whole and with the restructuring of his society. "The relations between men must change in order that a true change of society, a true rebirth, may take place."[325] This goal represents in essence the aims of the Labor Zionist movement and its teachings about land, labor, and Hebrew culture, which Buber called Hebrew Humanism.

In later years Buber developed these ideas in greater depth and scope, which I will consider in the next section. Here I merely want to call attention to the transition from his concept of Judaism as substance to Judaism as relation, which is the basic idea of his dialogical principle expounded in *I and Thou*. According to this principle, the Jewish people, like man in general, finds its fulfillment through the act of entering-into-relation with nature (in its ancient homeland), with fellowman (Jewish living together), and with God (in religious Hebrew humanism). What comes to life in these relations with things, men, and the Divine is the true community. As Buber moved away from the subjective, psychological view of reality toward a philosophical anthropology, he saw the divine aspect of communal life as the dominant factor in man's self-fulfillment. "The community," he wrote in 1923, "does not have its meaning in itself. It is the place where the Divine has not yet spent itself, the place of the coming theophany."[326] And when he looked for a sign of its manifestation, he said: "We are awaiting a theophany of which we know nothing but the place, and the place is called community."[327]

6
Essence of Communality

Three Movements of Fulfillment

The Way of Faith

The three tendencies of unity, deed, and the future in Buber's teaching of realization run through all three phases of his philosophy of Judaism, but with a different emphasis in each. In the first phase, realization centers on the *unification* of the duality in man's soul, in the second on the *act* of relating to God, while in the third the stress is on striving for the *future* or the messianic goal, which in essence is true communality. Buber finds it in Jewish Scripture and folk religion. As pointed out above, he started writing on the Bible long after he had already published his major essays in philosophy. As he says, he "had first to mature in the service of the Bible." This maturation is also reflected in his different treatment of the two fields. Of philosophy he notes, "I have no teaching but I carry on a conversation"[328]; of his "great experience of faith" he says, "I have received no tidings . . . but have gained experiences and insights."[329] In both fields he is the philosophizing man, but in the first he deals with philosophemes, ideas, concepts, theories, though not in closed systems, while in the second he seeks "to formulate the *theologoumena* of a folk-religion."[330] If his philosophical anthropology may be characterized as an ontology without metaphysics, his philosophy of Judaism is a religious teaching without theology—a teaching that points "the way" to the Jewish faith.[331] This is true particularly of the third phase of his writings on Judaism.

Buber derives the essence of Judaism from three major historical movements, from Prophecy, Hasidism, and Zionism, finding in each the fundamental tendency of Messianism as well as its counteracting forces. He describes this process

> as a struggle between the formative and the formless [which runs through] the history of Judaism and the history of great Jews. . . . The lot of the formative repeats itself eternally as victory and defeat. . . . The central persons who stand in the reality of mythos and Jewish history are the bearers and propagators of this one great proceeding.[332]

The essence of Judaism is thus to be sought in the life of the people and its leaders in the three movements in which the formative force breaks through the formless drive of the folk and tries to mold it into a true community. This is not a one-time act of establishing a communal image of a fixed order and norm. At times, the form and the image tend to become stagnant, lifeless, meaningless, as the formless drives constantly decompose them. However, the power of formation is not thereby destroyed, but remains latent until it reawakens and asserts itself in a twofold direction: to tame the formless and to renew the image. Formation is thus a transformation, and the struggle is an ongoing process of renewal. Although this struggle is between the masses and their great men who try to imbue them with the spirit of communality, the actual contest, as Buber sees it, is between these men and the official leadership—the priests, kings, scribes, rabbinites, nationalists, and many other experts, who want to perpetuate the established norm and order, even after their image has become meaningless. Within the masses it is a tension between the formative powers and the formless drives; in the contest between leaders it is a struggle of the forces of renewal against those of conservation.

Historical Conflict of Fulfillment

In Buber's view, the history of the Jewish people is a history of faith or of a religious community that may be traced in the footsteps of the prophets, from Moses to the "end of days." Israel is therefore not presented in a series of accomplishments, but as a process of fulfillment of its goal, not what it has been or is, but what it becomes and will be. "The religious character of the people consists exactly in this that it means something other than just what it is, that it should become something else, that it should become the true people, 'God's people.' "[333] This is what the prophet has in mind when he addresses the people, even when he speaks to it in a given historial situation. It is, furthermore, the source of tension between him and the official leaders, whether kings or priests, as they confront each other with a different outlook on the meaning of history. What one regards as failure, the other prophesies as fulfillment. The distinction is between what Buber calls history of power in the social-political sense of the state and history of God's way in the religious-political sense of the community. This is a cardinal distinction in his entire philosophy of Judaism. Therefore, in order to understand his interpretation of Prophecy, Hasidism, and Zionism, we must first clarify his dual approach to Jewish history.

Buber's fundamental idea is that God is not only the creator of nature and man, but also of peoples and history. The whole creation points to history, and history points to redemption. Since redemption is a dialogical act, a partnership between man and God, its fulfillment is not a one-time occurence, but an ongoing process in which God's word or speech is revealed in nature as well as in man. However, there is a difference between these two acts of revelation. In nature God's speech is constant, embracing all elements in their entirety, and may be apprehended by all who open themselves up to it. In human history, God's word is revealed in moments when man enters into relation with the Absolute (and only man is capable of this relation) through an act of his own decision, thus becoming a partner in redemption. Human history is therefore not a constant self-revealing process, as is nature, but one that must be revealed ever anew through man's active participation. Its renewal is the way of fulfillment, leading to the messianic goal. But man, being a free agent, may or may not follow this way.

What is the meaning of this revelation and how is it to be fulfilled? According to Buber's philosophical anthropology, man is not "the single one," but part of a community, not directly of mankind as a whole, but of a small community which, together with other small communities, is a constituent of humanity. Man's fulfillment therefore can come only through his participation in the building of the true community of his own people. The people one is a member of is not just "a sum of individuals . . . but something in existence beyond these and, moreover, something which is intended as such by God, and as such addressed by Him and responsible to Him,"[334] that is, to fulfill His demand to establish the true community. This demand, Buber says, was made of the people Israel at the very moment of its becoming a nation when it entered into a covenant with God at Sinai. Israel's uniqueness is that, of all nations, it alone was addressed by God as a people, not merely as individuals. Even before there was a people Israel, its progenitor Abraham was addressed as the father of a people: in his seed shall he become a blessing. However, as a people, Israel has not yet fulfilled its destiny, for it has not yet established itself as a true community, nor has it fulfilled its mission to serve, in this respect, as a paradigm to mankind as a whole.

The holy history of mankind, Buber holds, is the way of all nations toward the universal nation of nations. This is God's will on earth, the completion of His world creation. Each nation must take part in it, but Israel has been specifically commissioned to complete its own community. This is the real meaning of its chosenness. Its "election is entirely a demand."[335]

> Humanity is destined to become a single body . . . through the activities of men themselves. . . . A true humanity, that is, a people composed of peoples, must begin with a certain definite true people. . . . Only true peoples, each of whom lives in the light of righteousness, are capable of entering into upright relations with one another. The people Israel was commissioned to pave the way in this direction.[336]

This is the meaning of fulfillment in the history of Israel's faith in the arena of world history. Buber calls it history "from below," that is, emanating from man and people, who reach out to meet God in "a dialogue of action," but whom God gave freedom to "act for or against Him." There is another history which he calls "history from above," that is, when man assumes that he has been empowered by God to carry out a set of specific instructions to their successful conclusion. Success through the use of power is taken by man as a sign of God's commission: "Successes are revelations."[337] Man thus becomes a tool of a higher power without himself assuming responsibility for his deeds. This has been the history of kings and other potentates who have claimed divine authority for whatever action they may have perpetrated.

In "history from below" power is regarded as authorized by

God on condition that each one to whom it is entrusted assume the responsibility for its specific application. That is, while one may be become aware of God's intention through his experience with the divine encounter, the decision for its exact meaning is his own and so is the responsibility for carrying it out. "The meaning of history [from below] is not an idea which I can formulate independent of my personal life."[338] It is not a subjective idea originating in man's emotional or ideational reactions, because it does not depend on man alone, but on his relation with another, on his living experiences with others in reality. This is Buber's meaning of the "history of faith." As he defines it in another place, it is "the history of human participation, as far as is known to us, in that which has taken place between God and man. Accordingly, Israel's history of faith . . . is that which has taken place between God and Israel."[339] In "history from above" the action is represented as coming from God working itself out *through* man. In "history from below" the action takes place *between* God and man. The former knows only the power of temporary success, but the latter may go on its way to fulfillment even through failure and disappointment, for its spirit abides and asserts itself in great moments of the life of the people. It is this spirit which Buber seeks to uncover in the history of Judaism and the history of great Jews.

Prophecy

History Overcoming "History"

The conflict between the two historical views described in the preceding section has been operative from the earliest time of Israel's peoplehood to the present, but most strongly in the period of the classical prophets. Out of the tension between the prophet and the people and between the prophet and the king or priest, there grew a spiritual force which the prophets promulgated as the messianic idea. Buber regards this idea as the dialogical communication between God and the people, as a people, in the divine acts of creation, revelation, and redemption of humanity as a whole. Indeed, his philosophy of Judaism is an unfolding of this dialogue in its prophetic form, presaging an "era of history which refutes 'history,' " the latter meaning history of power.[340] As he examines Jewish experience in biblical times, he sees in it the conflict between the mass of people who want a king to rule over them, like all other nations, and the prophets who uphold God's covenant with Israel to be its only king and ruler. What is meant here is not an other-worldly existence, but the actual political life of the people in its own land, its basic structure being that of a political-religious community, with the human head of state serving only as "governor" entrusted by God and responsible to Him. Difficult as it may be for modern man to visualize the actual operation of this kind of state in national and international affairs, Buber presents it in all earnestness as the prophetic goal not only for Israel, but also for all other nations on earth. He is no religious romanticist, but one who sees reality as existing solely in man's relation to God, and who therefore draws its consequences in all walks of life. As already noted, he expects Judaism to establish itself as the paradigm of this reality.

While the messianic idea of fulfillment is a goal to be realized in the distant future, in actuality it is the spiritual force that activates the life of the people in its everyday interhuman and interpeople relations. It is the future acting at every moment of the present. Its goal is the "overcoming of history" or the fusion of "outer history" of surface successes with "inner history" of depth, which lacks success. The fusion is not to be postponed to the end of days, but must be an ongoing process in our daily lives. "A drop of messianic fulfillment must be mixed into every hour, or else it is godless despite all piety."[341] In the age of prophecy, both historical functions devolved on Israel as a body politic. The prophets demanded that the people live according to its original covenant with God, whereby it was made into a people, and also to strive toward the fulfillment of the task placed upon it by this covenant, namely, the realization of the true community in world history. What is the prophet's role in these functions, and how does the messianic idea grow out of it? Its proper perspective may be seen in the role Moses played in the drama of the covenant between God and Israel at Mount Sinai.

Moses, according to Buber, cannot be characterized strictly as prophet or priest, or a combination of both. His unique leadership has elevated him above this type of division of functions. Through his role in the formation of Israel as a people in the divine presence at Sinai, he originated the theopolitical idea of God's direct rule over this people as the first part (*Anfangsteil*) of God's Kingdom, later to be extended to all nations on earth.[342] This became Israel's goal in its ancestral land for which it had been prepared through its wandering in the desert. Combining the two spheres of religious leader and political legislator, Moses was the man most suited to translate the divine will into decisions of the moment as well as into lasting laws. But this kind of combination of powers is not transferable from person to person. Moses himself realized it when he was compelled before he died to allot the two spheres to different persons. He had to yield to "the historical way of mankind," the way of power history, and split the functions of his succession between the judge and the priest, who were in time replaced by the prophet and the king, respectively. In this division of functions, the king and his court priests tend to abolish God's direct kingship over Israel and the prophet tries to uphold it. But the prophet is not God's "viceregent" over the people, only His messenger who delivers the divine word to the earthly rulers, admonishing them to fulfill the people's covenant with God. Although in a sense he is a political man, he is not the messianic theopolitical figure who would himself carry out God's will, but one who must call on the king to do it. The prophet has no power in the face of the king, but this, says Buber, is the source of his strength. Even when his message fails to move the king, it penetrates into the very fabric of the people's consciousness and continues to demand its fulfillment; it turns into the messianic idea that realizes itself at every hour, whenever the people turns to God.

As Buber points out, in promulgating theopolitical rule the prophet does not vie with the king or priest in establishing a theocracy in the accepted sense of the word. Generally understood, a theocracy is the autonomous and unlimited rule of men over men derived from a divine authority and often passed on in hereditary succession. The ruler here is a person of a priestly caste who claims consecration from a deity. On the other hand, the prophet not only does not claim such powers for himself or for his anticipated Messiah, but also opposes its usurpation by any other human being. There is a difference in movement. The priest moves from man to God in order to wrest from Him an irrevocable decision. The prophet moves from God to man in order to confront the king and the people with God's word and to demand their decision. He does not bring them an oracle, but a message, and he wants them to choose. Neither does he present a rationally designed political plan forecasting the future. He speaks only of the historical situation in which the people finds itself at a given time and calls on it and its leaders to decide how to act in it with full responsibility toward the future. Since each decision also determines the next situation, the prophet places before the people the goal of the true community and calls for its realization "corresponding to the situation." Buber sums it up in one sentence, quoted above: "A drop of messianic fulfillment must be mixed into every hour, or else it is godless despite all piety."[343]

What has been said thus far of the prophetic view of historical reality is illustrated by Buber in his interpretation of Isaiah's encounter with Ahaz, and later with Hezekiah, in two critical moments of the kingdom of Judah. In both cases the prophet advises the king not to go through with his plan to form a pact with a powerful nation, Syria or Egypt, but to trust in God, the true king, who "will protect the community attached to Him."[344] This may sound utopian, Buber admits, but the historical reality of the situation, as seen by Isaiah, is that a small nation, such as Judah, must not ally itself with great powers or become involved in their wars of expansion and thus lose sight of its own independent historical course. From Isaiah's religious-political viewpoint, Israel must have confidence that its destiny to fulfill the task entrusted to it by God will be consummated; it means placing "history of faith" above "history of power."

> He who has dealings with the powers renounces the power of powers, that which empowers and disempowers, and forfeits its protection; but he who is confident and keeps still, thereby gains political insight and strength to hold fast against danger.[345]

This, says Buber, is the core of Isaiah's theopolitical teaching. To understand it more fully, we must recall Buber's view on the practice of power as a political principle, which he considers to be a main evil of modern society. The true community, he holds, cannot be realized under the dominance of power politics in national or international affairs. When, therefore, the prophet calls for trust in God, Who will protect the community that is faithful to Him, he "at the same time [calls for] trust in the inner strength and in the influence of a community that ventures to realize righteousness within itself and toward its surroundings." When leaders act with faith and responsibility toward this goal, without resorting to power politics, their "political decision . . . conforms to God's rule."[346] According to the prophetic teaching, then, Israel's history of faith is not preordained, but is a series of divine revelations that happens as each situation arises. Not the prophets alone but the people too participates in each revelation. Thus history is revelation, and revelation is history. If there will ever be a person who may perform the messianic function, he will act as God's viceregent on earth, when power and faith will be one in God's rule over nations. But this person will be a human being, not one who becomes God, but who stands in His presence and is responsible to Him. In this respect, the Messiah may be regarded as a political figure.

Development of Messianic Belief

In Buber's sketch of the history of faith, the messianic goal is not preestablished, but is a process of realization, the completion of creation through man's participation. The origin of the messianic belief, Buber points out, stems from Israel's acceptance of the rule of God when it became a people at Mount Sinai. In binding itself to the covenant, Israel committed itself to realize the divine kingship in its own midst and to help bring it into the world as a whole. This burden was borne by Moses as leader and legislator and was transmitted by him to his followers, the kings or priests, as they were all regarded as God's "viceregents" or "anointed ones" commissioned to lead the people to the fulfillment of its task. When these leaders, due to lack of spirit, failed in their mission, God sent His messengers, the prophets, to call them to responsibility. In a sense, the prophets continued the work begun by Moses, though not in the same capacity, as they did not possess the combined powers of leader and legislator. Like Moses, they were the bearers of the divine demand for the fulfillment of the people's task, yet, unlike him, they were not able to lead the people toward its realization. The latter function was taken over by the judges and kings, and when some of them broke God's covenant by serving other gods, there arose the idea of God's "anointed king," the *Mashiah* (the Hebrew word for "anointed"), who would appear at some future time as the true representative of the divine king on earth. This idea was cultivated by the prophets themselves out of their despair with the backsliding of the people and its rulers.

Buber traces the development of this idea among the classical prophets in great detail. But this need not detain us here, because our interest is not in his biblical exegesis, but in his concept of Messianism as such. "So long as God's kingdom has not been established," he says, "Judaism will never recognize a human being as the Messiah who has come." For "its waiting for the Messiah is the waiting for the true community," and this is to be realized by man. "It is man's task to establish God's power in the terrestrial world."[347] Buber does not consider the fulfillment of the messianic goal to be the burden of a single individual, no matter how greatly endowed with the divine spirit, but rather the function of the people Israel as a whole. However, since the people did not fulfill its function during its national existence in its ancient land, there may now be individual Jews elected to do its work. Buber refers to the Second Isaiah, 49:3, which he translates "Mein Knecht bist du, das Israel du, mit dem ich prangen darf" ("My servant art thou, thou who art Israel, with whom I will shine forth"),[348] giving it the interpretation that God now addresses Himself not only to the people, but also to individuals to carry out the divine task, and that whoever responds to God's call is His servant embodying the truth of Israel's existence. The prophetic image of the Messiah is thus extended to all those who may become God's servants. Indeed, this is the culmination of all prophecy.[349]

The Suffering Servant

Of all the descriptions of the suffering servant of God, whether as individual or as corporate body, found in the prophetic books, Buber portrays his quality of suffering with greatest finality, especially in his interpretation of the messianic allusions in the Second Isaiah. There is not one Messiah, he says, but many messianic figures who are essentially followers of the servant's way, each chosen by God to perform the task which Israel had failed to do. While they are chosen for the same purpose as Israel was, they do not replace it but stand in a special relationship with it. Buber calls it the paradox of the two servants (corporate and individual) which cannot be resolved but must be accepted as intended in "the messianic mystery of the Second Isaiah." He finds the same paradox in the relationship between the anonymous servant, who is the corporate body of Israel, and the prophet, who announces it, speaking as if he himself were that anonymous body.

Buber differentiates three stages in the way of the suffering servant—prophecy, affliction, and action—which emerged out of the prophet's failure to overcome the people's resistance to the divine call. In the first stage the prophet is like an arrow which is powerless because it must remain hidden in the quiver; not realizing its purpose, he suffers from his helplessness, yet continues to admonish and protest. In the second stage, which is one of quietude, the prophet becomes aware of the meaning of his affliction and submits to it as God's will. In the third stage he is sent forth like an arrow hurled from the quiver to bring the divine order for Israel and the nations. These are not periods in the life of a single person, but of the messianic goal passing from a condition of powerlessness, in which the prophet can only protest and demand, but not lead, to one of awareness of a call to action, but suffering because, being hidden in the quiver, he is unable to act, and finally, having come out of the quiver, to a period of active leadership. In the last stage the leader is the "completed man" (Meshullam), who embodies the "reality of Israel in its purity: . . . Jeshurun, the upright people, [is incorporated] in the reality of Meshullam, the completed man."[350] The highest type of God's servant grew out of the prophetic line and became the "anointed prophets" (Nabi-Mashiah), instead of the "anointed kings" (Melekh-Hamashiah). They are not Israel's redeemers or the bearers of its sins, for God alone is the bearer and redeemer of the people. Buber might say with the Talmudic sage, "Israel has no Messiah" or anointed king to rule over it, because God is its king and redeemer.[351]

The messianic men are truly God's servants in the same sense as the prophets were, with the added function of leadership: "The suffering nabi is the antecedent type of the acting Messiah." As a group they represent Israel, interceding on its behalf with God, but mainly as the nucleus of "the true Israel." The nabi-mashiah "is Israel as servant."[352] Perhaps here the paradox of the two servants may be considered resolved. The true Israel and the true servant are one and the same. Also the paradox of the prophet who calls himself servant when the people is intended, may find its resolution in the nabi-mashiah, who is both the announcer and the leader, the one who demands and fulfills, combining in his person his own task and that of the people. If we recall what Buber said to his young hearers in the first of his "Three Speeches on Judaism," we shall see how his idea of the messianic men took shape even then. He said:

When we have thus confirmed ourselves in our deepest self-knowledge, when we have said yes to ourselves, to our whole Jewish existence, then we no longer feel as single ones, then every single one of us feels as a people, for he feels the people in himself.[353]

The messianic idea played a dominant role also in Buber's approach to Hasidism and Zionism, which we shall examine next.

Hasidism

The Teaching

"Historically," Buber writes, "Hasidism arose in answer to the crisis of Messaianism."[354] The crisis came toward the end of the seventeenth century after the collapse of the Sabbatai Zvi movement. The massses who had flocked under its banner saw the futility of trying to realize the messianic age through the advent of a single human being at a specified time. They had just emerged from their catastrophe of 1648–1649 in the Polish Ukraine and, having been disillusioned with the pretender-Messiah, they sought a new meaning of redemption in their every-day life.[355] This was offered by the Hasidic movement, which was founded by Israel Baal-Shem-Tov in the first half of the eighteenth century. The essence of its teachings is that redemption is not to be sought in some distant future, but here and now in every situation by hallowing each act of ordinary life, by turning all life of man with man and with nature toward God. This may not be accomplished according to a premeditated plan conceived by a single human being of superior powers, but by all men, and without plan, each according to his own ability. Buber therefore sees in Hasidism a renewal of the messianic idea of the age of the prophets: many men can be the servants of God by helping to bring His Kingdom on earth. He takes up this theme again, with all its earmarks of the "suffering servant," in his exposition of the Hasidic teachings. In his *Origin and Meaning of Hasidism* he writes:

It is a mistake to regard Jewish Messianism as belief in an event happening once and for all at the end of time and in a single human figure created as the center of this event. The end of time is bound up with present life by the certainty of the cooperative power which is accorded to man, to the generations of men. . . . [There is] a series of "servants of God" arising from generation to generation, who lowly and despised bear and cleanse the dross of the world.[356]

These men do not function openly "in the light of recognizable history," but in hiddenness, "in the dimness of an inaccessible, personal act of suffering, of which only distorted information or none at all reaches outside." None of them is the Messiah, but all are forerunners who possess messianic power and who represent the messianic idea of the "end of time," as the idea of all time and beyond the times. "This is the suffering Messiah who ever again endures deadly torment for the sake of God."[357] His hiddenness is not feigned secrecy, but the essence of his work, which he performs without knowledge except that he is the servant of God. If this hiddenness were torn apart, a counteraction would set in. "Messianic self-announcement is the undoing of Messiahship." How is all this manifested in the Hasidic movement? What is being redeemed, how are the suffering servants able to help, and what is the meaning of their suffering?

We have already noted that Buber's method is selective, not all-embracing. In Hasidism as in Scripture, he singles out those teachings and recorded ways of life which go to the core of the movement insofar as they reveal the Jewish idea of redemption. Indeed, all his writings on Hasidism center on this idea. Moreover, in bringing it to light, he addresses himself to the crisis of modern man out of the same world outlook that characterizes his works on the dialogical principle. He regards Hasidism as an attempt to realize the true dialogue between God and man through man's relation with fellowmen and with nature.

> I consider the truth of Hasidism [he says] vitally important for Jews, Christians, and other men, and at this particular hour more important than ever before. For now is the hour when we are in danger of forgetting for what purpose we are on earth, and I know of no other teaching that reminds us of this so forcibly.[358]

The Hasidic message is twofold, "the teaching and the way." In each Buber enters not as a mere observer, but as one who wants "to learn the teaching and to follow the way," that is, to experience its truth and to gauge his own life by it. This does not mean that he embraced Hasidism as his personal mode of life. As he writes of his experience with the movement,

> Certainly, I could not become a Hasid. It would have been an unpermissible masquerading had I adopted the Hasidic manner of life—I who had an entirely different approach to Jewish tradition, since I had to distinguish in my innermost being between what is commanded me and what is not commanded me. It was necessary for me to absorb into my own existence as much as I could of what had been experienced there in the past, namely, the realization of that dialogue with being whose possibility my thought had shown me.[359]

Around the time Buber came into personal contact with the movement, he considered it to be in its state of decline. True, he found that "every Hasidic community still bears in it a germ of the Kingdom of God"[360]; but it had splintered into disparate groups, and in order to penetrate its essence he had to look into the lives of past generations as recorded in the written and oral traditions of the zaddikim. He found these best represented in what he termed the "legendary anecdote," which he collected and published among his other Hasidic works. "This form," he says, "has enabled me to present Hasidic life so that it is at the same time apparent as reality and comprehensible as teaching. Even where I had to let theory speak, I could relate it back to life."[361] He did not convert the Hasidic message into "solid concepts" or transmit it as "speculative theology," but presented it as "the lived life of seven generations," in his capacity as its "late-born interpreter."[362] In what follows, then, I will present Buber's theoretical interpretation of the Hasidic meaning of redemption and how he found it exemplified in the life of the Hasidim.

To understand the Hasidic speculative teachings, we must consider another crisis that loomed in the Western world at the time, with which Hasidism, to be sure, had no direct contact, but nevertheless provided an answer. Buber calls this crisis "the tendency of the Western spirit toward monological life," which, he says, was intensified by Spinoza in his attempt to remove God from any personal relation with man.[363] By his desire to "purify" God of any blemish of the attribute "person," Spinoza undermined the Jewish teaching that God is open to man's address. For this, says Buber, is the chief contribution Israel has made to Western religious thinking—"not that it taught the one real God, . . . but that it showed that this God can be addressed in reality, that one can say Thou to Him, can stand face to face with Him, can hold discourse with Him."[364] What happens when this prime relationship is denied is that, instead of speaking with God, man speaks to himself and only makes believe that he speaks to God. Monologue replaces dialogue. In practical life it means that a religious deed through which man may have consecrated his life to God now becomes an impersonal cult, a fixed ritual, independent of the prime relation between God and man. Or, on the human side, it means that the soul has made itself an independent vehicle of ecstasy or devotion and wants to have communion with God without relation to the world. The soul thus makes believe that the world has vanished, but, in reality, so has its God when it tries to reach Him through sheer ecstasy. Spinoza acknowledged that such ecstatic, world-free communion with God lacks all reality in man's personal life; but rather than bring the world into the act of man's relation with the Divine, he denied the possibility of speech between them altogether. He made the world "the place of God" instead of "the place of the meeting with God."[365]

The Cosmic Drama of Redemption

The Baal-Shem-Tov and his followers, says Buber, replied to Spinoza's contention, without knowing its source, by reaffirming Israel's age-old view that the world is not "the place of God," but God is the "place of the world," and that He "dwells in" it. God's "dwelling-in," as taught by Hasidism, means that there are divine sparks of His presence in everything in the world and that man is called upon to redeem them by coming into contact with them. The meaning of redemption can be understood only in connection with the other two elements of the "triad of world-time," as Buber calls it, namely, creation and revelation. It centers on the meaning of reality, man's loss of relation to it, and his renewal of this relation. "The essence of the Hasidic message," Buber states, "consists in founding a renewed relation to reality" in Jewish life, which had been shattered in the wake of the Sabbatian-Frankish tragedy.[366] Yet Hasidism did not create new religious dogmas or precepts and did not establish a new cult. It has remained fully within the fold of Talmudic tradition, precepts, and observances, but with a different emphasis on its fundamental spirit, which expresses itself primarily in the Jewish teaching of redemption. It has created, as Buber says, "a new *illumination* of the teachings and precepts," gave them "a new meaning," and renewed "their vitality without changing their matter."[367] This renewal found expression in a new approach to two traditions, the Kabbalah and rabbinic law, the first representing a teaching of cosmic dimension, and the second a way of inner life. Both were fused by the Hasidim "into a reality of life and community."[368]

Buber describes the basic concepts of Kabbalah insofar as he considers them decisive for Hasidism. Of prime importance is the distinction he draws between the two on the matter of *gnosis*. The problem which gives rise to every form of gnosis is how to reconcile the existence of a conditioned, imperfect world, which is full of contradictions, with the existence of God, Who is infinite, perfect, and unconditioned. The gnostic explanation is that there is a prime duality of beings, such as God and the world, good and evil, light and darkness, or any other pair of positive and negative forces contending against each other in the very heart of the cosmos. In the contest between God and world, the latter holds the godhood imprisoned, hidden from us, and it is up to us to "unveil" the realms of God through a system of mystic knowledge that transforms man into spirit and unites him with the deity, which is man's salvation. In this process the world is completely denied.[369] Kabbalah rejected the gnostic absolute dualism, but introduced a dualism into the divine unity itself and at the same time retained the gnostic scheme of secret knowledge and mystic acts, whereby the world contradictions into which the divine unity has descended may be removed. Kabbalah thus aimed at "seeing through the contradiction of being and removing itself from it."[370]

While Hasidism accepts the Kabbalah's view of an upper and a lower world, it does not seek to abolish the world of contradiction, but rather to redeem it. It rejects the gnostic way of knowing as an instrument of redemption, and promulgates the biblical "knowing," which is a mutuality of relation between man and God.[371] The second aspect of Kabbalah which Hasidism has transformed deals with man's influence on the destiny of the Divine in the act of redemption. Hasidism rejects the magic elements implied in the Kabbalistic mystery of prayer in prescribed formulas and fixed procedures of intention (specified *kavanot*) as mediators between God and man. Instead, it teaches that the essence of intention *(kavana)* or the force of its influence is that man directs himself to God with his whole being in response to the divine demand at any moment, but without any preconceived knowledge of its specific meaning. Kabbalah approaches God with certitude, claiming precise knowledge of how to elicit His help on specific occasions. Hasidism does not claim this kind of knowledge, but reaches out to the Divine with trembling, anticipating but never sure of a response, only trusting in its Presence. Therefore, Hasidism does not require esoteric powers as Kabbalah does; the simple ignorant man as well as the learned can come near God if he goes out to meet Him in true piety, in real trust.

Buber maintains that, on the whole, Hasidism has engaged in Kabbalistic speculations only marginally, and only as it concerns the problem of redemption of Israel from Exile. It has accepted the Kabbalistic view that this problem relates to the Divine Presence itself being in exile, but adapted its terminology ("contraction," "emanation," "cleaving," etc.) to its own view that man's relation to God is essentially of a dialogical character. Hasidism holds that God is wholly transcendent to the world yet takes part in its destiny, or that "God's destiny in the world" is determined by His own will and not through a duality, whether external or internal to His Being. God, Who himself is a nondual and nonrelational unity, willed the coming into being of an other that strives to enter-into-relation with Him, to know and to love Him. This is the Hasidic meaning of "contraction" *(tsimtsum)* and "emanation" *(atsilut)*: God contracts Himself to make room for otherness and to allow certain spheres to emanate from Him and become manifest in creation, formation, and making—in various material and spiritual forms of life. The mystery of the *tsimtsum* is that while God withdraws to allow room for others, His divine Presence, the *Shekhina,* is not withdrawn. He is the "place" and center of the world, dwells in His acts of allowing things to come into existence through His emanations, which descend from the highest to the lowest spheres, from the pure sphere of separation (world of ideas) to the spheres of creation (spirit), formation (soul), and making (corporeal life), the last being the limit of their transformation. As the highest emanation descends in the corporeal sphere, God's wave breaks and the divine sparks of the first creation *(Adam Kadmon)* scatters and becomes imprisoned in the shells *(kelipot)* of the things of our earthly existence. This is what is meant by God's exile. The divine Presence banishes itself from one sphere to another, from one shell to the next, until it reaches its destiny in the world. This is its furthest exile, its indwelling in all things on earth. God's *Shekhina* then wants to be redeemed from Exile as Israel wants to be redeemed from its exile.

What has been described here in terms of divine emanations following God's contraction is the same as the divine acts of creation and revelation. God is revealed through the sparks of His creation, and redemption is the "lifting of the sparks" out of their imprisonment in the shells and helping them to regain their divine origin. Man has a part in it because, of all creatures, he embodies the principle of freedom to decide for direction to God, a principle inherent in the mystery of God's contraction—the "mystery of *tsimtsum*." In the very act of making room for otherness God sets the other free and independent of His will, limited only by one's own action and its consequences. In contrast to traditional Kabbalah on the meaning of lifting the sparks, redeeming the *Shekhina,* and man's role in this process, Hasidism sees the world through man's relationship with God. Man is the highest creature descended from Adam Kadmon— that primordial anthropological being out of whose sense organs the world of things was made.[372] As a microcosm, man possesses the divine spark of Adam Kadmon's soul, and as the inheritor of the original freedom he is called upon to work for the redemption of the human soul as well as of the divine Presence from exile. He is the only one who can enter into relation with God and, since God's contraction made both relation and freedom possible, he must enter into free relation with God to redeem His contraction.

> Here man, this forlorn man, is by his prime meaning God's helper. For his sake, . . . for the sake of him who chooses God, who can choose God, the world was created. Its shells are here so that he may penetrate them to the kernel. The spheres have been removed from one another so that he may bring them nearer to each other. Createdness waits for him. God waits for him. From him, from "below," the impulse to redemption must proceed. Grace is God's *answer.*[373]

Thus Buber presents the Hasidic teaching of man's role in the act of redemption in line with his own concept of the dialogical principle of relation, or perhaps he derives this principle from his experiences with Hasidic lore and through his delving into its Kabbalistic speculations. Whether or not his interpretation is entirely in conformity with the original Hasidic sources may be a subject for debate, particularly with regard to its gnostic and pantheistic elements. But this is not our concern here. As said, Buber selected out of Hasidic lore, which is far from monolithic, those Kabbalistic contents which he regarded as most representative of pure Hasidism, that is, purified of gnostic Sabbatianism. According to him, Kabbalah has been overcome "as it made its way into the primal Jewish conception of dialogical life; this is the important work of Hasidism."[374] By putting the responsibility of redemption on man, it has become the ethos of Kabbalah. It changed the Sabbatian idea of "entering in sin" into a teaching of "hallowing the everyday." That is, the sinful is not an outside existence to be entered into in order to be eliminated, but an incompleteness in all conditioned beings which may be redeemed by directing them to God.[375] This is the same as Buber's "double-directed relation" of mutuality between the Infinite and the finite which impels man to take part in leading the world toward redemption. Speaking in the Hasidic-Kabbalistic vein, Buber states: "God has confined Himself before the world, He set it free; now destiny is grounded in its freedom. That is the mystery of man."[376]

The Way of the Hasidim

Basically, Buber says, Hasidism is a way of life; its teachings only provide a commentary. He saw in this movement a great attempt to renew in the diaspora the Jewish communal efforts toward the realization of God's Kingdom. A knowledge of the character of this movement, its leaders and their relationship with their followers as well as among themselves will give us insight into its direction toward the goal. In its social aspect, a community of Hasidim consists of all the adherents of a certain zaddik or Rebbe who stands at the center as their teacher and guide in secular as well as spiritual matters.[377] It has no geographical boundaries as far as the membership is concerned, although each community is identified by the town or village where the zaddik resides or originates from. The entire movement may thus be regarded as one large community constituted as an association of small societies, without, however, any recognized leader standing at the head of an overall body, except that the movement centers in the person and teachings of its founder, Rabbi Israel Baal-Shem-Tov. At the same time, the Hasidic community is part of the general body politic of Israel in its diversified local and national communities, whose spiritual heads are the Rabbis or Ravs, usually of the opposition or *Mitnagdim*.[378]

The role of the zaddik is of paramount importance in the life of each Hasid and of the Hasidic community. Buber delineates him in the following ideal traits. He is a man who perfects himself in the Torah; he is the man in whom the Hasidic teaching is fulfilled. In him the task of salvation is more concentrated than in any other man; in his person the transcendental responsibility in this direction assumes an "organic existence." In him God wants to be known, loved, wanted. He is the realization of the archetype of man, to which earthly man aspires. He bears the prayers from below upward and brings down the holy spirit from above. All his actions are for the sake of unifying the *Shekhina* with God. In him the world renews itself constantly through the turning of all things toward God.

The community of a zaddik's followers is structured in three layers, each standing in a particular relation to him. First, there is the general following, the mass of people, rich and poor, learned and unlearned, who do not reside in the zaddik's vicinity but "journey" to him on special occasions to hear him "say Torah" at a Sabbath "third meal," on holidays, or to receive his blessing on personal and business matters. His influence over them is great, and their loyalty to him is unquestionable. The second layer consists of those who live in his neighborhood, town, or village, and close enough to join with him at daily services. This is the section of the community that stands in close relation to the zaddik in his chief task of bringing the people's devotion *(yihud)* to God in prayer. The place is the house of worship. This task, however, is not just the work of the zaddik alone, but of every participant individually and jointly. The zaddik does not stand here like a priest officiating at a fixed ritual of salvation, but rather as one who takes part in prayer together with all the others, though in a more concentrated way than the rest. He is the one who directs his prayer to God with the highest degree of intention *(kavana),* with the "cleaving" *(devekut)* of his soul to God, and with the highest enthusiasm *(hitlahavut).* Performed in this manner, prayer becomes an act of divinity, in which everyone is to participate to the best of his spiritual strength. This is the act of devotion *(yihud)* whereby man moves toward redemption, not a redemption of a "soul" or a spiritual "self," but of actual man in his everyday life. The "lifting of the sparks" out of the shells, of which the Kabbalah speaks, means for Hasidism a dedication, a hallowing of every facet of earthly life by directing it to God. The divine sparks are reunited with their origin not by denying the world, but by releasing them from their imprisonment in the "shells," so that their divine immanence may emerge. This is the task of every man who joins with the zaddik in prayer and deeds: "to affirm for God's sake the world and himself and by this very means transform them both."[379] The greater the "intention" and the "cleaving" in prayer, the higher the sparks are lifted and the nearer they come to their origin. This is the meaning of "turning" *(teshuva),* when man turns to God not only with his "good impulse," but also with his "evil impulse," even with the sparks "that dwell in sin." Quoting a saying of the Baal-Shem, "In the hour when on account of sin you carry out the turning, you raise the sparks that were in it into the upper world,"[380] Buber explains that this does not mean, as it does in Kabbalah, that the divine sparks which dwell in the things and in man, even in his sinful state, are released *from* their corporeal existence; it means, rather, that they are consecrated *within* their corporeal state by directing the whole of man's being to God. It means, moreover, that there is no basic separation of the "profane" from the "sacred"; all acts of human life here on earth can be made holy when they are dedicated to God in earnest, with "intention" and "cleaving" to Him. Summing up the Hasidic way, Buber writes:

> There is no separation within the human world between the high and the low; to each the highest is open, each life has its approach to reality, each kind its eternal right, from each thing a way leads to God, and each way that leads to God is *the* way.[381]

A Parting of the Ways

The third layer of the Hasidic community is the intimate circle of disciples who come from far and near to live for various lengths of time at the zaddik's abode and to learn from him and with him the way to God. Here is where the zaddik exerts his greatest influence and here also is where he shows his particular bent of character and mode of thinking. In this respect, Buber distinguishes two types of zaddikim, one "the leader" and the other "the teacher," which he portrays in the two main characters of his narrative *For the Sake of Heaven,* in the zaddik of Lublin and the zaddik of Pshysha, respectively.

The theme of the narrative is redemption, the time is the period of the Napoleonic wars, and the place is the academy of the zaddik Yaakov-Yizkhak, called the Seer of Lublin, where another man by the same name, Yaakov-Yizkhak, known as the Yehudi, spent many years as the former's disciple before he established a community of his own, as the zaddik of Pshysha.[382] The wars waged by Napoleon were interpreted by the Seer as the "Wars of Gog and Magog," prophesied by Ezekiel (38–39) and considered in Talmudic-Midrashic literature as the days of the "birth-pangs of the Messiah."[383] According to traditional belief, "Gog and Magog" is the personification of evil that will in time to come subdue all the nations and establish his rule over the world; then God will cause him to be defeated and the Messiah son of David will come to rule the world in peace and justice. The wars of Gog and Magog were thus conceived as an inevitable stage in the messianic era, and the Seer therefore sided with Napoleon, who, personifying Gog and Magog, would conquer the world and, after being defeated through divine intervention, would usher in the days of the Messiah. In order to hasten the coming of those days, the Seer sought to influence the course of events through special Kabbalistic powers and also tried to engage in this enterprise the aid of his disciples and other zaddikim who came under his influence. But his most faithful disciple, the Yehudi, did not accept his views and, while he did not engage in active opposition, gained many sympathizers for his own idea of messianic redemption.[384]

Of particular significance in this conflict of ideas is the popular belief that there will be a second or rather secondary Messiah, the son of Joseph, who will lead the battle against Gog and Magog and prepare the world for the advent of the primary Messiah, son of David.[385] The Seer and the Yehudi did not differ on the basic Hasidic teachings expounded by the former in his academy in Lublin nor on the role of Messiah son of David, but only on the functions of Messiah son of Joseph. The Seer thought of him as a particular man endowed with divine powers to fight the evil forces in the current history of nations, as exemplified by Napoleon Bonaparte. The Yehudi saw him not as a single person, but as a type of man—many men, who serve God with their whole being and bear their suffering in silence, like the arrow hidden in the quiver, realizing the messianic goal in everyday life in every generation. Their prototype is Messiah son of Joseph, "the suffering Messiah who ever again endures mortal agony for the sake of God."[386] The Seer's way is that of an eschatological Messiah, whose coming may be hastened by the use of certain mystic powers. The Yehudi's way is that of ongoing acts by many men of faith and dedication at all times; for him "God marches to His victory by the path of our defeats."[387]

Buber looks at the Yehudi as the embodiment of his own idea of Messianism as a history of faith in contrast to the political view represented by the Seer. For him the Yehudi is

> the image of the suffering Messiah that appears from genera-
> tion to generation and wanders from martyrdom and death to
> martyrdom and death, and has shown up in the latest folk
> tradition of Judaism. In Hasidism . . . it is still being told of
> this or that Master, who died a violent or premature death,
> that he was Messiah son of Joseph.[388]

And so it was told of the Yehudi. According to one legend, which Buber adapted for his narrative, the Yehudi died a premature death for the sake of Heaven.[389] When the Napoleonic enterprise failed, the Seer summoned his disciple to "bring him a message from Heaven" on what to do next. The Yehudi knew that such a venture, when undertaken outside the Holy Land of Israel, would mean his death,[390] but being a faithful Hasid, he could not refuse martyrdom for the sake of the community. He prepared himself by prayer and fasting and died quietly with words of the Psalmist on his lips: "Laden with Thy yoke. . . . Suffering Thy pain. . . . The only ones to declare Thy one-ness."[391]

Does this signify the failure or success of the Hasidic movement? Buber would say it failed when it tried to go the way of the history of power, but made great strides on the way of the history of faith. It set out to build a "concrete communal life" within the "compulsory community" of the House of Israel, but its strength was sapped by the onslaught of Rabbinism as much as by its own growing cult of zaddik worship, a degeneration of ritual, and an involvement in power politics with the state authorities. Buber feels that Hasidism, like Judaism as a whole, "failed and had to fail" because, after thousands of years of isolation, it began in modern times to accommodate itself to the outside Western world and was thus unable to create something new of its own. At the same time, he notes (in 1916) an awakening of the creative urge in many Jewish souls which will grow and bear fruit, if the people will renew its power of religiosity; "and this," he says, "is what I mean by Palestine [Eretz Israel]."[392] This is how Buber views the messianic vision of the Second Isaiah being realized through the prophecy of the First Isaiah in the House of God in Zion.

Zionism

Building the True Community

In all his writings on Judaism, whether on the Jewish renaissance, the renewal of its prime force, the fulfillment of the unconditioned, the restructuring of its social order, its regeneration as a people, its mission among the nations, or its realization of the messianic idea, Buber has always pointed to Zion as the land where all these aspirations can be made fully possible and real. The following passages, selected from his first to the last speeches on Judaism over a period of almost five decades, testify to his deep involvement in the Zionist idea.

> The Jew is not the same now as he was before: he has gone through all Heaven and Hell of the Occident and has suffered damage in his soul; but his primal force has remained unhurt, indeed, it has been purified. When it touches its motherly soil it will become creative again. The Jew can truly fulfill his mission among the nations only . . . when he realizes what his religiosity has taught him of old: by sinking his roots in his homeland.[393]

> [We] want to build for the spirit a sound dwelling, the house of community. . . . [For this] we need our own materials, our own soil. We want to build not as individuals but as a people.[394]

> Zionism is the conscious will of the Jewish renaissance [that] wants to fulfill itself.[395]

In order to be able to start the formative work of our people freely, we need a free place, where we can create in our own manner and with our own powers, independently of others from without and within. . . . We need Zion.[396]

The [true] way leads through Zion to the renewal of society.[397]

The saving of a people—this is the only meaning of the establishment of Zion. This saving does not take the form of a struggle for liberation, but a redemption in freedom, . . . in order that [this people] may participate truly in the work of mankind.[398]

It may be noted that Buber had been estranged from Jewishness when he was carried away by "the whirl of the age" in his student days, and that he was reawakened to it by the Zionist idea. As he later described this stage of his early days, he said he had lived in

a world of confusion, a mythical habitation of roving souls with the fullness of spiritual agility but without Judaism, and thus without humanity. My first impulse toward my liberation came from Zionism.[399]

For a few years he occupied an official position in the World Zionist Organization, but soon found himself in disagreement with the leadership on basic policies and, after Herzl died in 1904, he withdrew from active participation. However, he remained a lifelong adherent of the Zionist movement and a fervent supporter of its cause, in the light in which he saw it. This is not the place to enter upon his differences with fellow Zionists on matters of policy or practical issues. Our subject is the role of Zion in his philosophy of Judaism as the fulfillment of Israel's destiny to become a true community.

The paramount question, of course, is how Buber regards the national aim of the Jewish resettlement of Eretz Israel in modern times. What does he mean when he says, "We want to build not as individuals but as a people?" Inasmuch as the people is engaged in the rebuilding of its ancient homeland, it aims to become a territorial nation and must therefore contend with internal and external economic and political factors. How does Buber see its national aspirations in relation to its larger goal of

establishing itself as a true community? In his view the two must
go hand in hand. Israel, he says, must live in God's presence,
that is, fulfill its communal task in everyday affairs. When it
lived in other lands, this goal was a cherished ideal; now in its
own land it should be in a position to start its realization. This,
says Buber, will depend on what course of history Israel will
follow as a nation.

From Mount Sinai to Mount Zion

In the section on prophecy above, I discussed Buber's concept
of the history of faith as distinguished from the history of
nations. He makes the same distinction between Zionism and
nationalism. "Zionism," he says, "is something different than
Jewish nationalism. We are called Zionists and not Jewish
nationalists very rightly so, because Zion is more than nation"[400]; it is a place where something unique, something above
all nations, is to occur. What he really means is not that the Jews
should not establish themselves as a nation in Zion, but that they
should not strive to become "like all other nations," as some
branches of the movement want, because the Jewish people is
not on the same "side of history" as the other nations. What are
the two sides?

On one side is the history of nations who have elevated their
national being to an absolute and made it an object of worship.
Each nation claims absolute sovereignty refusing to recognize
any other sovereign above it. Each may have its own God
representing its national character, as in pagan times, or each
may claim the One God on its side and thus regard itself as the
only true nation. In this kind of world international relations are
determined by a play of power politics without mutual responsibility, which is characteristic of Western civilization, including
Russia.[401] Buber differentiates between national independence
and sovereignty or between legitimate and arbitrary nationalism.
A nation, he says, ought to seek independence from other
nations, but this implies mutual responsibility, which
sovereignty as such does not recognize, since it promotes group
egoism. Sovereignty considers itself a moral end in itself, responsible only to itself, and while it recognizes responsibility
between individuals at home and abroad, it assumes no responsibility toward other groups but its own. Speaking in dialogical
terms, a self-absolutized nation disclaims group responsibility

because it does not stand as a nation before the divine Absolute or the Supreme Sovereign of all nations, friend and foe alike.

On the other side is the history of a nation that recognizes its relationship to the divine Ruler, and this is the Jewish people, which faced the Absolute at its very inception as a nation at Mount Sinai. In that encounter the people was commissioned to establish itself as a true community under God's rule. This goal has not yet been attained, but it may be realized now at another mountain, Zion, where, in the words of Isaiah, all nations will come to receive the divine word from God himself. "The mountain of the House of God" in Jerusalem—Mount Zion—is to become "the Sinai of the nations."[402] It does not mean that the people Israel will redeem the world, but rather that it will build the true community in Zion as an example how other peoples may redeem themselves. This, as Buber sees it, is the essence of the Zionist goal, and if Israel is to remain faithful to this goal, it must not become involved in international power politics nor practice it within its own borders or in relation to its neighbors.

All this may sound like the preachment of a religious visionary or the talk of a theologian, but Buber is neither of these. He does not project a "spiritual" or "religious" goal to be attained in some preconceived way. On the contrary, he maintains that he is "speaking of the reality of history," where all that is done in truth abides, even when it suffers certain setbacks in the history of nations. The way must not differ from the goal. If the goal is to establish a nation in justice and truth, it must be evident at every step and not go contrary to it even for temporary ends, for that surely will lead to a false end. Buber saw this goal being realized in the Zionist collective settlements, which he regarded as the ground form of a true communal life and of a restructured society that he envisaged for all mankind.[403] At the same time, he found the Jewish Yishub wanting in its approach to the Arabs. In order to understand the nature of his critique in this regard, we must consider his view of Israel's place in the Orient in general.

Renewal in the East

Buber sees the Orient, from Asia Minor through China, as one spiritual entity which stands in contrast to the Occident. As a psychological type, the Oriental has pronounced motor faculties, experiences things through action, thinks in terms of doing, relates temporally more than spatially, comprehends the world inwardly in himself, where he finds its meaning as the meaning of his life. Out of his inwardness he builds a unified world the realization of which he regards as his primal task, as a religious task, as "the way." By contrast, the Occidental type has predominantly sensory faculties, experiences things mostly spatially in a multiplicity of separate, detached shapes, from which he tries to arrive at truth. His thinking is in images, forms, rather than deeds. None of the great religions originated in the Occident. Western civilizaton cannot find the meaning of life despite its most comprehensive knowledge, or its way to God despite its unswerving beliefs. The Orient, on the other hand, has the authentic way.

Of all the ancient peoples of the Orient, Buber considers the Jewish people as its most representative type. While the Jew has lived among the Western nations and has been greatly influenced by their culture, he has remained an Oriental. "On this overt or latent Orientalism, this foundation of the soil of the Jew," he says, "I build my faith in a new spiritual-religious creation of Judaism." This can be realized only after the Jew has returned to his ancient land, where his "great concepts of the drive for unity once grew."[404] Buber points to an "Asiatic crisis in our age," in that the leading nations of the Orient have surrendered partly to the European powers and failed to preserve their own spiritual heritage. Nevertheless, he believes that eventually Asia will reassert itself and start building itself up anew. In this reawakening, the Jewish people, with its Western skills and its original Eastern character, can serve as a link between Europe and Asia, and perhaps also fuse them into a new way of life. This, according to Buber, is the Zionist mission to mankind.

Now the Middle East has for a long time been dominated by the great Western powers, and there is also an indigent Arab population within the land and around it that tries to thwart the Jewish people's rebuilding of its homeland. While Buber acknowledges these difficulties, he does not take their stark political realities fully into account. Shortly after the ratification of the British Mandate over Palestine by the League of Nations in 1922, he gave the following considered advice to his fellow Zionists, which he wrote down in the form of "Question and Answer."

Question: You say that we should not submit to European state politics [*Staatenpolitik*]. What if it determines our fate in Eretz Israel, whether we submit to it or not? You say we would make an alliance with the Orient and take an active part in its regeneration. What if the Orient does not want to ally itself with us? What positive politics do you recommend?

Answer: Land politics.

Question: What do you understand by that?

Answer: To direct all efforts within our power toward the rebuilding of the land. Not just the nation in the land . . . but the land, truly and for its own sake. If we succeed in this, then we shall be invulnerable to European state politics and will become visible, trustworthy and welcome to the Orient as indispensable pioneers of its regeneration. . . .

Question: And what if despite all this, after we have fulfilled our function in the building of the land, we are "majorized" and despoiled of the fruits of our labor?

Answer: O, you of little faith! God does not deposit a letter of credit. But one who lends himself to Him without a promissory note is blessed.[405]

Buber is known to have dealt with many paradoxes, but this one he could not cope with, because he was confronted here by the dialectic of his own theory of the two sides of history. He left out one crucial question, namely, what if the "history of nations" does not let the "history of faith" come to expression at all? What if "this side" prevents the "other side" from building the land, even, as Buber recommends, for all the inhabitants thereof and as a pioneering example for the Orient as a whole? Buber was aware of the rising Arab nationalism in the Middle East, and he advised that it be given full recognition by the Zionist enterprise. This was basically the view of many leading figures in the Labor-Zionist movement, but they had a more realistic approach to its political outlook. As one of them, Enzo Sereni, observed: "The political reaction of the Arabs does not concern itself with the economic advantages brought about by Jews, which are evident and are not denied by the clever Arabs."[406] Yet Buber demanded of Zionism that it go on its way of the "history of faith," while Arab nationalism was going in the direction of the "history of nations," along the road of European power politics. For this dilemma he had no "positive politics to recommend."

There is yet another, more fundamental paradox involved in this issue, one that stems from Buber's own concept of the dialogical relation. In the final analyis, what Buber expects from the Zionists is that they establish a real dialogue with the Arabs.

This is indeed their aim, but Buber's way of doing it, that is, by showing the Arabs that they are benefiting from the Jewish enterprise, precludes genuine dialogue. In a very illuminating discussion with the psychologist Carl R. Rogers, Buber established his thesis that in a situation where one person comes to the other for help, there can be no dialogical encounter between them, because the two sides of the situation are not the same for both. The one who is helped is dependent on the giver, while the latter is independent of the receiver. Since dialogical relation is possible only between two mutually independent beings, "there remains a *decisive* difference between the two," says Buber. "A man wanting to help the other . . . [has the] active, helping attitude. . . . A man helped cannot think, cannot imagine helping another."[407] This is the paradox of the situation which has prevailed in Eretz Israel between the Jewish and Arab peoples ever since the advent of the Zionist settlements there. Buber could find no way out of it, because he summoned the Jewish *Yishub* to establish a dialogue with the Arab *Yishub,* that is, respond to its national aspirations and thus assume responsibility *"for* the other," but he did not apply the same measure *to* the other. For only when each side recognizes the national rights and interests of the other side can the situation be changed on *both sides* to allow for genuine dialogue. Buber was not unaware of the paradox of his argument,[408] but he tried to resolve it through the "history of faith" on the Jewish side alone. On the tenth anniversary of Israel's Independence he wrote: "I have accepted the form of the New Jewish communal being which came out of the war, the State of Israel, as my own. . . . The commandment to serve the spirit is now to be fulfilled by us in this State and through it."[409] As for the other side, he hoped that after the State of Israel had begun the renewal of the spirit of the Orient and shown the way, the Arab states would follow the same way. Only the two sides of history *taken together* will tell the outcome.

Buber saw Zionism in its messianic dimensions, as the fulfillment of Israel's goal as a people in its own land and of its mission to mankind. He therefore regarded every true Zionist as a forerunner of this fulfillment, as a Messiah son of Joseph or the "suffering Messiah": to suffer "for the sake of Heaven," even when faced with setbacks and failures. Undoubtedly, he considered himself, too, as one of these forerunners, suffering because he had failed to persuade the leadership of the movement to adopt his vision, and was at times even ridiculed and denounced by his opponents; yet he had to go on speaking, admonishing, demanding.[410]

Culmination of Fulfillment: Hebrew Humanism

Just as Buber regards the renewal of mankind as "humanism of faith," so he considers the renewal of the Jew and his Jewishness as "Hebrew humanism." This, in essence, sums up his philosophy of Judaism, whether in its Prophetic, Hasidic, or Zionist stages. "When forty years ago," he wrote in 1941, "a circle of young people, to which I belonged, began to direct the attention of Jewry in the German-speaking countries to the idea of a rebirth of the Jewish people and the Jewish person, we designated the goal of our endeavors as a Jewish renaissance." As he leared from his teacher Wilhelm Dilthey and from the philologist Konrad Burdach, the idea of renaissance signified to him and his friends that behind it "was the concept of an affirmation of man and of the community of men, the phoenix-like rebirth of the human being." When some ten years later he designed a program for a Jewish high school in Germany (which did not materialize because of the outbreak of World War I), he proposed that it be conducted in what he called the spirit of "Hebrew humanism." Subsequently he applied this term, rather than the earlier word "renaissance," to the needs of Jewish education in Eretz Israel and, as time went on, to "the true goal of the movement for the rebirth of the Jewish people."[411]

By rebirth, as has been emphasized time and again, Buber does not mean a return to bygone forms of Jewish life, but to its original foundations, to the essence of Jewishness reshaped in new forms, under new conditions. This is biblical humanism becoming Hebrew humanism, in the sense that the modern Jew accepts the biblical image of man as a normative value and realizes it as far as possible in his present-day life. The biblical image of the Jew and his Jewishness, as Buber sees it, is rooted in the uniqueness of Israel's election, a theme which runs through his entire philosophy of Judaism. Why, then, does he call it Hebrew humanism? The term "Hebrew" is understood here to mean the Hebrew language of biblical man, not as a literary form, but as lived life in its very mode of expression, structure, word formation, and rhythm—that which sets the norm between human and inhuman. This language itself speaks the essence of the people Israel. The word "humanism" signifies that man is not just a zoological being like the rest of the animal kingdom, but a being sui generis, a unique kind of being, a *humanitas,* or one who has specific tasks in life. Hebrew humanism, then, connotes the uniqueness of Israel, which was established at its very inception as a people in biblical times and has been transmitted through the Hebrew language, not as a so-called spiritual heritage of days gone by, but as a lived reality surpassing all temporal conditions. It is a valid norm for the Jew of today as it was in ancient days. This norm centers in Israel's election.

The idea that the Jews are a "chosen people" has been debated from every angle, theological, ethical, psychological, and national, with various degrees of its acceptance or rejection, depending on how a person debating this issue, if he is a Jew, relates himself to the other nations, or, if he is a Christian, relates himself to the people Israel. In contrast to these two approaches, Buber sets the issue within the framework of the Jewish people itself. His question is, how does a Jew consider himself elected in relation to his own people, that is, how can his people's election be considered indispensable to him as a *humanitas?* Buber does not view it as a theological issue in the sense that Israel is an instrument in a divine plan of universal salvation conceived at a certain point in history, which can be replaced by another instrument at some other time. While Israel's election took place in a historical moment at Sinai, it is not subject to the exigencies of time. The life of the people is subject to temporal changes, but not its election, which is an act of relation entered into with the Divine in the form of a covenant. The historical moment of this covenant may be renewed at various stages of the people's existence, but it is never abrogated. This is the meaning of Buber's call to Israel to renew itself or to return to its primal force of the covenant.

Neither is Israel's chosenness a nationalistic idea. It is often argued, Buber notes, that the election of Israel is no more singular than that of other nations. Each considers itself "chosen" in one respect or another. That may be so. But the Jewish people does not consider itself elected, as others do, because of special national qualities, such as the capacity to rule or save the world, but because its entire historical existence, whether in its ancient land or in the diaspora, *factually* is singular. Not only that, but its very doctrine of election is different from that of other nations. The essential thing that makes Israel's election singular is that it is "altogether a demanding one"—not a bestowal of unconditioned greatness or power, but a stern *demand*, on the fulfillment of which depends the people's entire future existence. The demand is that the Jewish people build the genuine community in truth and righteousness. "The biblical man," says Buber, "is the man who stands in the face of this election and this demand." He may accept it or reject it, struggle against it or submit to it, but he does not act as if it were not there. He feels it is his burden and if he does all he can to realize it, he is justified by it, as Job and Abraham were. "That is Hebrew humanity [*hebräische Humanität*]."[412]

The response to this demand is the responsibility of every Jew individually and collectively, because only by building the true community will the Jew realize his own *humanitas*. Just as the uniqueness of man lies in his responsibility to fulfill his tasks in life, to become human, so is the uniqueness of a people shown by its responsibility to realize its task, to become a true people. What singles out the Jewish people in this respect is not only that its task was revealed to it as a command, but also that the manner of its election and its life lived throughout its history are manifest in its striving as well as in its failings to fulfill the task. It is only the Jewish people that was chosen in an act of meeting as a people with the Divine. It thus became a people and religious community at the same time. This is a unique kind of revelation in that people and faith came into being as one, and that out of this oneness came forth the great values which the Jews have created. In modern times there has ensued a separation between people and faith. Only through a return to their original unity can there be a renewal of the Jew and his Jewishness. "Outside the unity and uniqueness of Israel there is no rebirth of its values."[413]

Approach to Jesus

"That Christianity," Buber writes, "has regarded and regards him [Jesus] as God and Savior, has always appeared to me as a most earnest fact, which I must seek to grasp for his sake and my own."[414] This statement is pivotal in Buber's approach to Jesus and to Christianity. What, exactly, does he "seek to grasp," and why does he put it as a problem for the sake of Jesus as well as for himself? What issue does he raise and to whom is it directed?

A preliminary clarification of these questions will place Buber's interest in Jesus in its proper perspective.

The main question that Buber raises is about the historical figure Jesus as he presents himself in the New Testament. That he was a Jew no one inside or outside the Church denies. But the point at issue, as Buber sees it, is the kind of faith he represents, whether the one he inherited from his Jewish ancestors or the one that the Church established, with him as its foundation. This does not mean to say that Buber proposes to enter into a polemic with Christianity about its Christological doctrines or any other aspect of its faith. He considers these matters the internal affairs of the Church, which, as he says, is for him "a most earnest fact," and which he holds in high esteem. What he does question is whether there cannot be a different view of Jesus, not as God and Savior, but as a Jew who spoke to his own people at a juncture of events when his message might have been of great import to them as Jews. To put the question in a personal way, as Buber conceives it: Can a Jew, who has been reared in, and is tied to, the faith of his fathers with all his heart and mind, find the same type of faith in Jesus of Nazareth? This is not the same as the problem of "Judaizing" or "de-Judaizing" the Church, which flared up at various periods of its history. For Buber does not try to bring Jesus' Jewishness into the Church, but to grasp it for himself as a Jew. In brief, the question here is not about *Jesus the Jew* in relation to the Church, but about *Buber the Jew* in relation to Jesus insofar as he may know him from the New Testament. The problem of "Judaizing" may be seen as a family dispute between Christians; the question about Jesus' Jewishness Buber presents as a family discussion between Jews, in which our philosopher expresses a particularly personal interest.

From his youth, Buber relates, he regarded Jesus as his "great brother," and this feeling gained strength as he studied the New Testament in the course of almost fifty years.[415] But in his viewing of Jesus, Buber does not mean the Christ of the Christian religion, but the man of Nazareth who lived and preached at a certain critical period of Jewish religious history and who cut out a path of his own, somewhat deviating but not removed from, or contrary to, the basic principles of the faith of his ancestors. Since Jesus lived and acted among his own people before the founding of Christianity and the formulation of its religious doctrines, Buber presents him as a person who entered into relation with God by rejuvenating the primary intent of the revelation which had been inherent in the Jewish faith of old, and not by founding a new faith with himself at its center. What is most important for Buber is Jesus' authentic spoken words which convey his "abiding in the immediacy of God, the great Devotio," and the message which he brought as one who had "come very near the 'Kingdom of God' in the earthly" world, rather than in some heavenly realm of a superworld.[416] The person Jesus the Jew is thus distinguished from the Person Jesus Christ of the Christian Trinity, and this "hypothetical" distinction, according to Buber, is grounded in two different modes of religious belief.[417]

Two Types of Faith

Buber differentiates two fundamental types of faith, one predominantly Jewish and the other predominantly Christian. The first is expressed in the teachings of the prophets, or the Jewish concept of *emunah,* and the second in Christian teachings derived from the Greek concept of *pistis.*[418] According to this theory, one type is a "trust in" someone, and the other an "acknowledgment that" something is true; but in either case, the man of faith is unable to give a reason for his trust or belief. In relationship to the Absolute or Unconditioned, the first type is *faith in* God, whose existence does not come into question, whereas the second type is *belief that* God exists. This distinction is not a rational one (although the second type has a logical connotation), because in both cases it is man as a whole who believes and not some faculty of his, such as reason or feeling. The difference lies rather in the kind of relationship that is established between the believer and that which is believed. Trust comes through a state of contact with the one who is trusted; acknowledgment comes as an acceptance of that which is recognized to be true. As can be readily seen, the distinction is here drawn along the lines of Buber's principle of dialogue: "faith in" is a state of communication in which man finds himself,[419] whereas "belief that" is an act of accepting the other prior to the state of communication. Either one may lead to the other, but the emphasis is on the primacy of one or the other. In the case of "faith in" the state is primary and thus decisive; in "belief that," the act of accepting is primary and decisive.[420]

Applied to the religious situation of relationship with the Unconditioned, Buber finds the first type of faith particularly expressed in Judaism, because its contact with the Absolute was originally that of a community as a whole, of which the individual was a part regardless of private belief. That is, the individual member of the community did not have first to accept the truth of the revelation in order to become a part of the religious group; he experienced the revelation together with the rest of his group at the same time that the latter became a religious community, namely, at the revelation at Sinai. What the individual of this community is called upon to do now, after that original experience, is "to hold fast to his faith," to stand firm and realize or fulfill it in everyday life.[421]

In early Christianity, Buber holds, the process was in reverse, from individual to community, for when the religious communities of the ancient world fell into decay, the primary condition of man was that of an isolated individual, spiritually speaking. Each individual, then, had to be personally converted to Christianity before he could join with others of the same belief to form a community of co-religionists. Even in mass conversions, Buber points out, it is never a people as a whole that has becomes converted to Christianity, but a collection of individuals, and there is always a separation between the two in that the individual becomes subject to Christian discipline while the nation as such does not. The Christian group relationship to God, he concludes, is not that of a "holy people," but of a "holy church." Christianity, therefore, looks to individuals for its primary relationship to the Unconditioned and regards its mission to convert them as the essence of its religious life from its very inception.

Jesus Not an Originator of a New Faith

On the basis of this distinction between the two types of faith, Buber proceeds to demonstrate that Jesus of Nazareth was a man of the highest faith of the first type, namely, "trust in," and that he was therefore not an originator of a new religion which after his death became known as Christianity. The main burden of this argument is that a man who is summoned to have *faith in* God is not asked to give up an old truth for a new one, but to renew and fulfill his old faith or trust to its highest possible primary intent. Such, Buber says, was the message of the prophets to their people Israel throughout its ancient history. On the other hand, a man who is called upon to *believe that* something is true, which was not true in his eyes before, or which he could not have believed to be true, is asked to give up his old belief, or his refusal to believe, and *accept* the new one as true, that is, to convert to a new truth. Jesus' ministry among his people, Buber maintains, was of the same nature as that of the prophets before him. He did not come to convert the people to a new truth, but to lead them by his teaching and example as a man of undaunted faith toward renewal of their basic trust in God, which the Jews, as a people, had affirmed at the revelation at Sinai.

A Word about Method

Buber derives this characterization of Jesus from what he considers to be his authentic sayings as recorded in the Synoptic Gospels. Like many modern Christian theologians, he draws a sharp distinction between the gospel *of* Jesus and the gospel *about* Jesus.[422] The latter, he holds, is primarily the work of the Evangelist John and the Apostle Paul, who present Jesus as a divine being sent from heaven to announce to the world a new truth to be sealed by his blood.

It is not my purpose here to examine the various positions of Christian theologians with regard to this kind of distinction in the person of Jesus in the New Testament. However, such a distinction is untenable when made by Buber on the ground that one of its aspects represents a specifically Jewish view of Jesus. For having decided that Jesus was a man of the Jewish type of "faith in," Buber selects those of his sayings which lend themselves to an interpretation of this type and tries to show that Jesus did not or could not, as a man of this type, become the founder of a new religion. But this kind of argument can neither affirm nor deny Jesus' divine nature, which, in the final analysis, is the pivotal point of New Testament exegesis. The cardinal question of this exegesis is not whether Jesus' sayings were in keeping with, or contrary to, contemporary or earlier Jewish traditions, but rather *who* was the person who pronounced them. That is, the question is not, as Buber presents it, whether Jesus *founded* a new faith, later known as Christianity, but whether he can be regarded as the *foundation* of this faith. For that one must take the New Testament as a unified whole. And since there is no other source outside the New Testament that would identify

Jesus as essentially Jewish, one cannot legitimately draw a distinction between a traditionally Jewish Jesus and a Christian Jesus, as Buber does, by the method of selection from the only source available, that is from the source of Christian doctrine which regards him as its foundation.

To be sure, Buber also uses the method of selection in his approach to the Old Testament, but there he acknowledges its unity, regardless of its diverse backgrounds and tendencies. He furthermore notes with approbation that Paul, too, "upheld the unity of the Hebrew Holy Scriptures."[423] But when he himself applies his method to the New Testament he seeks to establish two separate sources, one of Jewish tradition and another of Christian tradition, thus breaking up its unity as Holy Scripture. He often speaks of "the authentic text," "the Aramaic original," "the Greek translator," or "fragments of reading which cannot be restored,"[424] and the like, as if the evangelical gospels were based on an Aramaic original that was fundamentally of a Jewish religious character but was later changed either by the Greek translator or by Christian interpreters. Even if we were to accept the theory of an *Aramaic Ur-gospel* (since lost), which Buber seems to support, its original text still would be a gospel of Christian origin and, what is more important, it could not be restored except through the existing evangelical gospels.[425] In what follows I will discuss Buber's interpretation of Jesus' ministry according to the Synoptic Gospels as that of a person of the type of *faith in* God, his relationship to the Pharisees, and his eschatology and Messianism.

The Highest Type of Devotio

Jesus, says Buber, never claimed divinity for himself and never considered himself as a mediator between God and man. On the contrary, his relation to God was one of immediacy, and his mission was to serve Him with the highest intention, his whole heart directed to Him, which Buber characterizes by the term *devotio*, as the essential Jewish relationship to divine Providence. Commenting on Jesus' answer to the rich man (Mark 10:18), "Why do you call me good? No one is good but God alone," Buber writes:

> God teaches his teaching for all, but He also reveals his ways in immediacy to select men. One to whom it is revealed and who follows it thereby translates the teaching into per-

sonal concreteness and thereby also teaches "the way of
God" (Mark 12:14) in befitting human manner. Thus Jesus
knows himself as a fitting means of teaching the teachings of
the will of the good master; but he himself does not want to be
called good; no one is good but God alone.[426]

The emphasis here is that Jesus wanted only to direct his hearers
toward *faith in* God and not to have them *believe that* he himself
ought to be the object of worship. Thus Buber also interprets
Jesus' words (Mark 1:14), "The appointed time if fulfilled and
God's rule has come near. Turn and believe in the message" (to
use Buber's rendition),[427] to mean that Jesus "does not invite his
hearers to believe his word; he aims after the intrinsic value of
the message itself," that is, belief in God's message of his
approaching kingdom on earth. Jesus, according to Buber, calls
on the people to turn to God and renew their faith in Him, in
order to be prepared for the arrival of the new aeon. But if we
read Jesus' words in the full context of the event, the evangelist
does not convey Buber's meaning; nor did those who heard the
words take them in that sense, but rather in the sense of "A new
teaching!" (Mark 1:27).[428] The words "believe in the message,"
spoken by Jesus earlier (v. 14), could well mean *believe that* his
own message was true. Buber's interpretation that Jesus' message here was "an heirloom of the religiosity of Israel" the same
as Isaiah's, that is, the realization of the faith in God in the
totality of life, is not borne out by the context of the gospel.[429]

Another example of Buber's exegesis of Jesus' meaning of
faith refers to the narrative about the boy who was possessed by
a demon and was brought by his father to the "Teacher" to be
cured, since the disciples had proved unable to do it (Mark
9:14–29). The text reads:

> And he [the father] said . . . "If you can do anything, have
> pity on us and help us." And Jesus said to him, "If you can!
> All things are possible to him who believes." Immediately the
> father of the child cried out and said, "I believe; help my
> unbelief!" [vv. 21–24].

Buber says that Jesus' words "to him who believes" refer to
Jesus' own belief and not to that of the boy's father, for "only
the faith which Jesus knows as his own may at all be called faith
in the strict sense," and this kind of faith is also "accessible to

man as such"[430]; that is, this is *faith in* God by virtue of which one is "taken into the realm of God" and is possessed by its power, but does not possess God's power. Obviously, Buber puts his own meaning of faith into the words of Jesus, because for him (for Buber) true faith can mean only "faith in." Assuming that his exegesis of the above passage is plausible, there is another passage of a similar event, regarding a woman who was cured by merely touching the fringe of Jesus' garment, and to whom the Master said, "Take heart, my daughter; your faith has made you well" (Matt. 9:22). It is quite clear from the context that Jesus meant the woman's faith, not his own, namely, that she *believed that* he had the divine power to cure her and that that power was so potent that it was effective even through the fringe of his garment (cf. Mark 6:56).

On the other hand, Buber's claim that the Apostolic view of Jesus' ministry is cast in the mold of the primary "belief that" is not borne out by the text to which Buber himself refers, namely, The Epistle to the Hebrews. He elaborates on some verses of this epistle, notably the statement "Now faith is the assurance of things hoped for, the conviction of things not seen" (11:1), the second half of which he regards as characteristic of the Greek mode of thought. "He who has faith in the sense of The Epistle to the Hebrews," he writes, "has received proof of the existence of that, the existence of which does not enter into perception."[431] This may be so, but the text does not necessarily seek to establish that this type of belief is primary and therefore decisive for the believer. It may well be, in Buber's own view of the relationship between the two types, that this is a case where *faith in* God, whose existence is not questioned, leads to the *belief that* things not seen exist. For the "things not seen" in the text do not refer to the existence of God, but to an invisible order above (in the Platonic sense), which God created through Jesus and made visible in him (Heb. 1:2). What the author of this epistle refers to is the order of a divine High Priesthood in heaven which, though invisible, is more real than the Levitical order of priests on earth. His argument is based on the assumption of the superiority of a supersensuous heavenly existence over the sensuous earthly appearance. But the point is that this heavenly existence is *believed in,* rather than *believed that* it exists.

If we take The Epistle to the Hebrews in its entirety, it appears as an attempt by a Christian author,[432] a follower of Pauline doctrine, to convince the Jews that the Christian faith is not a deviation from the faith of their fathers, but rather a confirmation of it on a superior divine level, unheard of before, that is, in an entirely new revelation in the person Jesus. The author stresses *trust in* God, Who has sent Jesus Christ to atone for the people's sins, the same as He had commanded the priestly rites of atonement in the Temple, but in an entirely new experience through direct divine atonement. He calls for the continuity of Jewish *faith in* God, for faithful endurance to "hold our first trust firm to the end" (Heb. 3:14), and he tries to convince the people that the new event reaffirms their old faith with greater certainty since the sacrifice for atonement was now performed as a divine act, not by human hands. His aim is to renew the old faith in its original intent, "to teach you again the just principles of God's word" (5:12), as he finds it revealed in the divine priesthood of Melchizedek (Gen. 14:18–20), but which he now identifies with Jesus, "a High Priest forever" (Heb. 6:20). Thus the author of *Hebrews,* too, speaks of a renewal of the original intent of the faith of Israel and calls upon the people to hold fast and firm in it, but he challenges the very meaning of that intent as he transforms it not into a "belief that" but rather into a new "faith in," namely, *faith in* Jesus Christ. Thus we find both types of faith represented in the Synoptic Gospels as well as in the Epistles.

Jesus and the Pharisees

Buber presents Jesus as a man brought up in the traditions of the Jewish religion and deeply concerned with its way of life, but in the original intent of fulfillment of the divine revelation at Sinai. The main tenets of the Jewish faith were expressed at the time in the teachings of the Pharisees, and Jesus upheld them in principle. But, like many another Pharisee of his day, he was critical of the legalistic fixedness of their interpretation and manner of observance. Buber maintains that there was always an "inner dialectic" in Israel's spiritual history, in that the living reality of faith tended to become holy script, objectified, static law.[433] This was particularly pronounced during the time of Jesus and the Early Christians. Jesus, Buber says, took the position of those Pharisees who sought to uphold the primal character of the Torah as revelation and teaching, that the divine word spoken at Sinai be kept as a living force through the constant renewal of man's relation to God. "For the reality of faith of biblical and postbiblical Judaism, and also for the Jesus of the Sermon on the Mount," he says, "fulfillment of the Torah means to extend the perceived word over the entire dimension of human existence."[434] Therefore, what Jesus and other Pharisaic interpreters of the Torah fought against was routinization and congealment in the carrying out of God's revealed will. When Jesus spoke against the so-called Pharisees, he meant the same men whom the Pharisees themselves denounced as "painted" in the semblance of Pharisees.[435] But, says Buber, though having the true teaching of the Torah in common, Jesus and the Pharisees passed each other by without "either knowing the inner reality of the other."[436] Their difference was in the eschatological sphere. As long as Jesus stood on the Sinai tradition, he interpreted it as a true Pharisee without deviation. "But then," says Buber, "Sinai cannot satisfy him," and he seeks to realize the intention of the revelation as it would be in the end of days, that is, in the eschatology of God's rule. The Pharisees considered this a break in tradition, which must be continued as the historical preparation for God's rule on earth, and not as if it had already been established.

Another important difference between Jesus and the Pharisees, Buber finds, is their divergent views of man's striving toward the Absolute. He contrasts Jesus' saying, "You, therefore, must be perfect, as your heavenly Father is perfect" (Matt. 5:48), with what he regards as the authentic Jewish view expressed in Leviticus (19:2), "You shall be holy, for I the Lord your God am holy." Jesus, he says, transcends the human as he teaches that in eschatology of the Kingdom of God man can become perfect, like God. The Torah does not expect this. It teaches the people to realize their highest quality of holiness not in order to be like God, but because God, Who is holy, wills it for them. Again, Buber stresses the radical aspect of Jesus' saying (Matt. 19:21), "If you would be perfect, go, sell what you possess and give it to the poor, and you will have treasure in heaven; and come and follow me," to mean "follow Jesus on his eschatological way."[437]

In Jewish tradition, Buber indicates, there is the concept of completeness of man's relation to God, of walking wholeheartedly with Him, imitating the qualities attributed to Him, such as mercy, graciousness, and the like. Such, for example, is God's call to Abraham (Gen. 17:1), "Walk before me and be wholehearted;" or Solomon's admonition to the people (1 Kings

8:61), "Let your heart, therefore, be whole with the Lord our God to walk in his statutes and to keep his commandments."[438] It is thus not meant for man to seek divine perfection, not to speak of the possibility of attaining it, but rather to strive for fulfillment of his human way with God to the fullest extent possible. Jesus' call to perfection, Buber holds, issued from his "eschatological radicalism," which is contrary to Pharisaic teaching. Nevertheless, he regards this radicalism still within the confines of Jewish differences in the interpretation of the Torah, that is, the revealed will of God, and as part of the inner critical conditions of Judaism at the time. For basically Buber emphasizes Jesus' declaration that he did not come to abolish the Torah and the prophets, but to fulfill them (Matt. 5:17), and considers it sufficiently clear that the conflict between Jesus and those he designated as "Pharisees" was one of "teaching against teaching, the true unraveling of the Torah against its familiar, erroneous and misleading applications," as taught by the pseudo-Pharisees.[439] In essence, Buber says, Jesus taught the same basic principles as did the real Pharisees.

Eschatological Radicalism

As we have seen, Buber finds Jesus' radical deviation from the teachings of the Pharisees in the demand for man's perfection in the eschatological rule of God. This may well be in keeping with Buber's own understanding of eschatology, but may not at all reflect Jesus' understanding of it.

> For the "eschatological" hope—in Israel, . . . but not in Israel alone, [Buber states] . . . is first always historical hope; it becomes eschatologized only through growing historical disillusionment. In this process faith seizes upon the future as the unconditioned turning point of history, then as the unconditioned overcoming of history.[440]

For Buber, then, eschatology, like history, is continuous—no break with the past—and he therefore sees Jesus' radicalism as having come from his "enthusiasm of eschatological actuality . . . viewed from the point of view of Israel's faith, implying at the same time a supplement to it."[441] That is, Jesus is regarded here as a *Reformer* and not as a transformer of the Jewish faith, as one who puts his teaching against the teaching of other Pharisees, and not as one who seeks a real break with tradition.

Buber tries to find support for this hypothesis in both the content and form of Jesus' sayings insofar as they have parallels in the Torah and Talmud.[442] But the problem of Jesus' "eschatological radicalism," as Buber calls it, cannot be resolved from his statements in the Sermon on the Mount or his other preaching, even though parallels can be found for a good many of them in Jewish Scripture and Talmudic-Midrashic lore. For contrary to Buber's claim, it is not sufficiently clear from these statements that Jesus opposed only the pseudo-Pharisees and did not seek to change principles of Jewish tradition or, for that matter, put a break into history altogether. Jesus' declaration, on which Buber relies most, namely, that he came to fulfill the law and the prophets (Matt. 5:17), could mean, as, indeed, it was interpreted by Paul (Rom. 3:21–31) and as may be inferred from Luke (10:21–24), that he came to fulfill them in *his* own way and not in the original Jewish intent or, more pointedly, that he, Jesus, was the fulfillment, which his words "I have come . . . to fulfill them" could well signify.

The real issue, then, is the role that Jesus saw for himself in his eschatology. As Buber himself states, "He knew himself as the prophet of the coming Basilea and at the same time as its appointed human centre."[443] Or as Rudolf Bultmann phrases the issue more precisely:

Today it is commonly accepted that the reign of God which Jesus proclaimed is the eschatological reign. The only point in dispute is whether Jesus thought that the reign of God was immediately imminent, indeed already dawning in his exorcisms, or whether he thought that it was already present in his person—what today is called "realized eschatology."[444]

Buber tries to resolve this issue by assigning to Jesus a special place in the series of messianic persons who have been envisioned in the prophetic writings and who have come on the scene of the spiritual history of the Jewish people, and whom he identifies with the legendary figure of the Messiah son of Joseph.

Jesus and Messianism

Buber regards Jesus as one of the men divinely selected to

carry out a task in the history of the Jewish people and through it for mankind as a whole. An individual, like a people, he notes, may be called upon by God to become His servant and thus "incorporate" in himself the truth of Israel's existence, namely, to establish the true community or Kingdom of God. Such, he says, was the mission of the Second Isaiah and also of Jesus, who has come under the influence of this prophet and who "understands himself to be the bearer of the messianic conceal-ment."[445] The emphasis here is on the *concealment,* which is Buber's vision of the figure of the Messiah son of Joseph, who does not represent one person only, but a series of men, more specifically, all those who became or may become the "servants of the Lord" as the forerunners of messianic fulfillment in the end of days. The essence of their mission lies in their hidden-ness, like the arrow hidden in the quiver, not knowing when it may be released for action. " 'Messiah son of Joseph appears from generation to generation.' This," says Buber, "is the suffering Messiah who ever again endures deadly torment for the sake of God." Jesus, he says, was the "first one in the series [and] incomparably the purest, the most rightful, the most en-dowed with real messianic power."[446] The latest of this "au-tomessianic" series Buber considers to be Sabbatai Zvi (1626–1676), whose undoing, he says, was due to the fact that he stepped forth from his hiddenness and announced on his own the fulfillment of God's Kingdom. In Jewish tradition this is consid-ered an act of "forcing the End" *(dohek et hakets* or *mehashvei kitsin)* and is therefore contrary to God's will.[447]

The question, then, with regard to Jesus, as Buber sees him, is whether he revealed himself in his messianic mission and whether he wanted to "force the End." Buber maintains the latter was the case but is not clear, or not sure, about the former. He speaks of Jesus as one of those "men who, stepping out of the hiddenness of the servant of the Lord, . . . acknowledged their Messiahship in their souls and in their words," and yet he is one who "does not know without doubt whether he is destined to be taken out . . . [to] offer himself for that purpose."[448] Jesus, he says, asks his disciples, "in an hour in which the question ascends from the depth," who he is, and as a result of their answer there "happens the 'forcing of the End,' and it happens in highest innocence."[449] I can only say about this exegesis of Jesus' words and of the entire event that it is an unsatisfactory interpretation of the text. A man of Jesus' character, who is "endowed with real messianic power" and acknowledges it in his soul, as Buber portrays him, would not respond to the most decisive revelation in his career "in the highest innocence." Besides, it contradicts Buber's previous exposition of Jesus' ministry, in which Jesus is represented as having wavered about revealing himself (coming out of the quiver). But at the trial, in answer to the question "Who art thou?," "he imagines himself in his own person as the one who will be removed and afterwards sent again to an office of fulfillment," and thus replies, "Thou shalt see the one whom I shall become."[450] Buber is not certain whether this was a real self-revelation, but admits it as a strong possibility.

As for Buber's assumption that Jesus was the first of a series of the Jewish vision of messianic forerunners in the person of Messiah son of Joseph, there is nothing in the Synoptic Gospels that would support such an interpretation and it is therefore highly speculative at best. According to all the gospels, Jesus suffered death as a martyr without any intimation that he was the forerunner of another, higher than he, yet to come. The Jewish legendary Messiah son of Joseph, although his origin is a matter of debate, is conceived as one who is to pave the way for the "great redeemer" Messiah son of David. His special function is that of a warrior (also called *meshuah milhama*, anointed for war, and the "second Messiah") who will be killed in the war with Gog and Magog, after which the Messiah son of David, the Messiah of peace, will come.[451] Whatever may be the difference between Jewish and Christian ideas of the "suffering servant," there is no Jewish tradition that identifies him with the person Jesus. The distinction, which is a real one, cannot be translated into a difference between Christian and Jewish views about the messiahship of Jesus when the account of his ministry is taken exclusively from Christian sources. Buber may call Jesus his "great brother" out of personal, psychological considerations, but there is no basis for his so-called "standpoint of Judaism . . . [on Jesus'] real 'Messianic mystery.' "[452] All such interpretations are legitimate standpoints of Christianity, but not of Judaism.

Buber's Personal View

I regard Buber's view of the ministry of Jesus entirely personal on his part, which, as he himself noted, he had to grasp for his own sake. For ultimately, it is not a matter of "teaching against teaching" between Jesus and the Pharisees, as Buber maintains, but rather of interpretation against interpretation between Buber himself and Christian theologians. At the same time it should be pointed out that Buber did not consider himself a follower of Jesus. If he had lived in his days, he said, he "would not have been among his followers."[453] But it must also be pointed out that, contrary to some of his critics, the distinction which he draws between the two faiths is, as he says, "not uttered [as] a negative evaluation of Christianity." On the contrary, his evaluation of Jesus' role in Christian belief as such is altogether positive. The "significance [of the appearance of Jesus] . . . for the Gentiles," he states, "remains for me the true seriousness of Western history." Salvation "has come to the Gentiles through faith in Christ: they have found a God Who did not fail them in times when their world collapsed.[454] However, his own belief with regard to the Messiah is steeped in Jewish tradition, as attested in a letter he wrote in 1926:

> According to my belief, God does not reveal himself in men but only through men. According to my belief, the Messiah did not appear in a definite moment in history, but his appearance can only be the end of history. According to my belief, the redemption of the world did not occur nineteen hundred years ago, but we still live in the unredeemed world and await the redemption in which every one of us is called upon to participate in an inexplicable manner. Israel is the human community which is the bearer of this pure messianic expectation. . . . According to our, Israel's, belief, the redemption of the world is one with the completion of creation.[455]

It is from this standpoint that Buber approaches Christianity as distinguished from Judaism, the one emphasizing the Redeemer, the other redemption. What both have in common, "if we look at it concretely," he says, "is a Book and an expectation. For you the Book is a vestibule, for us it is a sanctuary. But in this space we must live together, and together listen to the voice that speaks in it."[456]

The Kingdom of God

Buber's philosophy of interhuman relation is the expression of an affirmation of life in every act of man's earthly existence. This may be best summed up in his vision of the Kingdom of God. When he speaks of man as a partner in the creation and redemption of the world, he means that man has been created for this purpose and can therefore fulfill himself only insofar as he goes in this direction. It does not mean that man actually took part in the beginning of creation: that remains a mystery. But inasmuch as creation is a constant divine act of bringing order out of chaos, of building a cosmos, man is destined to play a decisive role in it. This is his destiny and also his freedom: as he directs himself as an independent being to God and assumes responsibility, his freedom is attained.

The striving for relation with the Absolute manifests an incompleteness in man, which he hopes to fill through his act of relation with the Divine and with all creatures on earth. The world too is incomplete, and as man fulfills himself he also helps bring the world to completion. What is to be redeemed in nature, Buber emphasizes, is not a world soul, but all the things which have been called into being in creation, so that they become a whole, a universe, the ingathering of all the chaos into a cosmos. In the same sense, redemption in human history is not of man's soul but of the chaos in him, of the evil that hinders him from becoming human, a being-as-a-whole. It is not, however, redemption *from* evil through its annihilation, but redemption *of* evil, of the evil spirit, through sanctification, so that it may turn into a hallowed force for man's self-realization: evil turned into good.

It is God's will to complete His whole creation, tò realize His full revelation, and to redeem the all that needs to be redeemed. Buber calls it "the threefold chord of world-time" *(Der Drei-klang der Weltzeit).*[457] God's call to the world is *creation,* His call to man is *revelation,* and man's response and responsibility is *redemption.* All this is the Kingdom of God as it fulfills itself through communication between man and the Absolute. In human history it is to be accomplished through a "true folk-community," "from the communities of family, neighborhood, settlement to the totality" of a people and a humanity of peoples. "We are awaiting a theophany of which we know nothing but the place, and the place is called community."[458]

It is in the true community, then, that Buber seeks to resolve the crisis of modern man. The dialogical principle is actualized through the principle of communality, in which Buber sees all "the isolated moments of relation combine themselves in one conjoint world life." Now that we have scanned these isolated moments in their respective areas, we shall take another look at his world as a whole, how it is constituted in its scientific, technological, and religious dimensions.

The World Structure of a Religious Humanist

We may recall again that Buber declines to be identified as philosopher or theologian, but prefers to call himself "a philosophizing man." What disturbs him about the other two personages has an important bearing on his world outlook. Traditionally, the others are looked upon as metaphysicians dealing with supersensate "objects," the first going beyond the physical things of observation into a world of ideas or objects of pure understanding, and the second going beyond all objective reality to a supreme Being or the highest object of knowledge in existence. Buber does not address himself either to the philosopher or to the theologian, but to man himself who is the center of his attention, and that is what he means by calling himself "a philosophizing man." In other words, he does not investigate the areas of the philosopher-metaphysician or theologian-metaphysician, as such, but looks into the sources from which their world structures emanate, namely, the natural sciences, on the one hand, and religion, on the other, insofar as they pertain to the category *humanum*. His concern is the human aspect of science and technology as well as of religion, and in this regard his world outlook is a religious humanism which, for him, constitutes the Kingdom of God. In order to grasp the full implication of his outlook, we must know specifically wherein he differs from the other two world views.

A Unified World

The prevailing view among philosophers since ancient times, but especially among moderns since the days of Kant, is that we may know the world only if it can be grasped as a whole. For if we see merely the parts, there is no end to other parts that may be added to them in the course of our experience, and we can never hope to see a unified world as such. The problem here lies in the meaning we ascribe to the term "experience." When applied to the natural sciences, it means the observation of phenomena either directly through our eyes or through instruments, and the calculation of their measurements according to accepted standards within a coordinated schema in which the observed things function in correlation with each other. Such a correlation of phenomena is considered a rational view of reality—rational in the sense that they all stand in certain calculable *ratios* to each other. This is how the physical scientist sees things in the world, but he can never see the world as a whole, because his objects of experience never constitute the complete universe.

Now the philosopher may step in and try to go beyond the experience of the natural scientist and construct a complete system out of supersensate, unobservable objects, thus forming a world unity of a metaphysical nature. The difficulty with this kind of structure is that the philosopher finds himself hard-set in trying to fit the physical phenomena into it, and he ends up with a two-world view of reality. Man's striving for unity then appears a hopeless dream. With the development of modern science and its remarkable successes in probing nature in its innermost recesses, the metaphysical outlook has been greatly discredited and all but relegated to a shadowy existence. On the other hand, the promise held out by the scientist to produce a unified world system out of his observable data has not materialized. What has been most disturbing in this project is that the more the scientist tries to unify his objective data as a whole, the less chance has man of finding himself as a human being in such a scheme of things, and he feels more and more alienated from it. Even when his human existence is taken into account, it comes into purview in fragments or "bits" of information, and man becomes alienated even from himself. This condition has been widely recognized as the crisis of modern science. What is at stake is man's freedom as a human being.

New Meaning of Experience

When Buber examined the nature of this crisis, he was struck by the fact that both the philosopher and the scientist apply the term "experience" in a restricted sense, namely, as a perceptual awareness and its conceptual implications, whether derived from that awareness or superimposed on it. In contrast to this view of man's ability to gauge reality, Buber finds the human being capable also of a different experience, peculiar to him alone and to no other creature, and that is a spontaneous or living way of relating himself to reality with his being-as-a-whole, not just with one or another of his faculties. What Buber then finds wanting in the other two world views is an opportunity for man to gain this living experience in either one of their unified schemes. In the philosopher's metaphysical system man may find himself conceptually through his faculty of reason, but cannot experience it with his being-as-a-whole, because he cannot divest himself of his faculties of sense perception, which hinder him from living in that world. And in a scientifically unified world, if ever attainable, man could not find his place at all, because it would be constituted entirely of observable objects, leaving no room for a being who observes.

A Restructuring of Our View of Reality

Buber recognizes man as a world builder, but he does not propose to resolve the philosopher's metaphysical predicament, because he does not see any way of unifying a two-world scheme which has been set apart by an unbridgeable gap. However, he holds out much hope for the world of the natural scientist and points to the way of bringing it into harmony with a realistic view of one world.

Out of the same manifestations in reality man builds a different world according to one or the other kind of his experience. Through his partial experience of things, that is, when he himself does not act as a being-as-a-whole, he constructs an *ordered world,* such as we meet in the natural sciences and in the practical usage of our surroundings. And through his living experience with the same things, insofar as he enters into relation with them as one whole being with another, he learns to know the *world order* or the unified universe. These are not two worlds, but one and the same reality manifested through man's different relationship to it and hence differently ordered. Each order may pass into the other as man approaches reality in one way or the other. Thus all the elements that enter into the makeup of the ordered world—space, time, causality, direction, determination, and the like—may be transformed into living experiences with the world order, even applying the same terminology in both cases, as Buber has done frequently. The effect of this transformation through the act of living experience is a humanization of the natural sciences.

In the same vein Buber proposes a restructuring of human society in such a manner that each member may enter into a living experience with his fellow members and at the same time retain his position as an independent person. The problem here is of a technological nature, that is, of devising a communal apparatus whereby the "social principle," as Buber calls it, will predominate over the "political principle" and propel the membership toward their goal of establishing an ethically viable social structure.

Role of the Absolute

This restructuring of the scientific and technological outlook on reality is not yet the entire solution to the threefold crisis of modern man, as it harbors also the religious issue of our time. In Buber's view, "religion is essentially the act of holding fast to God" or "the self-binding of the human person to God." Barring some differences in emphasis, there is no dispute about this dictum among theologians. Where Buber departs from their interpretations has to do with the area of investigation. The theologian seeks to attain a knowledge of the nature of God, his attributes, his powers, and the like, and comes up with some concept of Him or an Idea which he juxtaposes to certain concepts of man and nature and their interaction. Buber, on the other hand, does not deal with the problem of God's nature, which for him is hidden and incomprehensible, but sees the heart of the religious issue in the "essential act" of man's entering into relation. That is, he does not investigate the nature of God, but of man's relation to Him. To gain a fuller understanding of this approach, we must bear in mind that Buber is a religious humanist, which signifies that for him the religious issue is a human problem and not one of God's essence or existence. God, he says, is not the Lord of religion, but the Lord of Being. Religion is the affair of the human being who seeks meaning in life and hopes to find it in his relationship with the divine Absolute. This is not a metaphysical question about the essence of the absolute Being whom man may meet, but rather an ontological question about the human being or about his ontic act of entering into relation. The subject of investigation, therefore, is the nature of this relationship on the human side and the role of the Absolute in it.

Completeness as a Frame of Reference

Every science, inasmuch as it deals with incomplete, change-able, and contingent events, must have a frame of reference which is itself complete and can thus serve as a constant or absolute for gauging the variables of those events. This holds true for Buber's science of religious relation as well as for the natural sciences. Man's experience with things of nature and fellowmen is of a variable, incomplete, and changeable charac-ter. What prospect does one have of ever reaching a state of completion in himself so that he may enter into relation with others as a being-as-a-whole and experience the world in its wholeness? Only when he goes forth to meet the divine Absolute and brings with him all his finite relational experiences as if to purify them in the divine Presence. For only in a meeting of this kind does man attain complete relation. According to the dialogical principle, man's preparation for a meeting with the absolute Thou consists of an ingathering of all his finite relational encounters within his own being. To try to meet God without them is a vain attempt. But neither can one meet fellowman in truth without ever relating oneself to God. This is the meaning of Buber's opening statement in part 3 of his essay *I and Thou:* "The extended lines of relation intersect in the eternal Thou."

The experience of completeness in the encounter with the Absolute, even though it may come at fleeting moments and pass as readily as it comes, has an abiding, constant power which permeates all finite relations and is reinforced with every new divine encounter. Meeting with the divine Absolute, then, is man's goal in his striving for self-fulfillment as a human being. This is his destiny in freedom.

Fulfillment and Redemption

This, in essence, is Buber's world view of a religious humanism, which he has developed out of Jewish sources and in the center of which he has placed the messianic goal of building a true community for all mankind. To be sure, in this view man's place in the world is that of its builder, similar to the role assigned to him by the natural sciences. However, in contrast to the latter, Buber does not see him as the "lonely self" in this enterprise, but as the partner of God. Man's experiencing of wholeness in himself and the world is an uninterrupted process, consummated at each moment he enters into relationship with God, yet realizable only through the principle of communality which he carries in his being as his unconditioned responsibility. As he builds the true community, he helps build and complete the Kingdom of God. The world, according to Buber, has not been redeemed at any definite point in history, but is being redeemed everywhere and at all times, inasmuch as the partnership between man and God is being actualized. The two partners, the finite and the Infinite, do not meet *in* man, but *between* him and the Absolute in their mutuality of dialogue, and this mutuality is redemption. In the very act of communication between man and God, as man turns and returns to Him, God redeems.

Appendix
The Principle of Dialogue in the Jewish Mode of Thought

Hermann Cohen's "Correlation" and Martin Buber's "Dialogical Relation"

There has been some dispute as to whether Buber borrowed Cohen's term "correlation" and converted it into "dialogue" without giving credit to its source. (See *Sh'ma: A Journal of Jewish Responsibility,* New York, January 11 and February 22, 1974.) The question is whether Buber knew of Cohen's "correlation" before he arrived at his own idea of relation in *I and Thou,* and if so, whether Cohen had developed it sufficiently for Buber to have been able to make use of it.

There is no evidence that Buber had read Cohen's major works before he first sketched his concept of "I and Thou" in 1916. In a letter of that year, addressed to his friend Gustav Landauer, Buber wrote that he had known Cohen only "from some *(allerdings nur einzelnen)* of his writings and from personal acquaintance" (see Martin Buber, *Briefwechsel* 1: 456). But even if he had read them, the idea of correlation was up to that year not developed by Cohen to signify dialogical relation, certainly not in Buber's meaning of the term. We find that Cohen first mentions "correlation" (only twice in passing) in his essay "Liebe und Gerechtigkeit in den Begriffen Gott und Mensch," which deals with the divine attributes, notably "love as the fundamental condition of the concept of God." Although he intimates the idea of immediate relation, his treatment is conceptual, which is totally different from Buber's idea of spontaneous experience. Buber later clarified this distinction in his essay concerning Cohen's "The Love of God and the Idea of Deity" (*Eclipse of God,* pp. 49 ff.).

We find another, more direct source of Cohen's antecedent reference to an I-Thou relation in one of his major works, *Aesthetik des reinen Gefühls* (Zweite Auflage, zweiter Teil, n.d., p. 23), in which he writes as follows:

> This I of poetry, therefore, demands everywhere also a Thou more than it does a He or an It. . . . In poetry, in this generally sentient language of art, the I harbors the postulate of Thou. The isolation of the I extends itself towards duality. But the I becomes a double I. The language of feeling is the language of Eros, and love demands the confrontation [*Konfrontation*] with the Thou; it does not tolerate its replacement as a He.

We have here some ingredients of Buber's principle of dialogue: "Thou" as differentiated from "He" and "It," "confrontation with Thou," even an "Inborn Thou." However, for Cohen the I-Thou relation is in the nature of a *union,* through love, of a double I—"an I in Thou, a Thou in I," a "unification of I and Thou in feeling . . . standing in danger of turning into passion" (ibid., p. 24). For Buber, the I-Thou relation is not a feeling, as such, but the ontic act of an I *meeting* a Thou (another), not their unification. In any event, there was no borrowing here, as we learn from Franz Rosenzweig's testimony on the subject.

Rosenzweig, to whom Buber had sent the proof sheets of his *I and Thou* for critical comment, undoubtedly had the above passage of Cohen's *Aesthetik* in mind when he wrote to Buber (in 1922):

> What happened to you is exactly the opposite of what happened to your co-discoverer Cohen (a veritable story *of those who entered the Garden!* [referring to "the four who entered heaven" to discover the divine secrets, Talmud Babli, *Hagiga* 14b]): He discovered I-Thou as the great exception to the rule and built for it a lean-to to his finished structure, always being mindful of not spoiling the latter. . . . You, on the other hand, have erected from the start a new structure, turned creation into chaos, in order to furnish the building-material, well enough, for the new building. . . . Cohen was

frightened by the discovery, you are *intoxicated* with it [Buber, *Briefwechsel* 2: 126].*

A third source is Cohen's last work, *Die Religion der Vernunft aus den Quellen des Judentums,* published in 1919, or four years prior to the publication of Buber's *I and Thou.* In this source, the concept "correlation" is developed fully and no doubt represents a unique dialogical relation between man and God, which, following Rosenzweig's dictum, was co-discovered by both Cohen and Buber, but independently of each other. This co-discovery, I would say, stems from the fact that both of them, though each in his own way, delved into the innermost spirit of the Jewish mode of thought. Hermann Cohen brought forth "the religion of reason out of the sources of Judaism"; Buber, looking into the same sources "from the Decalogue to Hasidism," found that "the basic teaching that fills the Hebrew Bible is that our life is a dialogue between above and below" *(On Judaism,* p. 215). Cohen, however, approached these sources from the viewpoint of Midrash Halakha (interpreting the Law), whereas Buber drew his inspiration primarily from Midrash Aggada (interpreting the Lore). A more fundamental difference between them lies in their respective starting points, hence also in procedure and development.

Cohen starts with the idea of God as the Supreme Being (theology), from which he derives the concept of correlation with man as a logical necessity in order to ascertain the separation between God and man without impairing their immediate relationship. Buber, on the other hand, starts with man (philosophical anthropology) as a category of creaturely being that enters into immediate relation with nature, fellowman, and God. The separation between man and God is an ontic reality, and their immediate relationship comes into existence as an act of dialogue. Therefore, in Buber's view man may reach God only when he first enters-into-relation with fellowman and nature, whereas according to Cohen it is the other way around: the condition of correlation with God first enables man to enter in correlation with fellowman, which is an unfolding of the "mean-

---

*Cf. Rivka Horwitz, "Exposition concerning the History of the Formation of Martin Buber's Book *I and Thou*" (see Bibliography below): "Indeed, all sources indicate that Buber reached the essence of his theory by himself" (p. 173).

ing and content of the general" correlation with God *(Religion der Vernunft,* chapter 8, 1–4). Nevertheless, Cohen too recognizes that "the correlation of man and God cannot be fulfilled when it is not first fulfilled in the entailed correlation of man with man" (ibid.).

Now that the question of "discovery" has been somewhat cleared up, it should be of interest to the historian of ideas to note that it was neither Hermann Cohen nor Martin Buber, but rather Friedrich Schleiermacher who first called attention to the unique Jewish experience of the dialogical relation between man and God. It may also be noted that Schleiermacher introduced the term "correlation" between God and the world in order to obviate their unification into an undifferentiated universe, much in the same sense as Cohen did. This Protestant theologian, who otherwise had very little good to say about *den Judaismus,* pointed out in his lecture "Ueber die Religionen" (1799) that the spirit of Judaism is permeated with "the dialogical" *(des Dialogischen).* In Judaism, he said, "the whole history . . . is represented as a dialogue [*ein Gespräch*] between God and man in word and deed. . . . It is from this viewpoint that the gift of prophecy is developed to such perfection in the Jewish religion as in none other" (Friedrich Schleiermacher, *Ueber die Religion,* Philosophische Bibliothek, 1961, p. 160). But whereas Schleiermacher regarded "this whole idea very childlike" and of no universal import because it did not provide for a human-divine mediator (this remark was commented on by Cohen in his aforementioned essay), Cohen and Buber regarded this non-mediated relationship, whether in correlation or in dialogue, as the essence and strength of the Jewish religion.

Notes

References to Buber's works are given in their original German titles, followed (in parentheses) by their published English translation in the folllowing abbreviations. If a citation is direct from the translation, the German title is omitted.

BH	*A Believing Humanism*	Moses	*Moses*
BMM	*Between Man and Man*	On Judaism	*On Judaism*
Daniel	*Daniel*	OMH	*Origin and Meaning of Hasidism*
EG	*Eclipse of God*		
FSH	*For the Sake of Heaven*	PF	*The Prophetic Faith*
G&E	*Good and Evil*	PU	*Paths in Utopia*
HMM	*Hasidism and Modern Man*	PW	*Pointing the Way*
I and Thou or I & T	*I and Thou* (Walter Kaufmann's translation)	TH 1	*Tales of the Hasidim: Early Masters*
I&P	*Israel and Palestine*	TH 2	*Tales of the Hasidim: Later Masters*
I&W	*Israel and the World*	TR	*Ten Rungs*
KG	*Kingship of God*	TTF	*Two Types of Faith*
KnM	*The Knowledge of Man*		

Part I. The Reality of Communication

Introduction

1. *Werke* 1: 275 (KnM 77).
2. Ibid., p. 594 (EG 123). *Hinweise,* p. 259 (PW 112).
3. Ibid., pp. 1111–13 *(The Philosophy of Martin Buber* 35–37).
4. Cf. "Urdistanz und Beziehung," *Werke* 1: 411 (KnM 59). I describe the act of entering into relation sometimes as "spontaneous experience," in order to emphasize that a human relationship must be an experience of some kind. Buber tries to avoid using the term "experience" in the I-Thou relation altogether. He also refrains from using the German word *Erlebnis* (living experience), as it connotes a psychological state, rather than an ontic act which is expressed in relation *(Beziehung).* Cf. *Werke* 1:81, 84–85, 152 *(I and Thou* 56, 59–60, 157), and *The Philosophy of Martin Buber,* pp. 711–12, on the term *Erlebnis.* Nevertheless, Buber speaks of his own "I-Thou experience" *(Ich-Du-Erfahrenen)* and his "one great experience of faith" *(eine grosse Glaubenserfahrung),* which he transmitted in philosophical discourse *(Werke* 1:1111; *The Philosophy of Martin Buber,* p. 689). In my overview of Buber's philosophy of interhuman relation at the end of this book ("The Kingdom of God" section), I use the term "living experience" to emphasize the essentially humanistic character of his philos-

ophy. By that I do not mean a "psychological" experience, but, as Buber intends, an ontic act of relation.

5. Twofold communication. The German text reads, "nach seiner zwiefältigen Haltung." The word *Haltung* is meant here as communication rather than attitude. Buber seeks to establish the ontological ground of man's relation with fellowman, nature, and God, not his psychological reaction to them, such as the word "attitude" may connote. The word *Haltung* is taken here in the sense of *sich zu einem halten,* to be associated or in communication with someone, to keep one's company. Buber uses the words *Kommunion* and *kommunizieren* in the same sense as the English word "communication." Cf. *Werke* 1: 392–93. See also PF 195. "The creation itself already means communication between Creator and creature (*Werke* 2: 442).

6. *Werke* 1: 201, 202 (BMM 27, 28). Cf. L. Feuerbach, "Grundzüge der Philosophie der Zukunft," no. 62, in *Kleine philosophische Schriften,* p. 169.

7. Cf. Frederick Copleston, *A History of Philosophy,* vol. 7, part 1, Fichte to Hegel, pp. 59–68.

8. Cf. PW 36, on the dialectic discussion of unity.

9. The distinction between explaining and understanding, the first applied to natural science and the second to cultural science, was first made by Wilhelm Dilthey in his studies of the *Geisteswissenschaften.* Buber, who was a student of Dilthey's at the University of Berlin and who regarded his master as the father of philosophical anthropology, does not make this distinction directly, but it is evident from his use of the term *verstehen* and from his methodology as a whole. Cf. Wilhelm Dilthey, *Die Philosophie des Lebens,* p. 136. "Die Natur erklären wir, das Seelenleben verstehen wir" ("Nature we explain, the life of the soul we understand"). See ibid., p. 3, Vorwort by Otto E. Bollnow. With this declaration, he says, Dilthey went decisively beyond spiritual scientific psychology toward "the methodological self-understanding of the sciences of the spirit." Cf. Buber, *Werke* 1: 317. A similar distinction is made by Nicolai Hartmann in his *Neue Wege der Ontologie,* p. 27, where he speaks of understanding with reference to knowledge of inner experience and of conceiving with reference to outer or material nature. Cf. Bernard Groethuysen, "Towards an Anthropological Philosophy," in *Philosophy and History: The Ernst Cassirer Festschrift,* p. 77. "If we wish to grasp self-knowledge in the sense of self-reflection, we must not identify knowledge with scientific knowledge, but must give it a much wider significance. 'Know thyself,' then, means not simply try to define yourself by concepts, try to determine the essential characteristics of the species 'Man,' but become conscious of yourself, live in the consciousness of yourself, understand yourself, come to experience yourself, be present to yourself, live in the awareness of your present, come to yourself." Cf. BMM 121–23.

10. *Werke* 1: 438–39 (KnM 163). "Hier tut sich uns die Vorhalle auf, aus der sich die Pforten der vier Potenzen in die Innenräume der Erkenntnis, der Liebe, der Kunst und des Glaubens öffnen." ("Here the vestibule is unlocked to us from which the gates of the four potencies open into the inner halls of cognition, love, art, and faith.")

11. *Werke* 1: 1075. (PW 83), on the artist's intuition.

12. KnM 67–68. See Appendix, pp. 181–82. In a discussion with Carl R. Rogers, Buber expands on his concepts of acceptance and confirmation and makes some fine distinctions between them. He states: "I would say every true existential relationship between two persons begins with acceptance. By acceptance I mean being able to tell . . . the other person that I accept him just as he is. . . . Well, so, but it is not yet what I mean by confirming the other. Because accepting, this is just accepting how he ever is in this moment, in this actuality of his. Confirming means, first of all, accepting the whole potentiality of the other . . . the person he has been . . . *created* to become."

13. *Werke* 1: 87–88, 419 *(I and Thou* 66).

14. Ibid., p. 89 (68). "This, however, is the sublime melancholy of our lot, that every Thou in our world must become an It."

15. Ibid., pp. 113, 114 (102–103).

16. Ibid., pp. 383–84 (BMM 184).

17. Cf. EG, "Religion and Philosophy," p. 27. Buber speaks there of philosophy and

philosophizing as looking away from concrete situations and of the philosopher as opposed to the religionist. However, it would be more correct to designate the former as metaphysician or philosophical scientist in contrast to whom Buber considers himself as a philosophical anthropologist *(der Philosoph der Anthropologie treibt)*. What Buber really objects to is the type of philosopher whose conceptual structure at best yields a religious tone but not true religion, a situation which, as Franz Rosenzweig had pointed out, was Buber's own position in his early stages of philosophical speculation. In his essay *I and Thou* and in his subsequent writings Buber developed into a "philosophizing man" to whom the field of philosophy is a living experience. Cf. PW, Foreword, p. xv.

18. *Werke* 1: 312 (BMM 121).

19. Ibid., p. 1111 *(The Philosophy of Martin Buber* 689).

20. In a letter to Maurice Friedman, Buber wrote: "I have no inclination to systematizing, but I am of course and by necessity a philosophizing man" (Maurice Friedman, *Martin Buber: The Life of Dialogue*, p. 161). Cf. Hermann Wein, *Realdialektik*, p. 19, "Zur Bedeutung der anthropologischen Methode": "There are various kinds of philosophizing. There is among others, besides speculative philosophizing, the philosophizing of spontaneous experience. This cannot mean experience of the individual subject. But there are the manifold experiences of men, and with men, which have been recounted by psychologists, sociologists and also poets, and beyond that also by philosophical spirits who are not bound by systems."

21. I&W, "The Two Foci of the Jewish Soul," pp. 30, 34.

22. *Nachlese*, p. 113 (BH 117).

Chapter 1

23. I have borrowed this analogy of the artist painting himself into his own painting of the universe from J. B. Priestly, *Man and Time*, p. 249, in which he shows how J. W. Dunne illustrates infinite regress of serial time.

24. Francis Bacon, *Novum Organum*, aphorism 68.

25. *Werke* 1, "Was ist das: Selbst-Widerspruch?" p. 125 *(I and Thou* 119). Cf. *Nachlese*, pp. 156–57 (BH 150–51), on psychological self-contradiction.

26. *Werke* 1, "Urdistanz und Beziehung," p. 413 (KnM 61).

27. Ibid.

28. *Nachlese*, "Über Religionswissenschaft," and "Philosophische und religiöse Weltanschauung," pp. 124–35 (BH 127–35). Cf. EG 128. The I-Thou is the architect of human existence in reality.

29. Ibid., p. 124 (127).

30. Some may regard a science of religious relation as empirical, but Buber is not an empiricist in the accepted sense or this term. His concept of relation, to use a Kantian term, is a priori or transcendental, that is, it makes knowledge possible. There is much in his thinking which had its inception in Kantian transcendental philosophy, but this subject is outside the scope of our present study.

31. Cf. Wilhelm Dilthey, *Die Philosophie des Lebens*, Vorwort by Otto Friedrich Bollnow, pp. 2–3. Dilthey considered the "explanatory" natural-scientific orientation of psychology as inadequate for a true "understanding" of man as a living being. He then developed what became known as a *geisteswissenschaftliche* ("spiritual-scientific") psychology. Its methodology exercised considerable influence on the subsequent development of the different sciences of man, especially philosophical anthropology. Buber was influenced by him, although he differed from him in some fundamentals. Cf. *The Philosophy of Martin Buber*, "Buber's Dialogical Thought," by Nathan Rotenstreich, pp. 118, on the influence of Dilthey's "Lebensphilosophie," and "Reply to My Critics," by Martin Buber, p. 702. Cf. Maurice Friedman, *Martin Buber*, pp. 34, 40.

32. BMM 77.

33. *Werke* 1: 415 (KnM 64).

34. Ibid., pp. 100–101 (*I and Thou* 84–85).

35. Ibid., p. 101.

36. Ibid., p. 128 (*I and Thou* 123). Cf. further p. 154 (160). "By its nature, the eternal Thou cannot become an It." See below, chapter 3, "Role of the Thou".

37. Ibid., "Der Mensch und sein Gebild," p. 438 (KnM 163).

38. Cf. *The Philosophy of Martin Buber,* p. 691. Ibid., "Martin Buber's Metaphysics," by Charles Hartshorne, pp. 49–68, and Buber's "Reply," p. 717. Buber writes: "You begin, dear Hartshorne, with the sentence, I am no metaphysician and I am one of the greatest metaphysicians. After attentive reading of your essay, I am more strongly yet convinced than at the beginning of the reading that we can make only the first half of your sentence the basis of an understanding." Hartshorne's argument is with reference to a God idea or "the appropriate 'idea' of the divine nature," which he identifies with "the idea of supreme Relatedness—Transcendental Relativity. . . . 'The absolute' . . . is 'relation' and 'relativity' " (pp. 58–59). In the first place, Buber does not speculate about "the divine nature," nor does he conceive of God as an "idea." Furthermore, his principle of relation is not a logical concept of relativity, as Hartshorne sees it. I discuss this matter in chap. 3, "The Absolute Person" section. On the other hand, Buber's "metacosmic relation" with reference to the world-order is much like the "Idea" of world-as-a-whole in Kant's "science of metaphysics." Kant, too, considers it a principle of relation and not an actual object. His world-idea and the other two ideas of reason (the soul and God) are patterned after his category of relation of the Understanding. For Buber, however, this does not apply to God, who cannot be defined or described conceptually or perceptually. Cf. Kant, *Kritik der reinen Vernunft* B392 and B435. See below, chapt. 3, "The Sign of the Between" section.

39. *Werke* 1: 146 (*I and Thou* 148–49).

40. PW, Foreword, p. xv.

41. Cf. *Philosophers Speak of God,* by Charles Hartshorne and William L. Reese, eds., pp. 325, 327.

42. Cf. W. K. C. Guthrie, *A History of Greek Philosophy* 2: 26, 50. Cf. Wilhelm Capelle, *Die Vorsokratiker,* pp. 163–64, Proömium, fr. 1. Cf. Werner Jaeger, *Die Theologie der frühen griechischen Denker,* "Parmenides' Mysterium des Seins," pp. 107, 115, on his "way" as salvation in keeping with "the religion of the mysteries."

43. Wilhelm Windelband, *Präludien* 1, "Von der Mystik unserer Zeit," p. 294.

44. *Werke* 1: 356 (BMM 160): "Human reason can be understood only in connection with human not-reason. The problem of philosophical anthropology is the problem of a specific wholeness and its specific inner connection."

45. I&W 30–31.

46. Sir Arthur Eddington, *Space, Time and Gravitation,* p. 192.

47. *Werke* 1: 317 (BMM 126).

48. Cf. Arnold Sommerfeld, "To Einstein's 70th Birthday," in *Albert Einstein: Philosopher-Scientist* 1: 105: "In the old question 'continuum versus discontinuity,' he [Einstein] has taken his position most decisively on the side of continuum. . . . By far the most of today's physicists consider Einstein's aim as unachievable." Cf. Albert Einstein, "Reply to Criticisms," ibid., 2: 686, on his adherence to the continuum as the only way "to conserve four-dimensionality."

49. Cf. ibid., 2: 471–72, Karl Menger, "Theory of Relativity and Geometry": "I venture to elaborate Minkowski's dictum that the laws of nature may find their most perfect expression in the statement of relations between world-lines . . . in some fairly general continuum." See above, note 39 and text.

50. Cf. A. d'Abro, *The Evolution of Scientific Thought from Newton to Einstein,* p. 274: "It is this four-dimensional field which acts as a *guiding influence* on bodies, constraining them along the geodesics of space-time."

51. Cf. Albert Einstein, *Essays in Science,* pp. 58, 110, on the difficulty of fitting matter into the gravitational field, since the latter is produced by matter. See my article "Einstein's Metamathematics," in *Philosophia Mathematica,* Winter 1973.

52. Cf. Henry Margenau, *The Nature of Physical Reality*, p. 81, on the physicist's view. "We hold with Kant that epistemology must precede ontology and that epistemology denotes the methodology of the cognitive process." This may be so from a metaphysical viewpoint. Cf. ibid., p. 75, on the metaphysical requirements of constructs. Cf. Buber, BMM 119–21, on Kant's question "What is Man?"

53. Cf. Albert Einstein, *Über die spezielle und allgemeine Relativitätstheorie*, no. 31, pp. 66–70, on the possibility of a finite and yet not limited world. Cf. A. d'Abro, *Evolution of Scientific Thought*, chap. 33, "The Finiteness of the Universe."

54. *Werke* 1: 146 (*I and Thou* 148).

55. Ibid., p. 160 (168).

56. This is not the place to discuss the various trends toward a "unified science." I take it here in the sense that all special sciences will eventually be able to explain the phenomena of their investigation within a framework of space, time, and causality. This is known as the thesis of the naturalists. Cf. Herbert Feigl, "Unity of Science and Unitary Science," in *Readings in the Philosophy of Science*, ed, Herbert Feigl and May Brodbeck, pp. 382–84. Cf. Henry Margenau, *Nature of Physical Reality* pp. 18–20. He argues against all notions "of essential unity of the sciences."

57. Albert Einstein, "The Fundaments of Theoretical Physics," in *Readings in the Philosophy of Science*, p. 253.

58. Moritz Schlick, "Philosophy of Organic Life," in *Readings of the Philosophy of Science*, p. 536.

59. Cf. *Werke* 1: 100–101 (*I and Thou* 83–84): "Each meeting signifies to you a world order." Further, "In this firm and profitable chronicle [temporal succession in the world of It], the moments of Thou appear as fanciful lyric-dramatic episodes . . . dangerously pulling to extremes, loosening the well-tested interconnections [that is, the causal connections of the ordered world]." Cf. EG 128. "Both together [I-Thou and I-It] build up human existence. . . . [But] the I-Thou relation remains the architect, for it is self-evident that it cannot be employed as assistant."

60. Cf. *Werke* 1: 97–99 (*I and Thou* 80–82). See ibid., p. 88 (67): "Relation is mutuality. My Thou acts on me, as I act on it." But the two do not determine or change each other. Rather, one is being aware of the other, which means that "he becomes present to me," or I am aware of him "in this special sense as 'personal making present.' " Cf. KnM 80. Cf. Carl F. von Weizsäcker, "I-Thou and I-It in the Contemporary Natural Sciences," *The Philosophy of Martin Buber*, pp. 603–607, on the inadequacy of science to address itself to the Thou or even to the I. It speaks only of the It, and the I-Thou relation may come into play in "a research institute . . . in the . . . exchange of ideas."

61. *Werke* 1: 1083 (PW 128), "Die Frage nach dem Erfolg."

62. I&W 133. See ibid., 125.

63. Henry Margenau, *Nature of Physical Reality*, pp. 18–20.

64. *Nachlese*, p. 118 (BH 121).

65. EG 133, on the argument against Jung's psychologism.

66. Cf. Henry Margenau, *Nature of Physical Reality*, chap. 18, p. 356. The uncertainty principle is "a basic innovation in our way of representing reality." Cf. A. d'Abro, *The Rise of the New Physics* 2, "Heisenberg's Uncertainty Principle," p. 654. It is of interest to note that, according to the principle of uncertainty, the classical law of causality is not operative in quantum mechanics. For an evaluation of this issue see Niels Bohr, "Discussion with Einstein," in *Albert Einstein: Philosopher-Scientist* 1: 207. Bohr favored this principle; Einstein opposed it. Another illustration of how Buber's concepts of "exclusiveness" and "mutuality" or reciprocity correspond in a broad sense to similar concepts in modern physics we find in Wolfgang Pauli's "Exclusion Principle," and in Max Born's "Reciprocity Postulate." Without going into an elaborate demonstration, suffice it to say that these principles are concerned with the *interaction* between elementary particles (electrons, protons, neutrons, etc.) in which each retains its independent state, similar to Buber's concept of the independent states of two beings in the mutuality of their interrelationships. Cf. Margenau, *Nature of Physical Reality*, chap.

20, "The Exclusion Principle." See d'Abro, *The New Physics* 2: 578–81, and Hermann Weyl, *The Theory of Groups and Quantum Mechanics*, "The Pauli Exclusion Principle," pp. 242–44.

67. *Werke* 1: 1111–12. "Aus einer philosophischen Rechenschaft" (*The Philosophy of Martin Buber*, pp. 689–90).

68. Ibid., p. 438 (KnM 163).

69. Ibid., p. 440 (165).

70. Ibid., p. 185 (BMM 12).

71. EG 3, 126. Cf. knM 148: "It is not for me to speak in general terms of the inner reality of him who refuses to believe in a transcendent being with whom he can communicate. I only have this to report: that I have met many men in the course of my life who have told me how, acting from the high conscience as men who had become guilty, they experienced themselves being seized by a higher power." Cf. *Nachlese*, "Religiöse Erziehung," p. 123 (BH 126). We cannot train someone to believe. We can only teach how faith is manifest if one really believes, that is, "if one questions himself, decides and puts himself to the test."

72. *Werke* 1: 113 (*I and Thou* 102). Cf. I&W 18.

73. Ibid., p. 112 (100). Man's freedom in relation to God will be discussed below under "Freedom and Dependence" and "Man's Way to His Goal."

Chapter 2

74. Ernst Cassirer, *Die Philosophie der Aufklärung*, p. 339.

75. Cf. Christopher Jencks and David Riesman, *The Academic Revolution*, p. 517. Cf. Jacques Barzun, *The American University*, pp. 38, 60.

76. Cf. Barzun, *American University*, p. 233.

77. "Dem Gemeinschaftlichen folgen," *Werke* 1: 463 (KnM 98). Cf. Aldous Huxley, "The Door of Perception," *Collected Essays*, pp. 327–36.

78. *Werke* 1: 465 (KnM 100).

79. "Pfade in Utopia," *Werke* 1: 850–51 (PU 14).

80. The size of community is a practical matter determined by factors of production, consumption, and management of internal affairs as well as contingent and historical developments. Its most essential aspect, however, is its openness rather than its intimacy. "A real community need not consist of people who are constantly in contact with one another; but it must consist of people who, being comrades, are open and ready for each other" (*Werke* 1: 987, PU 145).

81. *Werke* 1: 995 (PU 131).

82. Ibid.

83. Ibid., p. 994 (130).

84. Ibid., p. 353 (BMM 158).

85. PW, "What Is to be Done?" 109.

86. *Werke* 1: 1089–94: "The West cannot and need not give up 'modern civilization,' the East will not be able to isolate itself from it" (p. 1094, PW 137–38). Cf. ibid., p. 844 (PU 8).

87. Ibid., p. 997 (PU 132).

88. *Hinweise*, "Drei Sätze eines religiösen Sozialismus," p. 259 (PW 112).

89. *Werke* 1. "Wer redet," pp. 187–88, and "Religionsgespräche," p. 180 (BMM 6, 14): "Wir harren einer Theophanie, von der wir nichts wissen als den Ort, und der Ort heisst Gemeinschaft." ("We are awaiting a theophany of which we know nothing but the place, and the place is called community.")

90. *Hinweise*, "Geltung und Grenze des politischen Prinzips," p. 345 (PW 218).

91. *Werke* 1: 831 (BMM 116), I&W 20–21, 245, on the meaning of "return." The renewal is not just of the social structure but of man himself as a person, for the one is

inconceivable or rather impossible without the other. The renewal of mankind arises out of the yearning for personal unity.

92. PW 169.

93. Ibid., p. 168.

94. *Werke* 1: 402 (BMM 200–201).

95. Ibid., p. 401 (200).

96. Ibid., p. 824 (110).

97. PW 172.

98. *Hinweise,* "Hoffnung für diese Stunde," pp. 317–19 (PW 223–24). Cf. PW 213, 220, 236 and KnM 82.

99. *Werke* 1: 1065 (PW 187). The reference is to Isaiah's view of power exercised by the Judean king, who is only a governor appointed by God, the true king. This may be taken as Buber's own view, which is clear from the context. Cf. *Werke* 2: 492, n.2 (KG 15, n.2), on the use of the word "governor" rather than "deputy."

100. PW 137.

101. It should be pointed out that it is not always clear from Buber's statements whether "restructuring" is a means or an end, that is, whether it precedes the particular changes to be made or follows them as a result. I would judge from his discussion of the utopian idea that the "restructuring" is a means which realizes itself as an end. "The 'utopian' socialists," he writes, "have aspired more and more to a restructuring of society," by which he has in mind a transformation of man and his conditions as a way of overcoming both his individual atomization and his collective loneliness. Cf. PU 14.

102. *Werke* 1: 852 (PU 15).

103. Cf. PW 190. Buber does not claim prophetic powers, but considers himself a "social thinker" in the prophetic tradition.

104. Massimo Salvadori, ed., *Modern Socialism,* pp. 147, 146.

105. Cf. PU 88. This notion of "development," Buber says, was also Marx's view in the days prior to his "Communist Manifesto" (p. 95).

106. *Werke* 1: 884 (PU 43): "Wir sehen hier . . . dass seine [Kropotkin's] 'Anarchie,' wie die Proudhons, in Wahrheit Akratie ist, nicht Regierungslosigkeit, sondern Herrschaftslosigkeit."

107. PW 174.

108. *Werke* 1, "Zwischen Gesellschaft und Staat," p. 1019 (PW 174).

109. Massimo Salvadori, *Modern Socialism,* pp. 165, 169.

110. *Werke* 1: 1019.

111. Ibid. (PW 174–75). Buber's concept of "political surplus" is analogous to Marx's "surplus value." For Marx it is not value, but surplus value, when converted into capital as production for the sake of production only, that creates an oppressive capitalist class. Similarly, for Buber it is not political power as such, but its surplus, when converted into power for the sake of power, that creates an oppressive government. There, an accumulation of "surplus value"; here, an accumulation of "surplus power." Cf. Karl Marx, *Capital,* "Conversion of Surplus-Value into Capital," pp. 634–36.

112. BMM 91: "I give my left hand to the rebel and my right hand to the heretic: forward! But I do not trust them. They know how to die, but that is not enough."

113. PW 175–76.

114. Ibid., p. 176.

115. Ibid., pp. 218, 235.

116. Ibid., "The Demand of the Spirit and Historical Reality," pp. 185, 191.

117. Ibid., p. 176.

118. BMM 111.

119. *Werke* 1: 1061–62 (PW 183–84).

120. PW 179, 191.

121. BMM 116, PW 188.

122. *Werke* 1: 108 (*I and Thou* 95).

123. "The 21st Century: Mystery of Life," television program (CBS), Sunday, February 26, 1967, 6:00 P.M. See also "On Pollution," Sunday, March 23, 1969.

124. "Geneticist Looks at the Year 2000," *The New York Times,* February 13, 1967, p. 1. Cf. Victor K. McElheny, " 'Genetic Engineering' Is a Rapidly Advancing Science," *The New York Times,* December 15, 1975, p. 37. Note Dr. Robert Sinsheimer's warning: Molecular biologists must avoid contributing "to the inventory of tragic results already caused by, for example, radium, asbestos, thalidomide, vinyl chloride, etc."

125. *Werke* 1, "Die Frage an den Einzelnen," p. 259 (BMM 78).

126. Cf. KnM 180–81. In a discussion with Carl R. Rogers about the psychotherapy of "a person that people call, or want to call, a bad person," Buber states: "I would say there is not as we generally think in the soul of a man good and evil opposed. There is again and again in different manners a polarity, and the poles are not good and evil, but rather yes and no, rather acceptance and refusal. . . . This polarity is very often directionless. It is a chaotic state. We could bring a cosmic note into it. We can help put order, put a shape into this. Because I think the good, what we may call the good, is always only direction. Not a substance."

127. TR 93, "The 'Way' of the Wicked." "It is written: 'Let the wicked forsake his way' [Isaiah 55:7]. Does the wicked have a way? What he has is a mire, not a way. Now what is meant is this: let the wicked leave his 'way,' that is, his illusion of having a way."

128. *Werke* 1: 260 (BMM 78–79).

129. TR 95: "He who still harbors an Evil Inclination has a great advantage, for he can serve God with it. He can gather all his passion and warmth and pour them into the service of God. . . . What counts is to restrain the blaze in the hour of desire and let it flow into the hours of prayer and service."

130. *Werke* 2, "Die Wege, Psalm 1," p. 984 (G&E 51). The Hebrew word for sinner is *hotei,* meaning literally "one who has missed the mark." Buber emphasizes this meaning by designating the sinners as "those who miss the way again and again." Cf. TR 92–93, comment on Psalm 1:6. "It is written: . . . 'for the Lord regardeth the way of the righteous; but the way of the wicked shall perish.' " Comment: "The ways of the righteous . . . are all one way and that is the way. But the ways of the wicked . . . are nothing but many ways of losing the one way." Cf. further comments on Psalm 73 in *Werke* 2: 971 (G&E 31). The psalmist does not place the good as the opposite of the wicked. The latter are two types of men, whereas the good is not a type of men at all ("there are no 'good men' in the world"), but a condition which man, any man including the wicked, may attain by coming near to God, i.e., by entering-into-relation with reality, human as well as divine. What the psalmist has recognized, Buber points out, is that in order for man to come near to God he must have a "pure heart" or rather purity of heart, of which he is capable as long as he lives. The wicked, however, persist in "separating" themselves from reality and are lost, or as the psalmist says, "Those who *distance* themselves from Thee shall perish; Thou hast cut off those who *separate* themselves from Thee" (Psalm 73:27). Note that the underscored words are in the Hebrew original *rehekecha* and *zoneh,* respectively. The first means "distancing" and the second may be translated as "separating" (as Rashi explains). Thus not only is the way of the wicked lost, as in Psalm 1, but they also perish because they persist in their distancing and separation.

131. *Werke* 3, "Der Weg des Menschen nach der chassidischen Lehre," p. 720 (HMM 141): "God does not say, 'This is a way to me and this is not.' Rather he says, 'Everything you do can be a way to me, only when you do it so that it leads to me.' "

132. Cf. PW 211, on the spheres of wholeness and division in man. "When, and insofar as, man becomes whole, he becomes God's and gives to God; he gives to God just his wholeness." Good means to take from the sphere of wholeness and give it to the sphere of division. Failure to decide for direction is called inertia, which Buber terms "the root of all evil."

133. *Werke* 1, "Moral und Religion," p. 191 (BMM 18). The conflict is between the "once-for-all" and "the dialogical power of the situation . . . of the unanticipated moment."

134. *Werke* 1, "Zwiesprache," pp. 208–10 (BMM 34–36). Which is the real spiritual act, Buber asks, to engage in contemplation of lofty ideas or to respond to fellowman in actual dialogue? He raises this question in reply to "the opponent," who would relegate the spirit to leisure-time dialectics and who wondered how "the manager of a huge technical enterprise could practice 'dialogical responsibility,' " that is, enter into I-Thou relationships with his employees. "Yes," says Buber, "he is exactly the one I mean, the one in the factory, the one in the shop, the one in the office . . . man. . . . Dialogue is not an affair of spiritual luxury. . . . It is the business of creation, of the creature, and that is man, of whom I speak." See also "Die Grundbewegungen," ibid., p. 195 (BMM 21).

135. Ibid., "Verantwortung," pp. 189–90 (BMM 16–17).

136. PW 95, BMM 166.

137. *Werke* 1, "Schuld und Schuldgefühle," p. 486 (KnM 132). Buber discusses in detail the problem of overcoming guilt not only through psychotherapy, which aims at the removal of the guilt feeling, but also through an existential act, which the guilty person alone can perform.

138. EG 87.

139. *Werke* 1, "Das Problem des Menschen," pp. 363–64 (BMM 166). Cf. *Werke* 3: 136 (HMM 172). When we fail to respond whenever and wherever we are summoned by others, we become conscious of the fact that "our life does not participate in true fulfilled existence." We have missed something. But we can find it only "there where we stand," in every situation which is allotted to us every day and demands essential fulfillment.

140. Ibid. 1, "Dem Gemeinschaftlichen folgen," pp. 471–73 (KnM 106–109). "But he who existentially knows no Thou will never succeed in knowing a We" (KnM 108). Cf. Dieter Wyss, *Depth Psychology: A Critical History*, p. 404. "The 'We' as the ontological absolute." Discussion of M. Buber, M. Scheler, K. Löwith, E. Michel, P. Christian.

141. Ibid., p. 474 (109), 128. Cf. *Hinweise*, p. 259 (PW 112) and *Werke* 1: 180 (BMM 7), on the relation of the community to the divine.

142. Ibid., p. 188 (BMM 15).

143. Ibid., p. 1086 (PW 131).

144. *Werke* 2: 941–42 (PW 206). Inner transformation means surpassing one's present factual state. Turning is not a return to a former innocent stage of life, but rather a return to the right way of life, which one has neglected to follow. This is the meaning of *teshuva* (return) as it was taught by the prophets of Israel.

145. Ibid., pp. 139, 129, 130.

146. Ibid., p. 136.

147. I&W 181–82.

148. *Werke* 1: 575 (EG 95).

149. Ibid., p. 577 (97).

150. Ibid.

151. Ibid., pp. 577–78 (98).

152. *Werke* 2: "Moses," p. 215 *(Moses* 188).

153. *Werke* 1: 797 (BMM 92–93).

154. *Werke* 2: 216 *(Moses* 188): "Dass hier ewigem Spruch ewiger Widerspruch entgegentritt."

155. Ibid., p. 217 (189).

156. Ibid.

157. *Werke* 1: 796 (BMM 92).

158. Lamentations 5: 21. CF. *Siddur (Standard Jewish prayerbook),* the prayer at the return of the Torah scroll to the ark.

159. *Nachlese,* p. 157 (BH 52).

160. Ibid.

161. *The Philosophy of Martin Buber,* "Reply to My Critics," Ethics, pp. 717–18, 721.

162. *Der Jude und sein Judentum,* p. 69. Cf. EG 18: "Only an absolute can give quality of absoluteness to an obligation." Its bearer is the individual "in the depth of any genuine solitude, . . . even beyond all social existence." Cf. *Nachlese,* pp. 233–39 (BH 205–10, "On the Ethics of Political Decision."

Chapter 3

163. EG 123.

164. Cf. *Nachlese,* p. 124 (BH 127): "Religion, however, is not human thought about the Divine; that it becomes as and when it passes into theology. . . . ('Theology,' in truth, is a 'latent' metaphysic)."

165. Cf. Karl Löwith, *From Hegel to Nietzsche,* p. 192: "The importance of eternity to Nietzsche's philosophy"; p. 195: " 'Beyond man and time,' Nietzsche sought to transcend the whole 'fact of man' together with time, and escape the dereliction of the modern world."

166. Jean-Paul Sartre, *Being and Nothingness,* p. 89: "Human reality is its own surpassing toward what it lacks." See p. 566: "Man fundamentally is the desire to be God."

167. Cf. Thomas J. J. Altizer, "The Sacred and the Profane," in *Radical Theology,* pp. 151–52: "Total redemption" is in "the possibility of an End that transcends the Beginning." Cf. Altizer, "Nirvana and the Kingdom of God," in *New Theology No. 1,* ed. Martin Marty and Dean G. Peerman, pp. 165–66. As "the Kingdom of God . . . breaks into time in our midst," "the world of 'history,' 'nature,' and 'being' is brought to an end." I have discussed the four philosophers of the God-is-dead movement at length in my book *Philosophy and Technology,* pp. 95–139.

168. Buber, *Begegnung: Autobiographische Fragmente,* p. 16. Cf. *Werke* 1: 327–28, 342, and *The Philosophy of Martin Buber,* pp. 11–12.

169. *Der Jude und sein Judentum,* p. 810.

170. *Begegnung,* pp. 16, 19 *(The Philosophy of Martin Buber,* pp. 11, 13).

171. Ibid., p. 19.

172. *Werke* 1: 329 (BMM 136–37).

173. Ibid., pp. 343–49 (149–56). Buber says that Nietzsche was under the influence of the eighteenth-century French naturalists and that he may be called "a mystic of the Enlightenment" (p. 349).

174. Ibid., p. 349. Cf. Löwith, *Hegel to Nietzsche,* p. 319: "He [Nietzsche's man] must rely on himself as upon a rope stretched over the abyss of nothingness, extended into emptiness. . . . Danger is his 'vocation.' "

175. Ibid., p. 350. Cf. EG 110 and PW 160: "We already literally find in Nietzsche the 'intention of training a ruling caste—the future masters of the earth'; he did not foresee that it would be the men without restraint—those who drag the masses along with them—who would most readily appropriate his intention." Cf. Löwith, *Hegel to Nietzsche,* p. 198: "Nietzsche is alien both to the 'national' and the 'social' [of the Nationalist Socialist movement]. . . . But this does not contradict the obvious fact that Nietzsche became a catalyst of the 'movement,' and determined its ideology in a decisive way. The attempt to unburden Nietzsche of his intellectual 'guilt,' or even to claim his support *against* what he brought about is as unfounded as the reverse effort to make him the advocate of a matter over which he sits in judgment."

176. Ibid., p. 346 (BMM 150).

177. Ibid., p. 588 (EG 111).

178. EG 69–70.

179. Ibid., p. 67.

180. *Der Jude und sein Judentum,* p. 173 *(On Judaism* 214).

181. *Werke* 1: 511–12 (EG 14).

182. Ibid., p. 520 (23–24). Cf. Solomon Ibn Gabirol, *Keter Malkhut* (The Royal Crown), no. 7: "Thou art the Light Supreme, and the eyes of the pure shall behold Thee; but the clouds of sin eclipse Thee from the eyes of the sinners."

183. *Werke* 1: 188 (BMM 15).

184. Ibid., p. 129 *(I and Thou* 124).

185. Ibid. (125).

186. Ibid., pp. 130–31 (127). "In the relation to God, unconditioned exclusiveness and unconditioned inclusiveness are one. . . . In the relation everything in included" (p. 130).

187. Ibid. Cf. *Bereshith Rabba* 68.4 (Vayetse): "God is called 'place' *(Makom),* because He is the place of the world but the world is not His place." Cf. *Baba Bathra* 25a: "God's Presence is in every place."

188. Benedict de Spinoza, *Ethics,* part 2, prop. 47, note.

189. Ibid., part 5, prop. 36, corollary: "Hence it follows that God, in so far as he loves himself, loves man, and consequently, that the love of God toward men, and the intellectual love of the mind toward God are identical." Cf. Buber, *Werke* 1: 326, 512–14 (BMM 134–35, EG 15–18).

190. *Werke* 1: 132, 383–84 *(I and Thou* 128, BMM 184).

191. Cf. TH 2: 225. The Yehudi: "I understood what is told of our father Abraham; that he explored the sun, the moon, and the stars, and did not find him, and how in this very not-finding the presence of God was revealed to him. For three months I mulled over this realization. Then I explored until I reached the truth of not-finding."

192. *Werke* 1: 133, 537 *(I and Thou* 130, EG 44–45): "I-Thou finds its highest intensity and radiance in the religious reality, in which the unconfined Existent *(das uneinge-schränkt Seiende)* becomes, as absolute person, my partner." Cf. I&W 37: "God wills to have need of man."

193. I&W 33. Cf. *Werke* 1: 384 (BMM 184–85), on Max Scheler's concept of a "becoming God" *(Gotteswerdung)* and Eckhart's view of God "born" eternally in the human soul. In his early years Buber was influenced by Eckhart, but he abandoned him completely when his own ideas ripened in a dialogical world view.

194. *Werke* 1: 596 (EG 126). Prayer, in its deepest sense, is asking for the manifestation of the divine Presence and it therefore presupposes man's readiness, his unreserved spontaneity, for the Presence. Cf. TH 1: 289. The Maggid of Konitz once prayed: "Lord, I stand before you like a messenger boy, and wait for you to tell me where to go."

195. Ibid., p. 134 *(I and Thou* 131).

196. Ibid., pp. 135–36 (134–35). Cf. Hans Jonas, *The Gnostic Religion,* p. 61, on the Gnostic idea of "restoring the Unity." "The universal (metaphysical) and the individual (mystical) aspects of the idea of unity" meet in the "action-patterns of each soul's potential experience, and unification within *is* union with the One."

197. Ibid., pp. 137–38 (136). According to a certain Upanishad, Indra, the prince of gods, came to Pradshapati, the creative spirit, to learn how to find the Self. After centuries of apprenticeship he received the right information: "When one rests bounded in deep dreamless sleep, this is the Self, this is the immortal, the secured, the All-being!" When Indra protested that in such a situation there is no distinction between the I and the beings, no knowledge of one's self, as it sinks into annihilation, Pradshapati retorted: "This, my Lord, is exactly the situation." Cf. Walter Stace, *The Teachings of the Mystics,* pp. 33–34. Uddalaka says to his son Svetaketu: "In the beginning there was Existence alone—One only, without a second. . . . Out of himself he projected the universe. . . . All that is has its self in him alone. . . . He is the truth. He is the Self. And that, Svetaketu, that art thou."

198. Immanuel Kant, *Kritik der reinen Vernunft,* "Kritik aller Theologie," p. 596.

199. *Werke* 1: 145 *(I and Thou* 147–48).

200. *Der Jude und sein Judentum,* p. 204 (I&W 32).

201. *Werke* 1: 145 *(I and Thou* 148).

202. Ibid., p. 147 (150).

203. Ibid., p. 148 (151).

204. The influence of the ontological argument for the existence of God, from its prototype in Augustine to its modifications in Anselm and Descartes, has reached through the ages into our own modes of thinking and our orientation in reality. Cf. Johannes Hessen, *Augustins Metaphysik der Erkenntnis,* "Die Geschichte des augus-

tinischen Gottesbeweises," pp. 135–70.

205. *Werke* 1: 166 (*I and Thou* 178): "Everything tells you that full mutuality is not inherent in men's life with each other. It is a grace for which one must always be prepared and which one can never be sure of attaining."

206. *Der Jude und sein Judentum,* pp. 191–92 (I&W 18).

207. *Werke* 1: 154 (*I and Thou* 160).

208. I&W 27.

209. EG 74–75.

210. *Nachlese,* pp. 108–109 (BH 113–14). There is no other revelation but the meeting of Divine and human, in which the human actually takes part. "We cannot therefore understand anything that issues from the factual revelation directly or indirectly (be it through written or oral tradition). . . . There is nothing but the certainty that we take part in the revelation."

211. *Werke* 1, "Die Zeichen," p. 183 (BMM 11).

212. Ibid. (10).

213. Ibid., "Wer redet?" p. 188 (BMM 15): "When we emerge out of it [the night of confrontation] into the new life and there begin to receive the signs, what can we know of that which—of the one who gives them to us?"

214. EG 15: "This is true of those moments of our daily life in which we become aware of the reality that is absolutely independent of us, whether it be as power or as glory, no less than of the hours of great revelation of which only a halting record has been handed down to us."

215. *Werke* 1, "Elemente des Zwischenmenschlichen," p. 283 (KnM 84).

216. Kant, *Introduction to Logic,* p. 15.

217. *Werke* 1: 309 (BMM 118). Cf. Kant, *Anthropologie.*

218. Buber regards this proposition as a misconception of a theological interpretation of the biblical account of creation. CF. *Werke* 1: 388 (BMM 188).

219. *Werke* 1: 133 (*I and Thou* 130).

220. Ibid., p. 230 (BMM 52).

221. Ibid., pp. 157–60 (*I and Thou* 165–68). Cf. OMH 117, on the Hasidic idea of the "value of human action, the influence of the acting man on the destiny of the universe, even on its guiding forces."

222. Ibid., p. 170 (182).

223. Ibid., p. 169 (181).

224. Ibid., pp. 169–70 (181–82). The question whether relation may be attributed to God without contradicting His unity and perfection, i.e., without relativizing Him, was raised by Maimonides. His answer was that "relation" as applied to God must be understood as God acting relative to His creatures but not as being acted on by them. Cf. *The Guide for the Perplexed,* part 1, chaps. 52–53.

225. Ibid.

226. Ralph T. Flewelling, "Personalism," in *Twentieth Century Philosophy,* ed. Dagobert D. Runes, p. 324.

227. William Stern, "Selbsdarstellung," in *Die Philosophie der Gegenwart in Selbstdarstellungen,* p. 162.

228. *Werke* 2: 410 (PF 164–65). In the Jewish way of thinking, the concept "person" is not applicable to God, for logically it leads to a trinitarian view, as in the case of Christianity, which is grounded in this concept. Buber tried his best to circumvent this difficulty by applying the term "person" to the divine Absolute only indirectly and very cautiously.

229. I&W 51.

230. EG 127.

231. *Werke* 1: 158 (*I and Thou* 166–67): "Even though we, earthly beings, never look at God without the world, but only look at the world in God, yet as we look we form eternally God's countenance [*Gottes Gestalt*]."

232. *The Philosophy of Martin Buber,* p. 689.

Part II. Judaism: A Living Experience of Relation

Introduction

233. *Der Jude und sein Judentum,* "An der Wende," p. 144; "Die vierte Rede," p. 173. This volume will henceforth be referred to as J&J *(On Judaism).*

234. Ibid., p. 165.

235. Ibid., pp. 172, 173 *(On Judaism* 212, 215).

236. Cf. *Werke* 3, "Mein Weg zum Chassidismus," p. 962 (HMM 24, 50).

237. J&J, "Der Glaube des Judentums," p. 190 (I&W 16). See p. 558, on the word "Israel" in preference to "Judaism."

238. OMH 22.

239. *The Philosophy of Martin Buber,* p. 701. See also pp. 691, 694, 744, on the ontological core of dialogue.

240. *Werke* 1: 1113, on the theologoumena of religion, and J&J, p. 187: "What I thus seek to formulate is theologoumena of a folk religion." Cf. I&W 13, on "theological concepts" and "nontheological material from which I drew those concepts."

241. *The Philosophy of Martin Buber,* p. 729. See also pp. 639, 703.

242. Ibid., p. 744.

243. Ibid., p. 731: "The tapestry, which my work is seen as, 'is woven of elective strands.' . . . I have not made use of a filter; I became a filter." See pp. 732, 737. Selecting from Jewish sources and interpreting according to his own experiences and insights was the method used by Philo in his allegorical exegesis of the Bible, especially as he tried to make Scripture fit into Greek philosophical concepts. Cf. Hans Lewy, *Three Jewish Philosophers,* p. 16, on Philo's "right of selection." In modern times, the same method was used by Nachman Krochmal in his *Moreh Nebuchei Hazman,* as he selected from biblical sources only what he regarded as necessary for his interpretation of the cyclical process of Jewish history (but not the history of the Jewish people). Cf. *Kitvei Rabbi Nachman Krochmal* (The writings of Rabbi Nachman Krochmal). Edited with Introduction by Simon Rawidowicz. Editor's Introduction, pp. 125–26.

244. *Werke* 2: 1095, 1096. Cf. *The Philosophy of Martin Buber,* James Muilenburg, "Buber as an Interpreter of the Bible," pp. 383–84, and "Replies to My Critics," p. 726.

245. *Werke* 2: 242 (PF 6).

246. J. Fang, *Hilbert,* p. 100.

247. *Moses,* Preface, p. 9.

248. *Werke* 2, "Der Glaube der Propheten," Vorwort, p. 235. This Foreword is not given in the translation, *The Prophetic Faith,* first published in 1949. It is also missing in the First Harper Torchbook Edition, 1960.

249. *The Philosophy of Martin Buber,* p. 726.

250. KG 17.

251. *Werke* 2: 13 *(Moses* 8).

252. Ibid., p. 19 (16).

253. Ibid.

254. Ibid., p. 117 (102).

255. Ibid., p. 18 (15).

256. *Werke* 2, "Die Sprache der Botschaft," pp. 1096, 1095.

257. Ibid., pp. 1096–97.

258. *Moses* 14.

259. CF. J&J, pp. 141, 142, on intuition as a reliable vehicle for selecting, sifting, and interpreting the Bible *(On Judaism* 172–73).

260. Cf. *Werke* 2: 719–20 (TTF 92), on "the *Lishma* doctrine."

261. Cf. *Werke* 2, Vorwort, p. 7, and J&J, "Eine Rede über Jugend und Religion," p. 141 *(On Judaism* 172).

262. Cf. Eisik Hirsch Weiss, *Dor Dor Vedorshav* (Hebrew), vol. 1, chapter 1.

263. J&J, "Pharisäertum," pp. 226, 227–28.

264. Ibid., p. 228: "Damage was done to Judaism not by Pharisaism becoming overdominant, but by its decay." A similar view of present-day rabbinic halakha is expressed by Eliezer Berkovits, who calls for a "return to the original halakhah, to rediscover it, and having rediscovered it, to restore it to its original function . . . for the sake of which God concluded this covenant of mutuality with Israel." "Halakhah in its original strength," he continues, "could solve such problems . . . that may be raised for Judaism in a modern state. . . . Halakhah in its present straightjacketed state cannot fulfill that function." See his article "Conversion 'According to Halakhah'—What Is it?" *Judaism*, Fall 1974, p. 478.

265. KG, Preface to First Edition, pp. 13–14.

266. Buber delivered his first "Three Speeches on Judaism" in 1909–1911, followed by other speeches in 1912–1914 and 1918, dealing with various aspects of the Jewish problematic, as will be discussed below.

267. J&J, "Der Glaube des Judentums," p. 190 (I&W 16). Cf. *Werke* 1: 297–98.

268. Cf. *Werke* 3, "Mein Weg zum Chassidismus," p. 965 (HMM 55). Cf. my book *An Analytical Interpretation of Martin Buber's "I and Thou," "Encounter with the Outside,"* and "Return to the Fold," pp. 5–10.

269. J&J, "Das Gestaltende: Nach einer Ansprache (1912)," p. 241.

270. Ibid., p. 243.

271. Ibid., p. 240, on the primal struggle between form and matter, "between the forming and the formless principles, . . . which goes on as an eternal process throughout the history of the spirit."

272. Ibid., p. 10 *(On Judaism* 12).

273. In his introductory remarks to his first three speeches on Judaism, Buber wrote: "These speeches . . . were spoken by a Jew to Jews, directed principally at a circle of young persons, out of an impulse of the most subjective mutual experience and in a sphere of the most intimate influence." *Drei Reden über das Judentum,* 1916, p. 7. First published in 1911.

274. *The Philosophy of Martin Buber,* pp. 717–18.

275. PW 157. In the biblical history of the Jewish people Buber differentiates five types of leaders, according to the different situations in which they exercised their leadership. Their common feature is that they aimed at certain goals, did not lead to successful achievement, but rather led the way. Cf. *Werke* 2, "Biblisches Führertum," p. 903. (I&W 119).

276. I&W 138.

277. BMM 110.

278. *Werke* 1: 1111 *(The Philosophy of Martin Buber* 689. See 690: "I am not merely bound to philosophical language, I am bound to philosophical method.")

279. There are altogether twelve "Speeches on Judaism" which Buber delivered on various occasions and published under different titles. The first three were published as *Drei Reden über das Judentum* (Frankfurt a/M, 1916). The next three were issued together with the first set and with "Der heilige Weg" and "Heruth" in a collection *Reden über das Judentum* (Frankfurt a/M, 1923). The last four were published as *An der Wende–Reden über das Judentum* (Köln, 1952).

Chapter 4

280. J&J, p. 279.

281. Ibid., p. 11 *(On Judaism* 13).

282. Ibid., p. 16.

283. This rationale of the existence of the Jewish people is worked out by Buber in his second speech on Judaism, "Das Judentum und die Menschheit," J&J, pp. 18–27 *(On Judaism* 22–23). Cf. ibid., Robert Weltsch, "Einleitung," p. xl. "Immer ist bei ihm Judentum und Menschentum eins" ("Judaism and humanity are always one for him").

284. J&J, p. 26 *(On Judaism* 32).

285. Ibid., p. 34 (42).
286. Ibid., p. 41 (50).
287. Buber regards early Christianity, in distinction from later Christianity, as imbued with Jewish religiosity.
288. J&J, pp. 45–46 (*On Judaism* 53–55).
289. *Daniel: Gespräche von der Verwirklichung.* In a letter to Buber (September 22, 1911), Hans Kohn raised some doubts about the realization of the three tendencies in Judaism and he hoped that the book (most likely *Daniel*) which Buber had promised to write would clear them up. See Martin Buber, *Briefwechsel aus sieben Jahrzehnten* 1: 299–300.
290. Ibid., "First Conversation," pp. 18–19.
291. *Werke* 1: 1030 (PW 38).
292. Cf. J&J, p. 53: "All that I have said about the Oriental applies to the Jew with particular distinctness."
293. *Werke* 1: pp. 1026, 1040, 1042 (PW 34, 48, 50).
294. J&J, p. 23 (*On Judaism* 28). Cf. ibid, p. 53, on the Jewish sense of realization of the I in contrast to the Chinese, Indian, and Persian concepts.
295. *The Philosophy of Martin Buber*, p. 721: "The call to 'realization' and 'deed' . . . fills the pages of . . . my early writings." Cf. Hugo Bergmann, *Hogé Hador* (Hebrew), p. 188: "Buber derived the basic vision of his philosophy, the unity-duality, from Judaism. There is no doubt that the culmination of his philosophy, namely, God as the ever-present Thou, contains the Jewish view of God. . . . On the other hand, from his philosophy Buber interprets Judaism, for he does not see Israel's great contribution to the world to be the belief in unity, but its message that God is one to whom it is possible to say Thou." Cf. OMH 91.
296. J&J, p. 69 (*On Judaism* 83).
297. Ibid., p. 4 (4–5).
298. Ibid. p. 56 (67). On Buber's concept of decision see *Werke* 1: 191, 208–10 (BMM 18, 34–36); *Werke* 2: 984 (G&E 51).
299. Ibid., p. 57 (69).
300. Ibid., p. 65 (79).
301. Ibid., pp. 69–70 (84–85). Cf. *Sifra on Leviticus* ("Holiness" 174): "Holy. You shall be separated unto me. If you sanctify yourselves I shall consider it as if you sanctified me, and if you don't sanctify yourselves I shall consider it as if you didn't sanctify me."
302. Ibid., p. 72 (87).
303. Ibid., p. 73 (88).
304. Ibid., p. 66 (80).
305. Ibid., p. 78 (94).
306. Ibid., p. 46 (55): To fulfill "the tendency of the future . . . in our personal life . . . we must loosen our soul from the drive for purposes [*Zwecke*] and direct it toward the goal [*Ziel*], so that it may be capable of serving the future." Cf. ibid., pp. 10–11 (11–12): "Where is there a godly fervor of Jews that would chase them out of the social drives after purpose into a genuine life, into a life that *bears witness* to God?" Cf. "China and Us," PW 124: "We have begun to learn . . . that success is of no consequence, . . . i.e., the validity of the man who sets an end for himself, carries this end into effect, accumulates the necessary means of power and succeeds with these means of power: the typical modern Western man." Cf. *Nachlese*, p. 211.
307. Ibid., p. 82 (99).
308. Ibid., p. 78 (95).
309. Ibid., pp. 84–85 (103).
310. Ibid., p. 88 (106).
311. Cf. ibid., p. 203 (I&W 30), "Die Brennpunkte der jüdischen Seele." One center of the Jewish soul is "the primal experience that God is entirely transcendent to man, is entirely beyond his grasp."
312. Ibid., p. 77 (92).
313. Ibid., Vorrede, p. 4.

Chapter 5

314. In the English translation *On Judaism,* the 1923 collection of speeches (called in the original "Die frühen Reden") are called "The Early Addresses (1909–1918)" and the 1951 collection (called in the original "An der Wende (1951)") are called "The Later Addresses (1939–1951)."

315. *Werke* 2: "Zum Abschluss," p. 1175.

316. *Werke* 1, "Zur Geschichte des dialogischen Prinzips," pp. 297–98 (BMM 215). The idea of I-Thou relation took hold of Buber much earlier, in 1905, when he absorbed the Hasidic tradition into his own mode of thinking (ibid., p. 297).

317. *Werke* 1, Nachwort, p. 161 (*I and Thou,* Afterword, 171).

318. Ibid., p. 299 (BMM 216ff.).

319. See my book *An Analytical Interpretation of Martin Buber's "I and Thou,"* chaps. 25, 26, 33, and 35.

320. *Werke* 1: 188 (BMM 15).

321. J&J, p. 90 *(On Judaism* 110).

322. Ibid., pp. 91–93 (112–17).

323. Ibid., p. 109 (133). The term "Israel" means here Judaism or the Jewish people. Buber often uses the word "Israel" in this sense, in preference to the word "Judaism." See above, note 237.

324. Ibid., p. 114 (139).

325. Ibid., p. 121 (146–47). Buber regarded the Labor Zionist pioneer and philosopher A. D. Gordon, who promulgated the principle of "religion of labor," as "A Bearer of the Realization." Cf. ibid., p. 456 (I&P 154).

326. *Nachlese,* p. 157 (BH 152).

327. *Werke* 1: 180 (BMM 7).

Chapter 6

328. *Werke* 1: 1114 (*The Philosophy of Martin Buber,* p. 693).

329. Ibid., p. 1111 (689).

330. J&J, p. 187 (I&W 13).

331. Ibid., p. 188. See above, "Ontology without Metaphysics" section. Cf. Über Religionswissenschaft," *Nachlese,* p. 124 (BH 127). Cf. *The Philosophy of Martin Buber,* p. 690: "The theological element . . . is the foundation of my thinking, but not as a derivative of anything traditional, as important as that also may be to me. It has, therefore, not been to 'theology,' but rather to the experience of faith that I owe the independence of my thought."

332. Ibid., p. 241.

333. Ibid., p. 167 (*On Judaism,* p. 207).

334. Ibid., p. 175 (216).

335. Ibid. Cf. *Werke* 2: 910, I&W 127, 138, 169, 250, *Moses* 105, PF 88, 102, 233.

336. Ibid., pp. 147–48 (I&W 186–87).

337. I&W 78–79.

338. Ibid., p. 82.

339. *Werke* 1: 657–58 (TTF 13). Cf. J&J 241.

340. *Werke* 2, "Geschehende Geschichte," pp. 1033–36. Cf. "Plato and Isaiah," I&W 104, 111.

341. J&J, p. 169 (*On Judaism* 209).

342. *Werke* 2: 456 (PF 208). See ibid., p. 378. Buber says the Second Isaiah shaped it into a monotheistic theology of world history.

343. See above, note 341. Cf. PW 112, on the realization of the goal "here and now," not in the beyond or in the distant future.

344. *Werke* 2: 378 (PF 135).

345. Ibid., p. 380 (137).

346. Ibid., pp. 378, 380 (135, 136).

347. J&J, p. 91 (*On Judaism* 111). This is in keeping with the Talmudic dictum: "Rabbi Yohanan said, 'The son of David will not come but in a generation that is either totally innocent or totally guilty' " (Sanhedrin 98a).

348. Ibid., p. 176 (218). Cf. *Werke* 2: 471, 478 (PF 223, 230), on this verse and other passages dealing with "God's servant." The standard translation is "Thou art my servant, Israel, in whom I will be glorified," which is interpreted to mean that Isaiah himself represented here the ideal Israel. Cf. *Isaiah* (London: Soncino Press, 1949). The same meaning is given by the biblical commentator "Metzudat David." Buber, too, surmises that Isaiah "saw himself at one point on the way," that is, the servant's way. Cf. Yoma 86a: "Whoever studies the Torah, if his ways are right and his deeds wholehearted, Scripture says of him, 'Thou art my servant, Israel, in whom I am glorified.' "

349. Cf. Sanhedrin 99a: "Rabbi Hiyya bar Abba said in the name of Rabbi Yohanan, 'All the prophets together did not prophesy but for the days of the Messiah.' "

350. *Werke* 2: 482 (PF 233). The reference is to Isaiah 44:2, "Jeshurun whom I have chosen," and 42:19, "Who is as blind as Meshullam and as blind as the servant of God?" Cf. ibid., pp. 480–81. Meshullam is called blind and deaf because he does not yet feel he is ready to serve.

351. Cf. Sanhedrin 99a: "Rabbi Hillel says, 'Israel has no Messiah.' " Rashi comments: "For The Holy One blessed be He will rule, and He alone will redeem them."

352. *Werke* 2: 481, 483 (PF 232, 234).

353. J&J, p. 17 (*On Judaism* 19–20).

354. *Werke* 3: 114 (TH 2, Introduction, 9).

355. On the catastrophe that befell the Jewish communities in the Ukraine in 1648–1649 see S. M. Dubnow, *History of the Jews in Russia and Poland* 1: 144.

356. *Werke* 3: 754 (OMH 107–108).

357. Ibid., p. 755 (109).

358. OMH, Author's Foreword, p. 22. Cf. HMM 27. See *Werke* 3: 741: "Ich spreche sie als solche gegen seinen Willen aus, weil die Welt ihrer heute sehr bedarf" ("I speak [of the Hasidic message], as such, against the will [of the Hasidim to speak to the world], because the world needs it today very much").

359. *Werke* 3: 936–37 and Vorwort (HMM 24).

360. Ibid., p. 88 (TH 1: 11). Cf. J&J, pp. 108, 278, 299–300. Cf. Gershom G. Scholem, *Major Trends in Jewish Mysticism*, pp. 325–26: "Hasidism as a living phenomenon is still with us. For all its decay it remains a living force in the lives of countless thousands of our people. . . . Beneath the superficial peculiarities of Hasidic life there subsists a stratum of positive value."

361. Ibid., p. 937 (HMM 26). Cf. OMH 27; *The Philosophy of Martin Buber*, p. 739; and Scholem, *Major Trends*, p. 326: "Among the factors which have made Hasidic writings more easily accessible to the layman . . . [is] their fondness for epigrams or aphorisms."

362. Ibid., p. 946 (41). Cf. Scholem, *Major Trends*, p. 338: "The new element [in Hasidism] must therefore not be sought on the theoretical and literary plane, but rather in the experience of an inner revival, in the spontaneity of feeling generated in sensitive minds by the encounter with the living incarnations of mysticism." "Classical Hasidism was not the product of some theory or other, not even of a Kabbalistic doctrine, but of direct, spontaneous religious experience" (p. 347). "In the place of the theoretical disquisition, or at least side by side with it, you get the Hasidic tale" (p. 349).

363. Ibid., p. 743 (OMH 92). Note: The opening sentence in this essay in the English translation, p. 90, should read "Twenty-three years before the Baal-Shem-Tov was born" instead of "Thirty-two years," etc. Spinoza died in 1677 and the Baal-Shem-Tov was born in 1700.

364. Ibid., p. 742 (91).

365. Ibid., p. 745 (95–96).
366. OMH 83 and 29.
367. *Werke* 3: 804 (OMH 115).
368. Ibid., p. 805 (117).
369. *Werke* 1, 596, 602–603 (EG 125, 136). See *Werke* 3: 806, n. 1 (OMH 119 note). Cf. *The Philosophy of Martin Buber*, pp. 716–17. Cf. Hans Jonas, *The Gnostic Religion*, pp. 34–35.
370. *Werke* 3: 844–45, 846 (OMH 175, 178). Cf. J&J, pp. 194–97 (I&W 21–24).
371. This is the gist of Buber's view of gnosis and the Hasidic reaction to it. Again, we must bear in mind that Buber selected certain aspects of gnosis which he found in Kabbalah but unacceptable according to his interpretation of the Hasidic concept of mutuality of relation. There are other gnostic views which also recognize mutuality of knowledge between man and God, although Buber would not accept their connotation of knowledge as such. Cf. Jonas, *Gnostic Religion*, p. 34.
372. See Scholem, *Major Trends*, p. 265, on the doctrine of *Adam Kadmon* as "a first configuration of the divine light which flows . . . into the primeval space of the *Tsimtsum*."
373. *Werke* 3: 809 (OMH 122–23).
374. J&J, p. 196 (I&W 24).
375. Cf. *The Philosophy of Martin Buber*, pp. 736, 737, 744. Cf. Scholem, *Major Trends*, pp. 315–16, on the Sabbatian-Kabbalistic teaching of entering sin in order to overcome it, and the extreme form it took in Frankism, which preached and practiced libertinism similar to the Carpocratian gnostics.
376. *Werke* 3: 809 (OMH 123).
377. On the social and religious background of the Hasidic movement see Salo W. Baron, *A Social and Religious History of the Jews* (1937) 2: 153–62. Cf. Simon Dubnow, *Toldot Hahasidut* (Hebrew) 1, Introduction.
378. On the conflict between the Hasidim and the Mitnagdim see Dubnow, *Toldot Hahasidut*, chap. 3.
379. HMM 127. Cf. *Werke* 3: 939, 940, 944–46 (HMM 31, 38–40): J&J, p. 72.
380. *The Philosophy of Martin Buber*, p. 737.
381. *Werke* 3: 828 (OMH 149). Cf. HMM, "The Life of the Hasidim,"
382. How the zaddik of Lublin got his name "Seer," see *For the Sake of Heaven*, p. 4, TH 1: 32, 303 ("His Gaze"). On the name "Yehudi," see FSH 20, TH 2: 33, 227 ("Elija"). In the German original, the book FSH is entitled *Gog und Magog: Eine Chronik (Werke* 3: 1001), which is more appropriate to the description of the events concerning the legends of the Messiah.
383. Cf. Joseph Klausner, *The Messianic Idea in Israel*, pp. 127–32, 375–76, 496–501.
384. By a system of Kabbalistic calculations the Seer arranged the celebration of a given Passover Seder in meticulous detail, each step to be taken at a specified moment, in precise order and manner, according to his instructions. All his followers and adherents, including the Yehudi, who was then the Rebbe in Pshysha, were to perform the Seder as directed by the Seer, so that all together they would bring about the victory of the Napoleonic armies in Russia. But something went wrong in Pshysha and the scheme failed throughout. The story concludes: "It was on the day after that Pesah night that Napoleon Bonaparte set forth from Paris upon that decisive campaign which put an end to his dominion." See FSH, "A *Seder* That Went Wrong," pp. 270–76.
385. Cf. Klausner, *Messianic Idea*, part 3, "Messiah Son of Joseph and the War with Gog and Magog," pp. 483–50.
386. OMH 109. This explains the title of the book, *For the Sake of Heaven*.
387. FSH 103.
388. *Werke* 2: 483 (PF 234).
389. Cf. *The Philosophy of Martin Buber*, p. 741, on "The mystery of the death of the 'holy Yehudi.' "
390. In Hasidic lore, the mystic act of forcing Heaven to reveal its secrets, when

performed outside of the Holy Land, is fraught with mortal danger. Few have tried it in the diaspora and remained alive. Thus it is related of the Baal-Shem-Tov that his pupil, the son of the mysterious Rabbi Adam, whom he had instructed in Kabbalah, persistently implored him to bring down the Angel of the Torah to reveal the secret of a particularly difficult passage. The Baal-Shem-Tov yielded twice. The first time, as a warning, the village was consumed by the Angel's fire. The second time, while the Baal-Shem-Tov managed to survive, his disciple died on the spot. Cf. *Shivhei HaBesht* (Hebrew), ed. S. A. Horodetsky, p. 16.

391. *Werke* 3, "Gog und Magog," p. 1233 (FSH 285). There are many striking similarities between the life and death of the Yehudi and those of Jesus, as Buber portrays them. He places them both within the panorama of the Jewish history of faith and, as we shall see later, he considers Jesus, too, as a suffering Messiah son of Joseph.

392. Cf. J&J, pp. 69, 77, 108, 299–300 *(On Judaism* 83, 92, 131–32, 184).

393. Ibid., p. 64 (77).

394. Ibid., p. 110 (134).

395. Ibid., p. 279.

396. Ibid., p. 705.

397. Ibid., p. 114.

398. Ibid., p. 706. Cf. pp. 260–61.

399. *Werke* 3: 966 (HMM 57).

400. J&J., "Rede auf dem xvi. Zionisten-Kongress in Basel" (1929), p. 521. Cf. I&W 214.

401. *Werke* 2: 1074 (I&W 203). Buber shows there how the idea of a deified absolute nation is presented with regard to "Holy Russia" in Dostoevsky's *The Possessed*.

402. Ibid., p. 1078 (I&W 207). Cf. I&P, Introduction, pp. 30–35; J&J, p. 318.

403. *Werke*, "Noch ein Experiment," pp. 981–92 (PU, "An Experiment that did not Fail," 139). Cf. J&J, p. 332, on the task of Jewish settlement in Eretz Israel.

404. J&J, p. 63 *(On Judaism* 76).

405. Ibid., p. 348. Cf. "Die Gegebenheiten für eine grossarabische Politik," *Die zionistische Bewegung*, by Adolf Böhm 2: 161.

406. Enzo Sereni, "Towards a New Orientation of Zionist Policy," *Jews and Arabs in Palestine*, p. 267. See ibid., "Problems of Jewish-Arab Rapproachment," by Moses Beilinson, and my "Summary" at the end of the book. Cf. my article "Jews, Arabs and Zionists in the Middle East," *The Jewish News* (Neward, N.J.) September 20, 1973.

407. KnM 176.

408. J&J, p. 331, and "From an Open Letter to Gandhi," I&W 227.

409. Ibid., p. 542.

410. Cf. Böhm, *Zionistische Bewegung*, 2: 295, n.2. Cf. *Towards Union in Palestine*, ed. M. Buber, J. L. Magnes, E. Simon; "Our Reply," by Martin Buber, p. 33.

411. J&J, pp. 732–33 (I&W 240–41).

412. Ibid., pp. 742–43 (251).

413. Ibid., p. 743 (252).

414. *Werke* 1: 657 (TTF 12).

415. Ibid.

416. *Werke* 3: 954 (OMH 247).

417. *Werke* 1: 726–27 (TTF 102–03), on the nature of the hypothesis of this argument.

418. Ibid., p. 656 (11).

419. On faith as a state of relation see BMM 12. Cf. EG 3, 126. On the meaning of the terms "contact" and "communication" in connection with this relation, see *The Philosophy of Martin Buber*, p. 705. See above, note 5.

420. *Werke* 1: 654 (TTF 8).

421. Ibid., pp. 669–70 (28–29).

422. Cf. Paul Tillich, *Perspectives on 19th and 20th Century Protestant Theology*, p. 223: "This is the classical formula of liberal theology: the gospel or message preached by Jesus contains nothing of the later message preached concerning Jesus." Tillich's own

view is "that the whole New Testament is unified, including the first three Gospels, in the statement that Jesus is the Christ, the bringer of the new aeon." Buber, it appears, has much in common with Adolf von Harnack on the subject of the gospel of Jesus and about Jesus, and with Albrecht Ritschl in interpreting Jesus as the "prophet" of man's self-realization in its communal aspect. Cf. Karl Barth, *Die protestantische Theologie im 19. Jahrhundert,* pp. 598–605.

423. J&J, p. 151 *(On Judaism* 167). Note: The English translation reads, "The unity of the Hebrew Scripture and the Gospel." The German original does not mention "the Gospel." It reads, "die Einheit der hebräischen Heiligen Schrift aufrecht erhalten."

424. TTF 17 n.1, 59 n.1, 18 n.1.

425. The existence of an Aramaic Ur-gospel which may have served as a common source for the gospels of Matthew, Mark, and Luke, was first suggested in a casual remark by Gotthold Ephraim Lessing in 1778. Cf. William R. Farmer, *The Synoptic Problem,* pp. 3f. See ibid., p. 15, on Friedrich Schleiermacher's Logia or a collection of Jesus' original sayings by Matthew, on the basis of which the latter wrote his Gospel.

426. *Werke* 1: 737 (TTF 115). Cf. *Werke* 3: 953–54 (OMH, Supplement, 246).

427. Ibid., p. 666 (24–25).

428. My quotations from the New Testament are from the Revised Standard Version, except where I quote Buber's German rendition in the English translation in his book TTF.

429. *Werke* 1: pp. 668–70 (TTF 27–29).

430. Ibid., p. 661, 663–64 (18, 20–21).

431. Ibid., p. 676 (37).

432. It is generally agreed among New Testament scholars that the Epistle to the Hebrews was not written by Paul. There is a view that its author was an Alexandrian Jew by the name Apollos. Cf. F. W. Farrar, *The Early Days of Christianity,* p. 167. It is of interest to note that recently (1963) the Reverend Andrew Q. Morton, a minister of The Church of Scotland who is also a mathematician, concluded from a computerized analysis of the original Greek of all the fourteen epistles which are attributed to Paul that only five of them (Rom. I & II, Cor., Gal., and Phil.) can be authenticated as coming from his hand. The other nine were written by at least five different authors. Cf. "Cleric Asserts Computer Proves Paul Wrote Only 5 of 14 Epistles," by Lawrence Fellows, *The New York Times,* November 7, 1963, pp. 1 & 13.

433. I&W 104, 111, on the "era of history which refutes 'history.' "

434. *Werke* 1: 692 (TTF 58).

435. Ibid., p. 695 (61–62). Buber refers to Sota 22b. It says there that the Rabbis taught that there were seven kinds of Pharisees who claimed to be following the Pharisaic manner of learning the Torah, but who were only simulating it. King Alexander Janai (second century), who persecuted the Pharisees, said to his wife, who had asked him to make peace with them lest they retaliate after his death: "Fear not the Pharisees or those who are not Pharisees, but only the painted ones who simulate the Pharisees."

436. Ibid.

437. Ibid., p. 693 (60).

438. Cf. ibid., p. 694. In the biblical reference, the Hebrew word for "whole" and "wholehearted" is *tamim.* Buber refers to Sabbath 133b. There we read: "Abba Shaul says, *v'anvehu* [Exod. 15:2, "This is my God and I will *glorify* Him"], be like Him: as He is merciful and gracious, so be you merciful and gracious." Rashi comments on the word *anvehu:* "It is like the words *ani* (I) *v'hu* (and He), I will make myself like Him to search his ways."

439. Ibid., p. 696 (63).

440. KG, Preface to the First Edition, p. 14.

441. TTF 76, in connection with Jesus' statement "Love your enemies," which is also taught in the Torah and the Talmud.

442. Ibid., p. 99: "In point of fact every true *reformatio* intends precisely that which found its strongest expression in the sayings of Jesus which begin with 'But I say unto you': to return to the original purity of the revelation."

443. *Werke* 1: 728.

444. Rudolf Bultmann, *History and Eschatology*, p. 31.

445. *Werke* 1: 731 (TTF 107).

446. *Werke* 3: 755 (OMH 109–10). This type is portrayed as the Yehudi in *For the Sake of Heaven.*

447. Ibid. Cf. Sanhedrin 97b: "Perish those who calculate the End, because they might say that since the End is due and he did not arrive, he would never come."

448. OMH 250. Maurice Friedman notes: "This does not mean that Martin Buber thinks that Jesus himself necessarily saw himself as the Messiah, though he did stand under the shadow of the Deutero-Isaianic servant of the Lord" (ibid. 110).

449. *Werke* 3: 957 (OMH 251).

450. TTF 108–09. Buber considers the High Priest's question, "Are you the Christ, the son of the Blessed?" and Jesus' answer, "I am," etc. (Mark 14:61–62) as inauthentic.

451. Cf. Sukkah 52a: "There will be mourning over Messiah son of Joseph who will be killed [in the war with Gog and Magog (Rashi)]. . . . God said to the Messiah son of David, 'Ask whatever you want of me and I will give it to you.' . . . When [the latter] saw that Messiah son of Joseph would be killed, he said, 'O Creator of the Universe, I ask of you nothing but life.' " There was also the belief of a Messiah son of Joseph among the Samaritans, who called him Taëb, meaning "he who returns" or "he who causes to return." He was regarded by them as a prophet who will restore the true law to its original meaning. Buber's conception of Jesus' messiahship fits this description—the restorer of the original intent of the Torah—though not as the Samaritans understood it. Cf. Klausner, *Messianic Idea*, p. 484. See above, note 442.

452. *Werke* 3: 956 (OMH 250–51). Cf. Joseph Klausner, *Historia Shel Habayit Hasheni* (Hebrew) 4: 265–66. While "Jesus was regarded as a Jew and not a Christian" (quoting Wellhausen), Klausner says, there was enough in his religious teachings that was contrary to Jewish tradition, and that served as a basis for the Christian idea of the Messiah.

453. J&J, p. 642 (PW, "Letter to Gandhi," p. 146). The specific reference is with regard to Jesus' teaching not to resist evil. "For I cannot have myself forbidden to resist evil," says Buber, "when I see it is about to destroy good."

454. *Werke* 3: 755, 955–56 (OMH 109, 249). Cf. Franz Freiherr von Hammerstein, *Das Messiasproblem bei Martin Buber*, p. 66. "Buber . . . has tried to set a course of religious dialogue in which both partners take each other in earnest. . . . He has tried first of all to understand his partner and to be understood by him."

455. Quoted by Franz von Hammerstein, *Das Messiasproblem*, p. 49, from a letter by Martin Buber to the Völkerversöhnungsbund (E.V.), one of the short-lived Jewish-Christian societies in Hamburg, dated July 16, 1926. The letter was printed by the society in its publication *Höre Israel!* no. 1, and again in no. 2. See ibid., p. 99 n.1. Cf. J&J, p. 210 (I&W 39). "We sense [*spüren*] redemption happening; and we notice [*verspüren*] the unredeemed world. No redeemer has appeared to us at a given point in history so that with him a new redeemed history began."

456. J&J, p. 211 (I&W 39).

457. Ibid., p. 197 (25). 458. Ibid., p. 153 (*On Judaism* 190): *Werke* 1: p. 180 (BMM 7).

458. Ibid., p. 153 (*On Judaism* 190); *Werke* 1: 180 (BMM 7).

Bibliography

This is only a selected bibliography. For a comprehensive listing of works by Martin Buber and about him in several languages the reader is referred to the following four sources:

A Bibliography of Martin Buber's Works. Compiled by Moshe Katanne. Jerusalem: Bialik Institute, 1958. Annotated in Hebrew.

"Bibliography of the Writings of Martin Buber." Compiled by Maurice Friedman. *The Philosophy of Martin Buber*. Edited by Paul Arthur Schilpp and Maurice Friedman. LaSalle, Ill: Open Court, 1967. The Library of Living Philosophers, vol. 12, pp. 747–86.

Kohn, Hans. *Martin Buber: Sein Werk und seine Zeit*. Köln: Joseph Melzer Verlag. Dritte Auflage, 1961. Nachtrag zur Bibliographiê, pp. 480–84.

Friedman, Maurice S. *Martin Buber: The Life of Dialogue*. Chicago: The University of Chicago Press, 1955. Bibliography, pp. 283–98.

Buber's Collected Works

A complete collection of essays and works which Buber chose for inclusion is several volumes is comprised in the following publications. (See his "Nachwort" in *Nachlese*, p. 261.)

Werke. München und Heidelberg: Kösel-Verlag und Verlag Lambert Schneider.
    Erster Band. *Schriften zur Philosophie*, 1962, 1128 pp.
    Zweiter Band. *Schriften zur Bibel*, 1964, 1229 pp.
    Dritter Band. *Schriften zum Chassidismus*, 1963, 1270 pp.

Der Jude und sein Judentum. Köln: Joseph Melzer Verlag, 1963, 837 pp.

Nachlese. Heidelberg: Lambert Schneider, 1966, 267 pp.

Hinweise. Zürich: Manesse Verlag, 1953, 380 pp.

Briefwechsel aus sieben Jahrzehnten. Heidelberg: Lambert Schneider.
    Band I: 1897–1918. Erste Auflage, 1972.
    Band II: 1918–1938. Erste Auflage, 1973.
    Band III: 1938–1965. Erste Auflage, 1975.

Buber's Essays in Separate Editions

German

Begegnung: Autobiographische Fragmente. Stuttgart: W. Kohlhammer, 2. Auflage, 1961.

Daniel: Gespräche von der Verwirklichung. Leipzig: Insel-Verlag, 1919.

Das dialogische Prinzip. Heidelberg: Lambert Schneider, 1962. Includes: Ich und Du, Zwiesprache, Die Frage an den Einzelnen, Elemente des Zwischenmenschlichen, Nachwort zu den Schriften über das dialogische Prinzip.

Das Problem des Menschen. Heidelberg: Lambert Schneider, 1961.

Der grosse Maggid und seine Nachfolge. Berlin: Schocken Verlag, 1937.

Der Mensch und sein Gebild. Heidelberg: Lambert Schneider, 1955.

Der heilige Weg. Frankfurt am Main: Rütten und Loening, 1919.

Der Weg des Menschen nach der chassidischen Lehre. Heidelberg: Lambert Schneider, 1962.

Einsichten. Wiesbaden: Insel-Verlag, 1953.

Ich und Du. Köln: Jakob Hegner Verlag, 1966.

Logos: Zwei Reden. Heidelberg: Lambert Schneider, 1962.

Reden über das Judentum. Gesamtausgabe. Frankfurt am Main: Rütten und Loening, 1923.

Schuld und Schuldegefühle. Heidelberg: Lambert Schneider, 1958.

Urdistanz und Beziehung. Heidelberg: Lambert Schneider, 1960.

Vom Geist des Judentums. Leipzig: Kurt Wolff Verlag, 1916.

"Wie kann Gemeinschaft werden?" *München ehrt Martin Buber.* München: Ner-Tamid-Verlag, 1961. Includes: Greeting by the Mayor Dr. Hans-Jochen Vogel; "Betrachtungen einer Philozionistin," by Paula Winkler (Mrs. Buber); "Martin Buber in München," Erinnerungen von Schalom Ben-Chorin.

Zwiesprache. Berlin: Schocken Verlag, 1934.

English Translations

A Believing Humanism: My Testament 1902–1965. Translated and with an Introduction and Explanatory Comments by Maurice Friedman. New York: Simon and Schuster, 1967. A volume of *Credo Perspectives.* Planned and Edited by Ruth Nanda Anshen.

Between Man and Man. With an Afterword by the author on "The History of the Dialogical Principle." Translated by Ronald Gregor Smith. Afterword translated by Maurice Friedman. London: Macmillan Paperbacks, 1965.

Daniel: Dialogues on Realization. Edited and Translated with an Introductory Essay by Maurice Friedman, New York: Holt, Rinehart & Winston, 1964. Also: First McGraw-Hill Paperback, 1965.

Eclipse of God: Studies in the Relation Between Religion and Philosophy. New York: Harper Torchbooks, 1957.

For the Sake of Heaven. Translated by Ludwig Lewisohn. Philadelphia: The Jewish Publication Society of America, 1946.

Good and Evil. New York: Charles Scribner's Sons, 1953.

Hasidism and Modern Man. Edited and translated by Maurice Friedman. New York: Harper Torchbooks, 1966.

I and Thou. Translated by Ronald Gregor Smith. Edinburgh: T. & T. Clark, 1937. Second Edition. With a Postscript by the author added. New York: Charles Scribner's Sons, 1958. A new translation, with a prologue and notes, by Walter Kaufmann. New York: Charles Scribner's Sons, 1970.

Israel and Palestine: The History of an Idea. Translated by Stanley Godman. New York: Farrar, Strauss and Young, 1952.

Israel and the World: Essays in a Time of Crisis. Translated by Greta Hort, O. Marx, I. M. Lask. New York: Schocken Books, 1948.

Kingship of God. Third, newly enlarged edition, Translated by Richard Scheimann. New York: Harper & Row, Publishers, 1967.

Moses: The Revelation and the Covenant. New York: Harper Torchbooks, 1958.

On Judaism. Edited by Nahum N. Glatzer. The Early Addresses, translated by Eva Jospe. The Later Addresses, translated by I. M. Lask, et. al. New York: Schocken Books, 1967.

On the Theater. *Martin Buber and the Theater.* Edited and Translated with Three Introductory Essays by Maurice Friedman. New York: Funk & Wagnalls, 1969.

Paths in Utopia. Translated by R. F. C. Hull. Boston: Beacon Press, 1960.

Pointing the way. Edited and Translated with an Introduction by Maurice Friedman. New York: Harper Torchbooks, 1963.

Tales of the Hasidim. Early Masters. Later Masters. 2 vols. Translated by Olga Marx. New York: Schocken Paperbacks, second printing, 1964.

The Knowledge of Man. Edited with an Introductory Essay by Maurice Friedman. Translated by Maurice Friedman and Ronald Gregor Smith. New York: Harper Torchbooks, 1965.

The Origin and Meaning of Hasidism. Edited and Translated by Maurice Friedman. New York: Harper Torchbooks, 1966.

The Prophetic Faith. Translated from the Hebrew by Carlyle Witton-Davies. New York: Harper Torchbooks, 1960.

Ten Rungs: Hasidic Sayings. Collected and Edited by Martin Buber. Translated by Olga Marx. New York: Schocken Books, 1962.

Two Types of Faith. Translated by Norman P. Goldhawk. New York: Harper Torchbooks, 1961.

Towards Union in Palestine: Essays on Zionism and Jewish-Arab Cooperation. Edited by M. Buber, J. L. Magnes, E. Simon. Jerusalem: IHUD (UNION) Association, 1957.

Books and Articles about Buber

Agus, Jacob. *Modern Philosophies of Judaism.* New York: Behrman's Jewish Book House, 1941, pp. 213–79.

Baillie, John. *Our Knowledge of God.* New York: Charles Scribner's Sons, 1939, pp. 161, 201–39.

Bergmann, Samuel Hugo. *Hogé Hador* (Hebrew). Tel Aviv: Hozaat "Mizpeh," 1935, pp. 179–93.

———. "Buber and Mysticism" (Hebrew). *Divre Iyyun: Dedicated to Mordehai Martin Buber on His Eightieth Birthday.* Jerusalem: The Magnes Press, Hebrew University, 1958, pp. 9–18; English summary, pp. 123–24.

———. *Faith and Reason: An Introduction to Modern Jewish Thought.* Translated and Edited by Alfred Jospe. New York: Schocken Books, 1972.

Berkovits, Eliezer. *Major Trends in Modern Philosophies of Judaism.* New York: Ktav Publishing House, 1974. Chapter 3, "Martin Buber's Religion of the Dialogue."

Blau, Joseph L. "Martin Buber's Religious Philosophy." *Review of Religion* 13 (1948): 48–64.

Böhm, Adolf. *Die zionistische Bewegung bis zum Ende des Weltkrieges.* Zweite erweiterte Auflage. Tel Aviv: Hozaat Ivrith, 1935. vol. 1, pp. 279–99, 522–40, 572; vol. 2, Jerusalem, 1937, pp. 295–96, 301–2.

Diamond, Malcolm L. *Martin Buber: Jewish Existentialist.* New York: Harper Torchbooks, 1960.

Downing, Christian R. "Guilt and Responsibility in the Thought of Martin Buber." *Judaism* 18, no. 2 (Winter 1969): pp. 53–63.

Friedman, Maurice. *Martin Buber: The Life of Dialogue.* Chicago: The University of Chicago Press, 1955. Paperback edition, Harper Torchbooks, 1960.

———. *Martin Buber: Encounter on the Narrow Ridge.* New York: McGraw-Hill Books, 1968.

———. "Martin Buber and Christian Thought." *The Review of Religion* 18, nos. 1–2 (November 1953): 31–43.

———. "Martin Buber's View of Biblical Faith." *The Journal of Bible and Religion* 22, no. 1 (January 1954), pp. 3–13.

———. "Revelation and Law in the Thought of Martin Buber." *Judaism* 3, no. 1 (Winter 1954): 9–19.

Goldschmidt, Hermann L. *Hermann Cohen und Martin Buber*. Geneva: Collection Migdal no. 4, 1946.

———. *Abschied von Martin Buber*. Köln & Olten: Jakob Hegner Verlag, 1966.

Herberg, Will. *The Writings of Martin Buber* (An Anthology). With an Introduction by the writer. New York: Meridian Books, 1965.

Horwitz, Rivka. "An Early Plan towards Martin Buber's 'I and Thou'" (Hebrew). *Iyyun: A Hebrew Philosophical Quarterly* (Jerusalem) 22, no. 4 (October 1971): 215–24; English summary, pp. 273–74.

———. "Exposition concerning the History of the Formation of Martin Buber's Book *I and Thou*" (Hebrew). *Divrei Ha-akademia Haleumit Hayisreelit Lamadaim* (Jerusalem, 1975) 5, no. 8, pp. 161–85.

Kaplan, Mordecai M. *The Purpose and Meaning of Jewish Existence*. Philadelphia: The Jewish Publication Society of America, 1964. "Martin Buber's Anti-Philosophic Rationale," pp. 257–86.

———. "Martin Buber: Theologian, Philosopher and Prophet." *Reconstructionist*, May 2, 1952.

Kohanski, Alexander S. *An Analytical Interpretation of Martin Buber's "I and Thou."* New York: Barron's Educational Series, 1975.

Kohn, Hans. *Martin Buber: Sein Werk und seine Zeit*. Köln: Joseph Melzer Verlag, Dritte Auflage, 1961.

Landauer, Gustav. *Zwang und Befreiung*. Köln: Verlag Jakob Hegner, 1968. "Martin Buber," pp. 156–71.

Lipzin, Solomon. *Germany's Stepchildren*. Philadelphia: The Jewish Publication Society of America, 1944. "Martin Buber," pp. 255–69.

Martin, Bernard. *Great Twentieth Century Jewish Philosophers*. Buber, Rosenzweig, Chestov. New York: Macmillan, 1969.

"Martin Buber on His Centennial. A Tribute and an Evaluation." *Judaism* 27, no. 2 (Spring 1978).

McCarthy, C. R. "Personal Freedom and Community Responsibility." *Catholic World*, June 1966, pp. 165–68.

Moore, Donald J. *Martin Buber: Prophet of Religious Secularism*. Philadelphia: The Jewish Publication Society of America, 1974.

Morgan, George W. "Martin Buber and Some of His Critics." *Judaism* 18, no. 2 (Spring 1969): 232–41.

Oliver, Roy. *The Wanderer and the Way: The Hebrew Tradition in the Writings of Martin Buber*. Ithaca, N.Y.: Cornell University Press, 1968.

Pfuetze, Paul E. "Martin Buber and Jewish Mysticism." *Religion and Life* 16 (1947): 553–67.

Potok, C. "Martin Buber and the Jews: His Interpretation of and Path to Hasidism." *Commentary*, March and September 1966.

Rosenzweig, Franz. *Kleinere Schriften*. Berlin: Schocken Verlag, 1937. "Die Bauleute. Über das Gesetz. An Martin Buber," pp. 106–21.

———. *Briefe*. Berlin: Schocken Verlag, 1935. List of letters to "Professor Dr. Martin Buber," p. 728.

———. *Franz Rosenzweig: His Life and Thought*. Presented by Nahum N. Glatzer. New York: Schocken Books, Published with Farrar, Straus and Young, 1953. See Index, "Buber, Martin," p. 381.

Schaffer, C. R. "Jewish View of Redemption." *Commonweal*, September 19, 1969, pp. 512–15, 574–75.

Scholem, Gershom G. "Martin Buber's Hasidism." *Commentary*, October 1961. Discussion, February 1962.

Simon, Ernst. "Martin Buber and Judaism" (Hebrew). *Divrei Iyyun: Dedicated to Mordehai Martin Buber on His Eightieth Birthday*. Jerusalem: Magnes Press—Hebrew University, 1958, pp. 19–56; English summary, pp. 120–23.

The Philosophy of Martin Buber. Edited by Paul Arthur Schilpp and Maurice Friedman. A Critical Analysis and Evaluation (by many authors). Buber's Autobiography. Buber's Reply to His Critics. LaSalle, Ill: Open Court, The Library of Living Philosophers, vol. 12, 1967.

Tillich, Paul. "Jewish Influences on Contemporary Christian Theology." *Cross Currents* 2, no. 3 (Spring 1952): 38–42.

———. "Martin Buber and Christian Thought." *Commentary*, June 1948, pp. 515–21.

Von Balthasar, Hans Urs. *Einsame Zwiesprache: Martin Buber und das Christentum*. Köln & Olten: Verlag Jakob Hegner, 1958.

Von Hammerstein, Franz, Freiherr. *Das Messiasproblem bei Martin Buber*. Stuttgart: Verlag W. Kohlhammer, 1958.

Weltsch, Robert. "Martin Buber 1930–1960." Nachwort, *Martin Buber: Sein Werk und seine Zeit*, by Hans Kohn. Dritte Auflage. Köln: Joseph Melzer Verlag, 1961, pp. 413–79.

Wood, R. E. *Martin Buber's Ontology*. Chicago: Northwestern University Press, 1969.

Woodhouse, Helen. "Martin Buber's 'I and Thou.'" *Philosophy* 20 (1945): 17–30:

General References Used in This Book

Abro, A. d'. *The Evolution of Scientific Thought from Newton to Einstein*. Second edition revised and enlarged. New York: Dover Publications, 1950.

————. *The Rise of the New Physics*. 2 vols. New York: Dover Publications, 1951.

Altizer, Thomas J. J. "Nirvana and Kingdom of God." In *New Theology No. 1*. Edited by Martin E. Marty and Dean G. Peerman. New York: The Macmillan Company, 1967.

———— and William Hamilton (eds.). *Radical Theology and the Death of God*. New York: The Bobbs-Merrill Company, 1966.

Aristotle. *The Basic Works of Aristotle*. Edited and with an Introduction by Richard McKeon. New York: Random House, 1941.

Bacon, Francis. "Novum Organum." In *The English Philosophers from Bacon to Mill*. Edited with an Introduction, by Edwin A. Burtt. New York: The Modern Library, 1939, pp. 24–123.

Baron, Salo Wittmayer. *A Social and Religious History of the Jews*. 3 vols. New York: Columbia University Press, 1937. Second edition revised and enlarged, Philadelphia: The Jewish Publication Society of America, vol. 1, 1952, and succeeding volumes.

Barth, Karl. *Die protestantische Theologie im 19. Jahrhundert*. Dritte Auflage. Zürich: Evangelischer Verlag, 1960.

Barzun, Jacques. *The American University: How It Runs. Where It Is Going*. New York: Harper & Row, 1968.

Bible (OT). Masoretic text in Hebrew. (NT) Revised Standard Version.

————. *The Torah (Mikraot Gedolot)*. 5 volumes with fifty-two commentaries and an additional volume of eight commentaries. Includes: *Midrash Hamekhilta* on Exodus, *Sifra* on Leviticus, and *Sifrê* on Numbers and Deuteronomy. New York: Shulsinger Bros., 1950.

Böhm, Adolf. *Die zionistische Bewegung 1918 bis 1925*. 2. Band. Jerusalem: Hozaat Ivrith, 1937.

Bultmann, Rudolf. *History and Eschatology: The Presence of Eternity*. New York: Harper Torchbooks, 1962.

Capelle, Wilhelm. *Die Vorsokratiker: Die Fragmente und Quellenberichte*. Übersetzt und eingeleitet von Wilhelm Capelle. Leipzig: Alfred Kröner Verlag, 1935.

Cassirer, Ernst. *Die Philosophie der Aufklärung*. Tübingen: Verlag von J.C.B. Mohr, 1932.

————. *An Essay on Man: An Introduction to a Philosophy of Human Culture*. New Haven: Yale University Press, 1964.

Cohen, Hermann. *Die Religion der Vernunft aus den Quellen des Judentums*. Leipzig: Gustav Fock, 1919.

————. *Religion of Reason out of the Sources of Judaism*. Translated with an Introduction by Simon Kaplan. New York: Frederick Ungar Publishing Co., 1972.

Dilthey, Wilhelm. *Die Philosophie des Lebens*. Aus seinen Schriften ausgewählt von Hermann Nohl. Mit Vorwort von Otto Friedrich Bollnow. Stuttgart: B.G. Teubner Verlagsgesellschaft, 1961.

Dubnow, S. M. *History of the Jews in Russia and Poland.* Translated from the Russian by I. Friedlaender. Philadelphia: The Jewish Publication Society of America, vol. 1, 1916; vol. 2, 1918; vol. 3, 1920.

————. *Toldot Hahasidut* (History of Hasidism). 2 vols. Tel Aviv, Hozaat "Dvir," 1930.

Eckhart. *Meister Eckhart.* A Modern Translation, by Raymond Bernard Blakney. New York: Harper Torchbooks, 1941.

Eddington, Sir Arthur. *Space, Time and Gravitation: An Outline of the General Theory of Relativity.* New York: Harper Torchbooks, 1959.

Einstein, Albert. *Essays in Science.* Translated from the German by Alan Harris. New York: Philosophical Library, 1934.

————. *Über die spezielle und allgemeine Relativitätstheorie* (Gemeinverständlich). 18. Auflage. Braunschweig: Friedr. Vieweg & Sohn, 1960.

Fang, J. *Hilbert.* Towards a Philosophy of Modern Mathematics II. Hauppauge, N.Y.: Paideia Press, 1970.

Farber, M. A. "Geneticist Looks to the Year 2000." *The New York Times,* February 13, 1967, p. 1.

Farmer, William R. *The Synoptic Problem.* New York: The Macmillan Company, 1964.

Farrar, F. W. *The Early Days of Christianity.* London: Cassell, Petter, Galpin & Co., 1882.

Feigl, Herbert, and Brodbeck, May (eds.). *Readings in the Philosophy of Science.* New York: Appleton-Century-Crofts, 1953.

Groethuysen, Bernard. *Philosophische Anthropologie.* München: Verlag von Oldenbourg, 1931.

————. "Towards an Anthropological Philosophy." In *Philosophy and History.* Essays presented to Ernst Cassirer. Edited by Raymond Klibansky and H. J. Paton. New York: Harper Torchbooks, 1963, pp. 77–89.

Guthrie, W. K. C. *A History of Greek Philosophy.* Vol. 2. Cambridge: At the University Press, 1965.

Hartmann, Nicolai. *Neue Wege der Ontologie.* Stuttgart: W. Kohlhammer, 1964.

Hartshorne, Charles, and Reese, William L. (eds.). *Philosophers Speak of God.* Chicago: University of Chicago Press, 1963.

"Harvard Overseers' Interim Report." *The New York Times,* September 19, 1969, pp. 1, 28.

Hessen, Johannes. *Augustins Metaphysik der Erkenntnis.* Zweite neubearbeitete Auflage. Leiden: E. J. Brill, 1960.

Horodetzky, S. A. (ed.). *Sefer Shivhei HaBesht* (Hebrew). Berlin: "Ajanoth" Hebr. Verlag, 1922.

Huxley, Aldous. *Brave New World Revisited.* New York: Harper & Brothers, 1958.

————. *Collected Essays*. New York: Harper & Brothers, 1959.

Ibn Gabirol, Solomon. *Selected Religious Poems of Solomon Ibn Gabirol*. From a Critical Text, edited by Israel Davidson. Philadelphia: The Jewish Publication Society of America, 1923.

Jaeger, Werner. *Die Theologie der frühen griechischen Denker*. Zürich: Europa Verlag, 1953.

————. *Aristotle*. Translated by Richard Robinson. Second edition. London: Oxford University Press, 1962.

Jencks, Christopher, and Riesman, David. *The Academic Revolution*. Garden City, N.Y.: Doubleday & Co., 1968.

Jonas, Hans. *The Gnostic Religion*. 2d ed., rev. Boston: Beacon Press, 1963.

Kant, Immanuel. *Anthropologie in pragmatischer Hinsicht*. Herausgegeben von J. H. v. Kirchmann. Berlin: Verlag von L. Heimann, 1869.

————. "Beantwortung der Frage: Was ist Aufklärung?" In *Immanuel Kants Schriften zur Logik und Metaphysik,* Berlin, 1870, pp. 109–19.

————. *Kritik der reinen Vernunft*. Philosophische Bibliothek 37a. Hamburg: Felix Meiner Verlag, 1956.

————. *Introduction to Logic*. Translated by Thomas Kingsmill Abbott. New York: Philosophical Library, 1963.

Klausner, Joseph. *Historia shel Habayit Hasheni* (History of the Second Commonwealth). Vol. 4. 2d ed., rev. and enl. Jerusalem: Ahiasaf, 1950.

————. *The Messianic Idea in Israel: From Its Beginning to the Completion of the Mishnah*. Translated from the third Hebrew edition by W. F. Stinespring. New York: The Macmillan Company, 1955.

Kohanski, Alexander S. *Philosophy and Technology*. New York: Philosophical Library, 1977.

————. "Einstein's Metamathematics." *Philosophia Mathematica* 10, no.2 (Winter 1973): 165–81.

————. "Jews, Arabs and Zionists in the Middle East." *The Jewish News,* Newark, N.J., September 20, 1973.

Landmann, Michael. *Philosophische Anthropologie*. Berlin: Walter De Gruyter, 1955.

Lewy, Hans (ed.). "Philo: Selections." In *Three Jewish Philosophers*. Philadelphia: The Jewish Publication Society of America. Second printing, 1961, pp. 29–112.

Löwith, Karl. *From Hegel to Nietzsche: The Revolution in Nineteenth-Century Thought*. Translated from the German by David E. Green. Garden City, N.Y.: Doubleday Anchor Books, 1967.

Maimonides, Moses. *The Guide for the Perplexed*. Translated by M. Friedländer. 2d ed., rev. London: George Routledge & Sons, 1942.

Margenau, Henry. *The Nature of Physical Reality*. New York: McGraw-Hill, 1950.

Marty, Martin, and Peerman, Dean G. (eds.). *New Theology No. 1.* New York: The Macmillan Company, 1967.

Marx, Karl. *Capital: A Critique of Political Economy*. Translated from the third German edition by Samuel Moore and Edward Aveling. Edited by Frederick Engels. Revised and amplified according to the fourth German edition by Ernst Untermann. New York: The Modern Library, 1936.

McLuhan, Marshall. *Understanding Media: The Extension of Man*. New York: A Signet Book, 1964.

Plato. *The Collected Dialogues*. Edited by Edith Hamilton and Huntington Cairns. New York: Pantheon Books, 1966.

Priestly, J. B. *Man and Time*. London: Aldus Books Limited, 1964.

Rawidowicz, Simon (ed.). *Kitvei Rabbi Nachman Krochmal* (The writings of Rabbi Nachman Krochmal). Edited with Introduction by Simon Rawidowicz. 2d enl. ed. Waltham, Mass.: Ararat Publishing Society (London), 1961.

Runes, Dagobert D. (ed.). *Twentieth Century Philosophy*. New York: Philosophical Library, 1947.

Salvadori, Massimo (ed.). *Modern Socialism*. New York: Harper Torchbooks, 1968.

Sartre, Jean-Paul. *Being and Nothingness*. Translated and with an Introduction by Hazel E. Barnes. New York: Philosophical Library, 1956.

————. *Literary and Philosophical Essays*. Translated from the French by Annette Michelson. New York: Collier Books, 1962.

Scholem, Gershom G. *Major Trends in Jewish Mysticism*. New York: Schocken Books, 1954.

Sereni, Enzo, and Asheri, R. E. (eds.). *Jews and Arabs in Palestine*. New York: Hechalutz Press, 1936.

Spinoza, Benedict de. "Ethics." *Philosophy of Benedict de Spinoza*. Translated from the Latin by R. H. M. Elwes. New York: Tudor Publishing Co., n.d.

Stace, Walter T. *The Teachings of the Mystics*. New York: A Mentor Book, 1960.

Stern, William. "Selbstdarstellung." In *Die Philosophie der Gegenwart in Selbstdarstellungen*. Herausgegeben von Raymund Schmidt. Leipzig: Verlag Felix Meiner, 1927, pp. 129–84.

Talmud Babli. Complete original text with standard commentaries. 4 vols. Berlin/New York: Hozaat Horeb, 1925.

"The 21st Century: What Are We Doing to Our World?" A transcript of a broadcast over CBS Television Network. Subject: On Pollution. Sunday, March 23, 1969.

Tillich, Paul. *Perspectives on 19th and 20th Century Protestant Theology*. Edited with an Introduction by Carl E. Braaten. New York: Harper & Row, 1967.

————. *Religionsphilosophie*. 2. Auflage. Stuttgart: W. Kohlhammer, 1962.

Wein, Hermann. *Realdialektik*. München: R. Oldenbourg Verlag, 1957.

Weiss, Eisik Hirsch. *Dor, Dor Vedorshav* (Each generation and its interpreters). A History of Oral Tradition. New York: Platt and Minkus, 1924.

Weltsch, Robert. "Einleitung." *Der Jude und sein Judentum,* by Martin Buber. Köln: Joseph Melzer, 1963.

Weyl, Hermann. *The Theory of Groups and Quantum Mechanics*. Translated from the second (revised) German edition by H. P. Robertson. New York: Dover Publications, 1950.

————. *Space—Time—Matter*. Translated from the German by Henry L. Brose. New York: Dover Publications, 1952.

Windelband, Wilhelm. *Präludien: Aufsätze und Reden zur Philosophie und ihrer Geschichte*. 9. Auflage. Band I/II. Tübingen: Verlag J. C. B. Mohr, 1924.

Wyss, Dieter. *Depth Psychology: A Critical History*. Translated by Gerald Onn. New York: W. W. Norton, 1966.

Index of Terminology

Buber was very meticulous about the use of terms in expressing his philosophical ideas. "I have learned in the course of my life to appreciate terms," he said. "When I find something that is essentially different from another thing, I want a new term. I want a new concept" (KnM 179). The following terms represent the basic vocabulary of his philosophical output. They are not defined, but rather described in their consistent usage in the context of his various writings. The references at the end of each term are to Buber's works in English translation. Page references to the present volume are given in the General Index.

Absolute. "A power which cannot be identified with any attribute accessible to the human understanding." We can make no statement about it in terms of concepts, images, or even ideas. If we express it in speech at all, we can only point to it as God (I&W 209).

Absolute Person (die absolute Person). In man's encounter with God, the Absolute may be designated as the Absolute Person, inasmuch as this kind of encounter can exist only between persons. The word "absolute" signifies that the divine Person is not relativized as in the case when one enters-into-relation with a human person (I&T 182, EG 60, 96–97).

Absolute Thou (das absolute Du, das ewige Du). Buber emphasizes that the Thou in the word pair I-Thou, when applied to God, cannot be turned into an It of the word pair I-It, as applied to objects of use. If any positive attribute may be given to the Absolute Thou it is that of Person, which by its nature is not an It (I&T 160–61).

Alienation (Verfremdung). When a man looks at the world either entirely as a structure of natural elements (of the It) or entirely as a construct of psychological factors (of the I), he cannot find himself as a human being in either case. Both aspects are mere abstractions, the first from objects of use, and the second from the subject or I. By thus splitting the I-It into two separate compartments, man falls into a hopeless contradiction between the knowing subject and the object known, and he feels alienated from the world as well as from himself. The point is that when one looks at the world apart from himself or at himself apart from the world, he sees neither in reality (that is, as a mutuality of interrelationship), but only ghosts, which frighten and alienate him (I&T 119–22). See *Escape*.

A Priori. This applies to man's striving toward relation before he actually enters into it. The striving is manifest in man from infancy. See *Inborn Thou*.

Art (Kunst). It is one of the four potencies of human communication, which expresses itself through the formation of an image of that which occurs between man and others in the act of relation. It is not an image of the artist's mind (the I) nor of the other in the relation (the Thou), but of the encounter, as such (KnM 165, I&T 60–62).

Being (Wesen, Sein). It is the living reality of one who enters into relation as a whole with another reality which is also taken as a whole. It is a subject who relates to another subject. Being, we might say, is a communicating entity. A solitary being is a contradiction in terms (KnM 59–60, BMM 50).

Being There (Dasein, da sein). To respond to another means "being there" when the other calls for communication. It means taking one's stand in the meeting of the I-Thou relation (BMM 166). See *Present*.

Between (Zwischen). When one enters into relation with another there occurs a "between" which was not there before the meeting took place. When one fails to respond to the other, there is no between, or no relation. Insofar as such failure has become prevalent in our time, Buber designates the modern age as that of "the crisis of the between" (KnM 77, 107, BMM 203, I&T 16).

Biblical Humanism. See *Hebrew Humanism*.

Category, Category of Being, Category Humanum (Kategorie, Kategorie des Seins, Kategorie Humanum) In Greek this term means "to say," "to speak" *(kategorein)* or generally that which may be stated about a thing (categorize it). When Buber applies this term to man, calling him "the category *humanum*," he means to point out that what we can say of man specifically, which differentiates him from all other creatures, is that he is the kind of being who *relates* to and *distances* from others—a capacity which no other creature has (KnM 59–60, 64). See *Relation, Distance.*

Cause and Effect, Causality (Ursache und Folge, Ursächlichkeit). These terms are not used in the same sense when applied to physical objects, on the one hand, and to relational occurrences, on the other. In the physical sciences, an effect follows a cause in the sense that the former depends on the latter inevitably, as the cause produces its effect of necessity. In a relational occurrence, on the other hand, one party in the relation does not depend on the other, for neither side brings the other into existence. There is a mutuality of interrelationship between them, that is, one affects the other, but neither side produces or is being produced by the other. The only product, which might be called an effect, that results from their meeting is the "between" which comes into existence as the relation occurs (I&T 81, 100, PW 125).

Chosen People (auserwähltes Volk). The Jewish people, Buber holds, has been chosen by God not for power or self-glorification, but for the long and arduous task of establishing a true community. Its election "is completely a demand" to build a community "of truth and righteousness." This does not imply a superiority over other nations, for in fact the Jewish people has fallen behind its task. "The choice means a charge imposed on them and nothing more," which is valid only insofar as it is being carried out in actuality *(On Judaism* 111, PF 88–89, 233, TTF 136, Moses 105).

Cognition, Knowledge (Erkenntnis, Kenntnis). It is a potency both of immediate knowledge of the other in an I-Thou relation and of mediated knowledge in an I-It connection. In the former one knows the other as a being as a whole, in the latter one knows him only in parts, as sense-perceptual images and intellectual concepts (KnM 163–64). See *Potencies.*

Collective, Collectivism (Kollektiv, Kollektivismus). An aggregate of individuals joined together for a given purpose of promoting a common interest, such as a labor union, a manufacturers' association, and the like, is called a collective. It may dissolve itself whenever its purpose is finished or found unattainable. In a collective the individual member has minimal responsibility as he is entirely subordinate to the functions of the group, which "devours his selfhood" (BMM 80, 110, PW 146, 225). See *Community.*

Communication (Kommunion, kommunizieren). It is the primary twofold act of relating to the world, either as I-Thou or as I-It. Buber uses the German word *Haltung*, which may be rendered into English as "communication" rather than "attitude." The latter term has a psychological implication which is contrary to Buber's intent. We might say, man *has* an attitude toward an other, but lives *in* communication with him (I&T 53, BMM 193).

Community, Communality (Gemeinschaft, Gemeinschaftlichkeit). It consists of persons who form an interrelationship in which each recognizes the other as an independent being, yet all are tied together *(verbunden)* in a living whole. "Community is an overcoming of *otherness* in living unity." Communality signifies the formative power of community, of which each person is an active bearer insofar as he relates himself to the Absolute Center (God). Community is the "place" in which the divine Presence is manifest (BMM 30–33, I&T 94, BH 151–52, PW 100, 102). See *Place*.

Confirming (Bestätigung, Bewährung). To confirm another is to accept him as is, without trying to change, dominate, or use him for one's own purposes. "Confirming means first of all accepting the whole potentiality of the other," that is, not only for what he is, but also for what he may become (KnM 71, 79, 182, BMM 34, 61).

Confirming the Meaning of Life. See *Meaning of Life*.

Conversation (Gespräch). A dialogue between persons who enter-into-relation with each other in truth, even when nothing is spoken in words (KnM 69, BMM 3–4, 34). See *Dialogue*.

Cosmos (Kosmos). In terms of the physical universe, cosmos is an abstract concept (or an idea) which cannot be put in visual form as a whole. It can only be formulated in mathematical equations or, at best, in terms of other concepts. But in living experience the cosmos is the All through which man-as-a-whole relates to the Absolute (I&T 103, 150, 163). See *Metacosmos, World*.

Creation (Schöpfung). Buber does not profess the doctrine of "creation out of nothing." To him creation of the world as such is a mystery, which man cannot fathom. Yet man may participate in creation through his activity of entering into relation with others and with the divine Absolute. In this sense creation continues constantly, as it manifests itself through speaking, for "God's act of creation is speech . . . and the same is true of each lived moment" of dialogue. Man participates in creation insofar as he helps bring order out of chaos or, to put it in religious terms, helps redeem the world (I&T 130, BMM 188). See *Redemption*.

Decision, To Decide (Entscheidung, sich entscheiden). This is the basic conscious act in choosing good and overcoming evil. The ability to decide stems from the potencies of relation. "Only one who is aware of relation and knows the presence of Thou is capable of decision." A lack of decision, then, is evil, which may come about through a refusal to enter into relation (refusing to respond to the other) or through missing the moment of the encounter when another calls for it. The first is an act of wickedness, the second just sinfulness (missing the mark) (I&T 100–101).

Destiny (Schicksal). Man is the kind of being who relates and that is his destiny. In order to fulfill himself he must decide to exercise his activity of relating, which is a free act of his inner potencies and not compelled by an outer force. "Destiny and freedom are vowed unto each other" (I&T 103–105). See *Category, Decision, Potencies, Freedom, Fate*.

Dialogue (Dialog, Zwiesprache). It means one person speaking with another. Its opposite is monologue or speaking in one's mind with oneself. In dialogue the other must be actual, not just a surmised other *(ein gedachter Andere)*, and the speaking must take place in an actual meeting between two beings, or subject with subject. True dialogue occurs when one enters into relation without holding himself back and speaks spontaneously without preconceived notions, but in direct response to the other, as and when the meeting takes place. Dialogue is essentially an act of turning to the other and listening to him exclusively, as if nothing else mattered at the moment (BMM 8–10, KnM 79, 85–88). See *Speech, Turning*.

Direction (Richtung, Gerichtetsein). It means basically a turning to God. Concomitantly, turning away from God is a lack of direction. Hence direction is identified with good, and a lack of it with evil. The first leads to man's self-fulfillment, the second to confusion and a meaningless life (BMM 79). See *Evil*.

Distance, Distancing (Distanz, Distanzierung). Man is the category of being who can enter-into-relation with another or be at a distance from him. Distance and relation are man's two primary movements, and thus the characteristic of his being human. Through distancing one separates the other as an object of experience and use, which is movement in the world of I-It (KnM 57). See *Category, Relation.*

Election of Israel. See *Chosen People.*

Encounter, The Over Against (Begegnung, das Gegenüber). Encounter means a meeting between two beings which happens spontaneously and expresses itself in an immediate response. Each meeting of this kind is unique; it does not repeat itself in the same manner even between the same two beings. In the encounter one stands "over against" the other to whom he responds. If there is no response, there is no real encounter (I&T 62, 162, 163). See *Meeting, Response.*

Escape. Failure to realize one's primary movement of relation is an escape from reality. Buber conceives it in terms of one's "Inborn Thou," which strives to express itself in a true I-Thou relation. When one sees his Inborn Thou not as the Thou of a real other who calls for an encounter, but as an image of his own I, he falls into self-contradiction (identifying the other with his own I), and this leads to alienation from the Self and from the World. See *Inborn Thou, Alienation.*

Evil (Übel). Evil may occur in two forms, as "wickedness," if one refuses to enter into relation with an other, or as "sin," if one simply misses the opportunity when it presents itself. There is a real problem of evil in the world of It, but the primary word pair I-It as such is not evil, as matter is not evil. Nor is man who speaks this primary word pair evil, but he is inclined toward good and evil (has "good and evil impulses"). He can turn his evil inclination to the service of God, and thus convert it into good (KnM 146, GE 95–97, 139). See *Direction.*

Experience (Erfahrung). Buber applies this term only to things which are used for various purposes in practical affairs, or even for theoretical understanding, that is, only in the world of It. The opposite of experience is relation *(Beziehung)* which pertains to I-Thou (I&T 55–56, 59–60, 157). See *Meeting, Relation, Communication.*

Faith (Glaube). This is man's highest potency of entering into relation, embracing also the other three potencies. It expresses itself as a trust in the Presence of God when one goes forth to meet Him through the fullness of one's being. Faith does not function when one tries to meet God through one's partial faculties, either perceptual or conceptual. "The fundamental experience of faith itself should be regarded as the highest degree of the reality of meeting." It is not to be considered as a feeling, but as an ontic act of man as a whole (I&W 29, BH 121, 126). See *Potencies*.

False Prophet (falscher Prophet). A diviner of fateful events who does not present alternatives for the people to choose from (PF 103).

Fate (Verhängnis). It is the concept of an outside blind force over which man has no control and which determines his entire life. In modern science it functions as causal necessity of natural law which is sometimes disguised in various modes of biological and historiographical determinations (I&T 106).

Freedom (Freiheit). Man is free when he decides to realize his category *humanum*, that is, his potencies of relation. He may accept or reject his being human. While he is, in a sense, determined as a creature with a duality of movement—relating and distancing—he is nevertheless free to decide for direction against chaos and confusion. His very act of decision is freedom (I&T 129–30, BMM 91–92, EG 68, 75–76). See *Destiny*.

Goal (Ziel). Man's goal is his self-fulfillment as a human being, to which he must strive throughout his life. Even though he may fail at certain instances, he must actualize some of it in everyday affairs, for the goal gives direction though it is never consummated (PW 128). See *Purpose*.

Good (das Gute). See *Direction*.

God (Gott). See *Absolute Thou*.

Guilt (Schuld). When one fails to respond to the call of an other, one is guilty of not fulfilling his category *humanum*. The guilt is not a feeling in him, but an actual "between" him and the other which is characterized as a breach of responsibility to that other. It is a violation of the order of being human which is to be realized through mutuality (KnM 132). See *Response*.

Hebrew Humanism (hebräischer Humanismus). The return of the Jewish people to the origin of its nature is "the true goal of the movement of its rebirth." The Hebrew language and *humanitas* (man as a unique creature) combine in playing a decisive role in it (I&W 241–45).

History of Faith (Glaubensgeschichte). It is the history of a people that recognizes the sovereignty of God and is responsible to His divine rule. This history is not preordained, but is a series of divine revelations going on in all generations. Israel's history of faith is expressed in its battling for the unique, true King against the idolatrous pseudo-kings (I&W 199, 224, KG 110–11).

Holy People (heiliges Volk). The people as a whole, with all its institutions, dedicated to the service of God, and therefore hallowed by Him *(Moses* 106–07).

Image of God (Gestalt Gottes, Antlitz). This is not to be taken literally as God's image or even as a concept of Him. It is the image of His revelation through the word as manifested in human perceptual and conceptual experiences. Ordinarily it assumes the form of cult and belief. In biblical language it is called "God's Countenance," of which man may have a living experience *(Erlebnis)* when he looks to God and the world together. It is "a mixture of Thou and It," of the Infinite and the finite (I&T 166).

Inborn Thou (das eingeborene Du). This is derived from observing an infant's reaction to its own body as if it were another being. This awareness of otherness within oneself Buber calls the "Inborn Thou," or the a priori principle of relation, "a priori" meaning that there is a striving toward an other before it is realized in an encounter. Since the activity of entering into relation never reaches completeness, the striving never ceases in a person's life. It manifests itself particularly in the striving for a meeting with the Absolute Thou, which holds forth the possibility of completion (I&T 78–79). See *A priori.*

Individual, The Singular, The Single One (Individuum, der Einzige, der Einzelne). As a unique being, man is designated "singular" *(der Einzige),* and in this respect he may also be regarded as an individual. But his individuality in itself is not the prime factor of his *humanum.* On the contrary, he realizes his human self only insofar as he relates with others in the formation of a community. The proper term for this kind of individual is person. If, however, he regards himself exclusively as an individual, without relation to others, he may be designated the "single one" *(der Einzelne),* which is a mere abstraction (EG 18, 127, BMM 70, 203). See *Person.*

Individualism (Individualismus). When each human self considers itself as the single one, existing as an individual for itself and makes his individuality the center of a world outlook, it is called individualism. Generally, the opposite of this is called collectivism, but in fact a collective is nothing but an aggregate of individuals, held together by an outside purpose. The real opposite of individualism is communality, or the force that holds human beings together from within (BMM 202). See *Collective, Community.*

Inertia (Trägheit). It is used in the same sense as in physics, that is, resistance to movement, but in the dialogical schema it means resistance to the movement of entering-into-relation. It also means a lack of decision and a state of being when one does not respond to the call of an other (the Thou). Inertia, thus, is at "the root of all evil" (I&W 18). See *Evil.*

Inner Awareness (innewerden). See *Observing.*

Intuition. In general, intuition is conceived as a faculty of knowledge whereby the knowing subject reaches the object known through an immediate fusion or identification with it. In this process the duality of subject-object is claimed to have been abolished. Buber does not hold this view, as he does not see any need for abolishing the duality or even for overcoming it. On the contrary, the duality is a prime condition of knowing in any form of cognition. For Buber, then, intuition is the state of the knowing subject when his "whole being becomes one in the act of knowing." That is, the oneness occurs within the subject himself and not as a fusion with the other. The other in this relationship is also a subject like his partner standing over against him in the meeting. "Intuition binds us with the world against us, . . . without being able to make us one with it" (PW 83, 86). See *Object.*

Jewish Question (die jüdische Frage). From the Jewish side, it is a question that a Jew ought to ask himself whether there is anything in him which identifies him with the Jewish people (*On Judaism* 13).

Kingdom of God (Königtum Gottes). The realization of an all-embracing rule of God over all nations on earth (KG 58). See *Theopolitics.*

Love (Liebe). It is one of the four potencies of communication and it stands out as the main feature of the category *humanum,* as it is exercised particularly in interhuman relations. Buber cautions against identifying love with the psychological property of feeling. Love may be accompanied by feeling, as all potencies are, but it is, like the others, an ontic act, creating a certain "between" man and fellowman. One takes his stand *in* love, as one does in all I-Thou relations. "Feelings dwell in man but man dwells in his love" (I&T 67–68).

Meaning of Life (Sinn des Lebens). Ultimately, meaning in all of man's endeavors issues from his relation with the Absolute Thou, from which all other relations receive their confirmation. This kind of meaning is therefore not a preconceived notion or concept which may be handed down in fixed tenets or formulas. It is bound up with each living experience *(Erlebnis)* in one's everyday affairs, great or small. "Everyone may confirm the received meaning only with the singleness of his being and singleness of his life" (I&T 158–60).

Meeting (Begegnung). One of the two ways of communicating with others takes place through an immediate confrontation, without premeditation or advance planning. This is called "meeting." "All real living is meeting" (I&T 62). See *Encounter, Dialogue*.

Metacosmos (Metakosmos). "Meta" in this word compound means "beyond," but as Buber understands it, it is not an entity which lies beyond our actual world but rather in a relation which man establishes between the world as he experiences it spontaneously and that which is not-world, or that of which he has no experience in itself. Taken as such, the Metacosmos is beyond human cognition, but in the sense of *meta*-cosmos, that is, as a relation between cosmos and *meta,* it is revealed in the human act of entering in relation. This signifies a primal duality of cosmos and not-cosmos as the ground of all acts of relation. It is the basis of the human twofold way of looking at reality, namely, that of distancing and relating (I&T 49, 165). See *Cosmos*.

Mystery, Mysterium, Mysticism (Geheimnis, Mysterium, Mystik). There are hidden things in man's way of looking at the world which cannot be explained or even articulated in speech. This is called a mystery, such as the mystery of divine creation or of the primary metacosmic duality. The term "mysterium" Buber reserves for the hiddenness of the Absolute. Man can only become aware of it through divine revelation when he enters into relation with the Absolute Thou. (Buber does not regard divine revelation as a one-time historical occurrence only.) "Mysticism," on the other hand, is a term used to designate a certain tendency in man to identify himself with the Absolute through some special faculty which he claims to possess apart from his ordinary perceptual and conceptual capacities. In this sense Buber cannot be described as a mystic, for he does not attribute to man such a capacity or even the need for an identification with God through other means. For him, God is the "great mysterium," transcendent to man, yet close to him when he (man) goes forth to meet Him through faith in His Presence (I&T 149, I&W 30–31). See *Faith, Revelation*.

Myth (Mythos). "The account of a divine event designated as a sensate reality. . . . It means: we must name as myth every story of a sensibly actual event which is perceived and presented as a divine event." Jewish myth does not describe God himself as sensate reality, but sensate events as having a divine source (*On Judaism* 95, 102–103).

Object (Gegenstand). We speak of an object of knowledge as that which the knowing subject perceives sensibly or grasps conceptually. This is a relationship of subject-object, mediated by the senses and the understanding. In the I-Thou relation, on the other hand, the Thou may not be spoken of as an object, because the act of knowing it is immediate, that is, not through a particular single faculty, but through one's being as a whole. This act is a relationship of subject-subject, meaning that what is known is an independent entity over against the I who relates to it (I&T 57–58). See *The Thou*.

Objective Reality (Wirklichkeit). By "objective" we usually mean the opposite of "subjective" or that which exists outside the knowing subject. However, in Buber's principle of dialogue the subject participates in establishing the nature of what is not-subject as an other, either in I-It or I-Thou. That is, the It or the Thou is not to be conceived as actually apart from the I in the word pair and vice versa. There is only one Thou which is completely set apart from the I, and that is the Absolute Thou, which Buber calls the "great *objectivum*." The Absolute Thou is completely transcendent to the human subject and, as such, is the only Objective Reality. "Life in the Face [in the meeting with the Divine Presence] is life in the One Reality, the only true '*objectivum*' " (I&T 167).

Observing, Viewing, Inner Awareness (beobachten, betrachten, innewerden). One may express his experience of communication in three ways: (1) state his observation of every phase of the thing seen; (2) give an overall view of its significant features; or (3) show his inner awareness of its presence and what it "says" to him. The first two ways are always expressly stated in spoken words and represent the world of I-It; the third way may be articulated in speech or intimated in silence, and represents the world of I-Thou (BMM 8–10).

Ordered World (geordnete Welt). See *World Order*.

Past (Vergangenheit). The contrast between past and future is manifest in two different ways in the act of communication. If we take the I-Thou relation as the main occurrence of human experience, the past is when man steps out of this relation and turns the Thou into an It, that is, into an object of observation and use or theoretical contemplation in terms of lapsed time. But in the original I-Thou encounter the lived experience is of a momentary character, a "present" which "is there" in a flash and is no longer "there" when the relational act ceases. It never repeats itself even with the same other, for entering in relation is an ever new experience (I&T 63–65). See *Present, Time*.

Person. The fundamental unit out of which a community is formed is called "person," signifying the human being as a whole who of his own accord enters into relation with other human beings and confirms their mutual existence. That is, a person is a coexistent *with* others and *with* the world. By contrast, an individual who knows only himself as "being thus," is one who lives *in* the world (BMM 177–79, I&T 112–15). See *Individual*.

Place (Ort). Apart from the physical meaning of this term, it means also the "between" where man meets fellowman in living relationship. On a higher level, "place" signifies "the true folk community" which is the center of human realization and where the divine Presence reveals itself in the life of man (I&T 81, BMM 7). See *Space*.

Potencies (Potenzen). Buber considers the acts of communication between man and others as potencies of the human being rather than his psychological or physiological faculties. There are four such potencies—cognition, art, love, and faith—each acting in its own specific manner and all together constituting the category *humanum* (KnM 163).

Present, Presentness, Meeting (Gegenwart, Vergegenwärtigung, Begegnung). The German word *gegen* in the word compound *Gegenwart* has a double meaning of being "present" and meeting someone "over against," whereby the person who enters this relationship "makes the other present" *(vergegenwärtigt)* in the encounter. In this sense, "present" is not a temporal concept, but means simply "being there" in the movement at the moment of meeting. Buber coined the word *Vergegnung* (a misencounter) as the opposite of "being there" or as "the failure of a real meeting between persons" (KnM 70–71, 78, I&T 63–64, 158, *Begegnung* 15–16). See *Being There*.

Primary Words (Grundworte). I-Thou and I-It are the primary words of communication. Actually, they are not to be taken as single words, but as word pairs, that is, the I cannot be singled out as a separate existent apart from the Thou or It. Man takes his stand in each word pair through his act of communication and it is only then that he can speak I together *with* the Thou or the It, but not without them (I&T 53–54). See *Speech, The I, The Thou, The It.*

Purpose (Zweck). A limited end of conditioned things set by man in order to gain temporal success, and using force when necessary in order to attain it *(On Judaism* 54). See *Goal.*

Reality, Actuality (Wirklichkeit). The German word *Wirklichkeit* stands for "reality" as well as for "actuality." It is in truth an act of realization which takes place between man and another when the two sides meet in mutual relationship, and that is, in the I-Thou encounter. It is not a fixed state given apart from man's potencies, for it is through those potencies that he first brings that state into reality. Reality is therefore neither in the I nor in the Thou (or It) but between them. The crisis of reality which we witness today Buber calls "the crisis of the between" (I&T 136–37, BMM 125, 205).

Redemption (Erlösung). Man may be redeemd as a whole, not just his soul or any aspect of his being. Indeed, redemption of man means his becoming a human being as a whole. Moreover, he cannot be redeemed partially or all alone but only insofar as he participates with his wholeness in the redemption of the world as such. Buber conceives it as the divine plan of the creation of man, namely, to have him as a partner in the redemption of the world. Redemption is not of man as an evil being (for he is neither good nor evil), but of his evil inclination by turning it into good. Man serves God with both inclinations, when he directs them to God (I&W 37). See *Creation, Evil.*

Relation (Beziehung). It is one of the two fundamental movements of communication and it refers specifically to the spontaneous experiences in I-Thou. The other movement (distancing) is man's experiences *(Erfahrung)* in I-It (I&T 56–57, KnM 67, 163). See *Distance, Experience.*

Religion, Religiosity (Religion, Religiosität). Buber considers the first as a passive acceptance of sacred teachings and accumulated customs transmitted through oral and written instruction, in contradistinction to the second, which he regards as an act of relating oneself to God. The second must be exercised as an inner power of man and renewed constantly in one's personal and communal life *(On Judaism* 80–81).

Response, Responsibility (Antwort, Verantwortung). A dialogical relation occurs when one person responds to another who calls for his attention. The call need not be in articulated speech but it is there nevertheless when one encounters the other. One may then turn to the other and confirm him or turn away from him and deny him. This is a matter of one's responsibility toward the other, which stems from the responsibility to God, in general, and this is at the root of redemption (BMM 61, 92). See *Redemption, Turning*.

Return (Umkehr). The way to Go Buber calls "direction." When one loses his way, that is, has sinned, he may return to it by deciding to resume direction to God. This does not mean starting again from a new state of sinlessness, but rather to return to the point on the way where one went astray and to resume direction. Return is possible only through a real turning toward God (I&W 19–20). See *Direction, Turning*.

Revelation (Offenbarung). The divine call to man to assume responsibility for fellowman and the world is what Buber designates as "revelation." That is, revelation is a summons to man to participate in redemption. By turning to this call man accepts his responsibility. But what is revealed is not a specific content, only a power of mutuality between the human and the divine, giving man the strength to exercise his potencies of relation (I&T 161, I&W 27). See *Creation, Redemption*.

Sin (Sünde). It is the alienation of the soul from God. Each man sins in his own situation as Adam did in his, but not because Adam sinned. In Jewish tradition, sin is man's disturbing the basic relation between him and God. Sin means inertia, withholding decision, being conditioned, being acted upon, in contradistinction to acting in direction to God (TTF 64, 157–58, *On Judaism* 82). See *Direction, Inertia*.

Space (Raum). In physical terms space is a measurable quantity of distance, determining extension, separation, and continuity. In the sense of I-Thou relation it means both exclusiveness and endurance. To say that a Thou appears in space is to indicate its exclusiveness and independence (in physical terms, separation) from an other being when it enters-into-relation with it. That is, in the relation the Thou endures as it is and is not limited by the other in the encounter (I&T 81). See *Place*.

Speech, Speaking (Sprache, reden). The very act of turning to another in relation is an act of speaking, even when not a word is uttered between them. Speech is also manifest in the act of turning away from the other. The first is the speaking of I-Thou, the second of I-It, both conceived as primary word pairs or speech. However, the essential character of speaking is dialogical, or true relation, and can be addressed only to an actual, living other. No one can truly speak to himself. In this respect, speech is not *in* man, but *between* man and man (I&T 151, BMM 199, KnM 68, 106, 117–18). See *Dialogue*.

Spirit (Geist). As in the entire dialogical process, spirit comes into existence through the act of entering into an I-Thou relation. Spirit is therefore not a substance to be found *in* man or outside of him, but between him and an other. In universal terms, it is the special kind of between which comes into being when man relates to that which is not-world, and is objectified in human experience when the Thou is turned into It. Then its force is diminished but not lost entirely; it persists in human life as long as man continues to strive for relation with the divine Absolute (I&T 99–100, BMM 191, PW 187). See *Metacosmos*.

Spirituality (Geistigkeit). When man tries to use the divine Thou for his own self-aggrandizement, spirit degenerates into a kind of spirituality, which is only pretense or make-believe, but not a real spiritual between. This happens mostly when one separates his life of the spirit from everyday affairs in personal and communal activities (I&T 100).

Subject, Subjectivity (Subjekt, Subjektivität). These two terms are differentiated in their application to the I in each of the two word pairs. In I-It the I is called "subject" and in the I-Thou it is called "subjectivity." Or, in the first the I is identified as individual and in the second as person (I&T 113). See *Individual, Person*.

The I (das Ich). The I is not an existent in itself apart from the two word pairs in which it is placed. Outside of them it is but an abstraction, which "is the veritable shibboleth of mankind." The I becomes actual only through communication with an other, especially a Thou. "Through the Thou a man becomes I," or "becoming *I*, I speak Thou." Moreover, the I in the I-Thou is not the same as the I in I-It. Only man who speaks either of the two word pairs is the same, except that in the I-Thou relation he speaks as a human being as a whole, and in the I-It communication he speaks partially through one faculty or another. Buber also distinguishes a state of "prior to becoming I" *(vorichhaft)* and one which "follows the becoming of I" *(nachichhaft)*. The I, as such, he calls "the property of being I" *(Ichhaftigkeit)* (I&T 62, 75–76, 79, 115, EG 127–28).

The It (das Es). This, too, does not have a separate existence outside the word pair I-It. The It in this pair stands for anything which may be observed, analyzed, classified, or even constructed theoretically, as it is always a combination of parts. The It appears as object only relative to man's experience with nature, and may be abstracted from the word pair as if it were able to exist as an entity by itself. In the natural sciences the It may be conceived as a simple element or a structure of elements within a given theoretical frame of reference free from self-contradiction. If contradiction sets in, the It loses its objective validity (I&T 87–89). "I-It finds its highest concentration and illumination in philosophical knowledge" (EG 45).

The Thou (das Du). It has a dual meaning which is derived from its position in the I-Thou relation. On the one hand, it stands for the other in the mutuality of relation with the I, and on the other hand, it exists in this mutuality as an independent being in its own right. Indeed, the I can enter into relation with the Thou only insofar as the latter is independent of it. Yet the Thou must not be thought of as if it were another I, because its position in the encounter is that of an other than I. Or, the I addresses the Thou as an "other" and the Thou is addressed, as such. However, inasmuch as the Thou is exclusive, it may be considered as an I when it, in its own right, addresses an other as its Thou. In that case it can be only a human being, for only man has this capacity of addressing. It should be pointed out that, according to the dialogical principle the I-Thou relation is not confined to man's encounter with fellowman, but extends to his meeting with any other being-as-a-whole, be it an animal, a plant, and even an inanimate being (I&T 61–63).

The Way (der Weg). It means specifically "the way to God," which can be only "one way" in the sense of direction, not many ways, which is a lack of direction. It consists of the moments of going forth to a meeting with the Absolute Thou, which is the Center of all particular I-Thou meetings. Man may go astray and lose his way, but he can always return to where he left off and go on without a real break in the continuity of his striving toward the goal. This continuity is manifest in a constant turning and returning to God, which is called in Hebrew *teshuva,* generally translated as repentance, but etymologically meaning actual returning (I&T 168). See *Return.*

Theopolitics (Theopolitik). This is a policy of a people as a whole that directs itself toward the establishment of a beginning of God's rule on earth at a certain time in a given land. God demanded this especially of the Jewish people when He made a covenant with it at Mount Sinai and promised to bring it back to the land of its fathers. Since then, Israel's national goal has been a striving "toward the realization of divine rulership" (KG 57).

Time (Zeit). This term may be applied to physical events as well as to relational occurrences, but in different connotations. In the former it deals with successive measurable intervals in physical space. In the latter it signifies moments of entering-into-relation, which are unique, nonsuccessive, and nonrepetitive, and thus not measurable. In this occurrence the dimension of time is of an intensive character rather than an extended interval. Buber also speaks of historical time, meaning a moment of divine revelation, which is also nonrepetitive, yet renewable in different forms each time man decides to go forth toward an encounter with the divine Being (I&T 81, 163, I&W 25, BMM 140–41.).

Turning (Kehre, Wendung, sich hinwenden). This is manifest in the I-Thou relation when one responds to an other, that is, "turns" to him as a partner in the meeting. This is possible if one does not hold himself back but goes out fully and openly toward the meeting. Turning is especially applicable in man's relation with God, when one has lost direction and must turn to the divine call in order to find his way. Buber sees the act of turning as the breaking of a crisis in the life of a person or a nation. "The power of turning that radically changes the situation, never reveals itself outside the crisis" (PW 237, BMM 22, I&W 245). See *Return.*

We (Wir). The We is an extension of the I in relation. It is a manifold togetherness of relationship between I and Thou. Hence one who does not relate to an other as Thou does not know the We. "Judaism," Buber notes, "rejects the 'We' of group egotism, but postulates that 'We' . . . which maintains genuine relations with other groups" *(On Judaism* 211, KnM 107–108, BMM 80).

World, Our World, Real World (Welt, unsere Welt, wirkliche Welt). When man distances himself from all that which is not-himself and sees everything as standing over against him, there emerges before him a totality which he calls world, separate and distinct from his I. However, distancing goes hand in hand with relation, in which the world is viewed as "our world" or a human world, though not as a subjective aspect of the I, but as the outcome of the human primary twofold communication with nature. The "real world" comes into man's purview when he goes forth to a meeting with the Absolute Thou, when he is in the Face of the "One Reality." In all its aspects, the world for Buber means "this world" of human life on earth and not something "beyond" (BMM 61–63, KnM 60–62). See *Objective Reality*.

World Order, Ordered World (Weltordnung, geordnete Welt). We usually conceive of the world in terms of space, time, and causality. In Buber's terminology, these concepts are not the same in what he designates as the "world order," which man knows through his living experience of entering-into-relation. Man may still speak in terms of space, time, and cause in this relation, but in the sense of his participation in creation, revelation, and redemption, which Buber calls "the threefold chord of world-time." The physical meaning of these terms apply only to the world of I-It, which Buber designates as the "ordered world," as it is conceived in the physicomathematical sciences, even in the fields of sociopolitical and psychological knowledge (I&T 82–85, 115, I&W 25). See *Space, Time, Cauase*.

General Index

273